Stolen Youth

Stolen Youth

The Politics of Israel's Detention of Palestinian Children

Catherine Cook, Adam Hanieh and Adah Kay

Pluto  Press

LONDON • STERLING, VIRGINIA

in association with

DCI

Defence for Children International
Palestine Section

First published 2004 by
Pluto Press
345 Archway Road, London N6 5AA
and 22883 Quicksilver Drive, Sterling, VA 20166–2012, USA

www.plutobooks.com

British Library Cataloguing in Publication Data
A catalogue record for this book is available from the British Library

ISBN   0 7453 2162 3 hardback
ISBN   0 7453 2161 5 paperback

Library of Congress Cataloging in Publication Data
Cook, Catherine, 1971-
   Stolen youth : the politics of Israel's detention of Palestinian
children / Catherine Cook, Adam Hanieh, and Adah Kay.
      p. cm.
Includes bibliographical references.
   ISBN 0–7453–2162–3 (hbk) — ISBN 0–7453–2161–5 (pbk)
   1. Juvenile detention—Israel. 2. Political prisoners—West Bank.
3. Political prisoners—Gaza Strip. 4. Children, Palestinian
Arab—Crimes against—Israel. 5. Children, Palestinian Arab—Legal
status, laws, etc.—Israel. I. Hanieh, Adam, 1972- II. Kay, Adah,
1943- III. Title.
   HV9192.2.A5 C66 2004
   365'.48'095694—dc22

                                                        2003019586

10   9   8   7   6   5   4   3   2   1

Designed and produced for Pluto Press by
Chase Publishing Services, Fortescue, Sidmouth, EX10 9QG, England
Typeset from disk by Stanford DTP Services, Northampton, England
Printed and bound in the European Union by
MPG Books, Bodmin, England

Contents

List of Figures and Tables

FIGURES

TABLES

BOXES

Preface

In October 2002, the authors of this book met at the headquarters of Defence for Children International/Palestine Section (DCI/PS) in Ramallah to discuss projects in support of Palestinian children's rights. Following this discussion, we decided to move forward on the idea of a book on Palestinian child prisoners that DCI/PS had been considering for some time.

Although drawing on the work of many local and international human rights organisations, the authors have attempted to present an analysis of how the practice of incarceration – particularly of children – fits into the overall system of occupation. This book thus approaches the issue of child prisoners from a political perspective. We examine the central role the arrest and detention of Palestinian children plays within the overall strategy of the Israeli occupation.

Each of the authors was a staff member or volunteer with DCI/PS at some stage between 1999 and 2003. During that period we developed a level of expertise on the issue through research and advocacy work and, most important, by learning from the experience of our colleagues, many of whom were former child prisoners themselves.

The work of DCI/PS began in 1992 as a local response to the gross and systematic violations of Palestinian children's rights resulting from Israel's occupation. A local human rights activist, Rifat Kassis, established a committee as part of the developing international child rights movement and through a belief in the importance of bringing the international movement to the local level. In June 1992, the local committee was granted approval to establish an independent section of the Geneva-based Defence for Children International, with a mandate to promote and defend children's rights in the Occupied Palestinian Territories.

Initially DCI/PS focused on offering legal aid to Palestinian child political prisoners, a response to the waves of child arrests that characterised the first Intifada. However, it was clear that a broader approach to the issues was needed, as the impact of imprisonment on children extended beyond the period of detention. Consequently, in 1994 the organisation launched a counselling project to work with released detainees and assist their reintegration into Palestinian society. Since then DCI/PS has complemented these programmes with wide-ranging advocacy efforts designed to increase international awareness and mobilise opposition to Israel's practice of imprisoning Palestinian children.

In September 2001 DCI/PS launched an international campaign, Freedom Now!, demanding the release of all Palestinian child political prisoners. The campaign has received broad international support from organisations and individuals around the world. This book should be viewed as a continuation of the basic aims of the campaign: to raise international awareness and understanding of the issue of Palestinian child political prisoners and secure their release.

The arrest of children within the context of military occupation prompted DCI/PS to adopt a comprehensive approach to the issue of Palestinian child rights, since imprisonment is not the sole trauma that Palestinian children will sustain during their childhoods. The very poor child rights situation in the Occupied Palestinian Territories (OPT) is a function of a political situation that results in simultaneous violations of children's rights on a daily basis and a low level of awareness and enforcement of children's rights, locally and internationally. Accordingly, as support for the organisation increased, its work expanded to include other spheres: documenting and addressing violations of children's rights on all levels and by all actors, working directly with children to empower them and provide a venue for their voices to be heard, building awareness among the local community of children's rights, developing the capacity of local professionals through training, working to institutionalise child rights within the legal system of the Palestinian Authority, and engaging in advocacy efforts at the international level.

This book is a culmination of, and testament to, the work of DCI/PS. At present, DCI/PS is the sole Palestinian child rights organisation and the only human rights group working specifically to offer legal advice and support for Palestinian children in detention. Much of the information and many of the case studies drawn upon in this book are based upon DCI/PS documentation.

For these and many other reasons, the authors owe a deep debt of gratitude to the tireless work of DCI/PS staff over the last ten years. This book would not have been possible without these individuals, in particular, George Abu Zulof, Nasser Atallah, Ayed Abueqtaish, Riad Za'qiq, Hashem Abu Mari'a, Museika Obeid, Khaled Quzmar, Renad Musleh, Sanaa Anfous, Samah Darwish, Ayyad Wafeq, Cat Hunter, Annelien Groten, Daoud Dirawi, Younis Daragmeh, Adnan Rabi and Mohammed Na'amneh. DCI/PS child rights attorney Daoud

Dirawi was at the forefront of the authors' minds while drafting the manuscript, as he was arrested, interrogated and severely tortured by Israeli authorities in February 2003. As of November 2003, he remained imprisoned without charge or trial under an administrative detention order.

It is hoped that the information and analysis presented in this book will help raise awareness of the extremely difficult circumstances in which DCI/PS staff operate. All of the royalties from this book go towards supporting the work of DCI/PS in defending Palestinian child detainees and working with children who have been released from prison.

Many other organisations have offered valuable support and advice in the writing of this book. Staff of Addameer Prisoners Support and Human Rights Association, one of the main organisations representing Palestinian detainees in the West Bank and Gaza Strip, read earlier chapters of this book and agreed to be interviewed, as did the Israeli organisation, Hamoked. The Israeli Information Centre for Human Rights in the Occupied Territories, B'Tselem, and Physicians for Human Rights Israel provided useful background information. The Gaza Community Mental Health Programme provided helpful access to their research on the psycho-social effects of imprisonment.

Much of the information about the experience of lawyers working within the military court system and with Palestinian detainees is drawn from interviews conducted with both Palestinian and Israeli lawyers. These lawyers work in extremely difficult conditions and this book is in part testament to their efforts. In particular, the authors would like to thank the attorneys Khaled Quzmar, Sahar Francis, Tamar Pelleg, Leah Tsemel and Andre Rosenthal for their time and patience. DCI/PS attorney Khaled Quzmar and Addameer attorney Sahar Francis spent many hours assisting the authors in understanding the complex and confusing system of military courts and orders.

The authors would like to thank the many individuals who read and contributed useful suggestions to earlier versions of the manuscript. Lori Allen, Roberta Cecchetti, Hanan Elmasu, Nadya Engler, Lisa Hajjar, Emma Hanieh, Ala Jaradat, Stephanie Koury, Cailin Mackenzie, Miryam Rashid and Omar Yassin all provided valuable input and support during the writing of this book. Peter Huff-Rouselle generously donated his time to edit the manuscript prior to submission to the publishers. We would also like to thank Bailasan and the Applied Research Institute-Jerusalem who supplied us with sketches and maps. While greatly appreciative of the assistance of these and others, the authors assume full responsibility for any errors.

Each of us has personally experienced daily life under occupation and it has left an indelible mark on our lives. This experience has increased our awareness of the challenges facing Palestinian civilians, particularly children, and engendered an immeasurable level of respect for Palestinians who continue to struggle for freedom with dignity in spite of repeated assaults on their humanity. We hope that this book will both contribute to the historical record and increase wider understanding of the just cause of the Palestinian struggle and the enormous obstacles Palestinian people face on a daily basis. The authors are absolutely convinced that the Palestinian people will one day triumph and be free.

Glossary

Administrative Detention: In Israel's case, the practice of detention without charge or trial. It is justified on the grounds of 'emergency' situations and based on 'secret' evidence that neither the detainee nor his/her attorney is allowed to review. In Israel and East Jerusalem administrative detention orders are issued by the Minister of Defense; in the West Bank and Gaza Strip they are issued by military commanders. An administrative detention order is issued for a specific period of detention, to a maximum of six months. The order can be renewed before expiration and continued indefinitely. Some detainees have been kept for years under administrative detention.

Areas A, B, and C: The Oslo Accords divided the West Bank into three categories. In Area A, the Palestinian Authority held full responsibility for internal security, public order and civil administration. In Area B, the Palestinian Authority held civil authority and responsibility for public order for Palestinians and Israel had overriding security control. In Area C, Israel held sole responsibility for security and public order and some control of civil issues was transferred to the Palestinian Authority. As of September 2000 Area A consisted of 17.2 per cent, Area B 23.8 per cent, and Area C 59 per cent. A similar division of powers occurred vis-à-vis the Gaza Strip. The Palestinian Authority controlled approximately two-thirds of the area, with Israel remaining in control of one-third. The Accords gave Israel ultimate security control over all areas, should it choose to exercise it.

'Best Interests' Principle: A major child rights principle that places a child's welfare above all other considerations in actions concerning children.

Canteen: A facility available in some Israeli prisons from which detainees can purchase a limited range of food and other necessities.

Checkpoint: A permanent or temporary roadblock staffed by Israeli soldiers through which individuals, who must present identification, must pass in order to cross from one area to another. Checkpoints are the means by which Israel controls movement of persons and goods in the OPT. They exist within the OPT and between these areas and Israel. Checkpoints are randomly closed and passage through many of them by Palestinian residents of the West Bank and Gaza Strip requires an Israeli-issued permit.

'Child': According to the UN Convention on the Rights of the Child, a child is any individual under the age of 18 years.

Child Rights: Child rights are a specific group of human rights afforded to persons under 18 years old. Like human rights, they are universal, meaning that they apply to *all* children everywhere. See Convention on the Rights of the Child (CRC) below.

Closed Military Zone: An area that the Israeli military has declared off-limits through a military order. Entrance to these areas is restricted for everyone including foreign journalists, diplomatic and UN staff.

Closure: An Israeli government policy, implemented by the military, in which checkpoints are placed around a particular area and all movement in and out is prevented. Closures can be temporary, lasting a few hours or days, or permanent. There is a permanent closure on the West Bank and Gaza Strip. Movement by Palestinian residents of these areas into Jerusalem or Israel is prohibited unless they possess a permit issued by the Israeli military.

Collaborator: A Palestinian recruited by the Israeli authorities to provide information on individuals or activities from amongst their community.

Committee Against Torture: The UN body charged with monitoring implementation of the UN Convention Against Torture by State Parties. Like the Committee on the Rights of the Child, its members are independent experts in their field, rather than representatives of their respective governments.

Convention on the Rights of the Child (CRC): A human rights treaty adopted by the United Nations General Assembly on 20 November 1989. The CRC outlines specific rights for children and provides measures of protection. It is the most widely ratified human rights treaty – only two countries, the United States and Somalia, have failed to ratify it. Implementation of the treaty by State Parties is monitored by the UN Committee on the Rights of the Child.

Curfew: A practice of the Israeli army in which residents of an area are forbidden from moving outside their houses for an indefinite period of time. The threat and use of force is used to implement curfews.

'Deprived of Liberty': An umbrella term used to refer to persons, including children, who are institutionalised, incarcerated, or otherwise forbidden from leaving a particular place by order of an administrative, judicial, or other public authority.

Detention Centre: A facility under the control of either the Israeli military or police to which children are taken immediately following their arrest. These are supposed to be temporary holding centres and are generally located in Israeli settlements, military camps or police stations.

Fourth Geneva Convention: One of four Geneva Conventions of 1949, it addresses the protection of civilian persons in time of war, armed conflict and occupation. It is a major cornerstone of international humanitarian law and a primary legal reference for Israel's occupation.

Held Pending Trial: Term for persons held in detention while awaiting completion of their trial.

Intifada: An Arabic word literally meaning 'shaking off' used to describe Palestinian uprisings against the Israeli occupation. The first Intifada began in 1987 and ended around 1993. The second Intifada began in September 2000 and is also referred to as the 'Al Aqsa' Intifada. Other smaller-scale uprisings throughout Palestinian history have also been referred to as Intifada.

Israel Defense Forces (IDF): Official name of the Israeli military. Given that many actions of the IDF are 'offensive' rather than 'defensive' in nature, many do not use this term, referring instead to the Israeli military or army.

Israel Prison Service (IPS): The body in charge of administering Israeli prisons under the control of the Ministry of Public Security. These prisons hold Israeli civilians as well as Palestinians accused of criminal and political offences.

Israel Security Agency (ISA): Also known as the Shabak or Shin Bet, and formerly titled General Security Service (GSS), the ISA is a domestic agency that reports directly to the Israeli Prime Minister. Details of its structure and activities are kept secret, but it is known that the ISA is responsible for intelligence gathering and covert operations in the OPT, recruitment of collaborators and interrogation of Palestinians in serious cases, among other activities. In practice, the ISA is the most senior body in the hierarchy of the Israeli occupation.

Israeli Civil Administration: The governing body responsible for functions related to civilian, rather than strictly military, matters vis-à-vis Israel's control of the OPT. It was established by the military in 1981, and, despite its name, operates under the control of the Israeli military.

Israeli Civil Law: The body of law applying to Israeli citizens, including Israeli settlers living in the OPT.

Israeli Military Intelligence: A branch of the Israeli army which is sometimes responsible for the interrogation of Palestinians.

Military Court: Courts operating in the OPT which enforce military orders and are presided over by a military judge. Except in extremely unusual circumstances, Palestinians arrested in the OPT and charged with a political offence are brought before one of these courts.

Military Government: The governing body established by Israel following its occupation of the West Bank and Gaza Strip in 1967.

Military Orders: Edicts issued by the Israeli Military Commander of the OPT that function as law and govern every aspect of Palestinian life. Military orders are issued under separate numbering systems for the West Bank and Gaza Strip, though the content is largely the same. Military orders become applicable immediately following their issuance and are frequently revised.

Military Prison: Prisons under the control of the Israeli Ministry of Defense.

NIS: Israeli currency, short for New Israel Shekel.

OPT: Occupied Palestinian Territories, a term used to refer to the Palestinian territories of the West Bank, East Jerusalem and Gaza Strip, occupied by Israel in 1967. Also referred to as the 'occupied territories'. Although East Jerusalem is occupied territory, Israel applies a different legal code there. Consequently, some general references to the OPT exclude East Jerusalem.

Oslo Accords and Oslo II: Oslo Accords refers to the numerous agreements signed between the Palestine Liberation Organisation and the Israeli government beginning with the signing of the *Declaration of Principles on Interim Self-Government Arrangements*, in

September 1993. *The Palestinian–Israeli Interim Agreement on the West Bank and Gaza Strip,* commonly referred to as Oslo II, was signed in September 1995.

Palestinian Authority (PA): A body established in 1994 to administer those areas from which Israel redeployed following the Oslo Accords. The leadership of the PA is intertwined with that of the Palestine Liberation Organisation (PLO) and is largely staffed by Palestinian returnees who had been living in exile prior to the Oslo Accords.

Permit System: Israel's system that requires Palestinians to apply for Israeli permission to undertake numerous tasks, including movement within and outside of the West Bank and Gaza Strip and into Jerusalem or Israel.

Post-Traumatic Stress Disorder (PTSD): A psychological disorder affecting those who have experienced severe traumatic episodes.

'Security' Prisoner: Term used by the Israeli authorities to describe a prisoner arrested for any action deemed likely to threaten Israel's security.

Settlements: Areas where Israeli citizens have settled in the OPT on confiscated and expropriated Palestinian land. Settlements are illegal under international law.

***Shabeh*:** An Arabic word referring to a particular form of torture, position abuse, in which prisoners are tied in painful positions, fettered to walls or small chairs that force them to contort and cramp their bodies for extended periods of time. Long-term damage to internal organs, joints and limbs can result from this form of abuse.

Part I
Framework and Context

1
Introduction

Three more people in masks came into the room. They blindfolded me, put a hood over my head...they kicked and slapped me. They beat me with a plastic pipe and whatever they could get their hands on. I couldn't see anything because I was blindfolded. I just felt the blows. That lasted ten to fifteen minutes...Later they stood me on a chair and told me to grab a pipe that was fixed to the wall. They removed the chair from under me and left me hanging in the air, with my handcuffed hands holding onto the pipe and the weight of my body, hanging in the air, drawing my hands downwards. They left the room.[1]

Isma'il Sabatin, 17 years old

They reached the detention centre at around 2 a.m. and Israeli soldiers took Rami directly to interrogation. During his interrogation Rami was severely kicked and punched by the soldiers, he was not allowed to sleep, and was tied to a small chair in a contorted position for a long time. He had ice-cold and hot water alternatively poured over his body. At one point during his interrogation Rami was forced to stand on one foot, and when the interrogator told him to confess and Rami refused, saying he had nothing to confess to, the interrogator began beating him on his standing leg. Another time they forced Rami to walk from one room to another, blindfolded, until he stumbled into some stairs and fell down.[2]

Concerning Rami Zaoul, 16 years old

The interrogations of 17-year-old Isma'il Sabatin and 16-year-old Rami Zaoul parallel those of the nearly 2,000 Palestinian children from the OPT whom the Israeli authorities have arrested over the last three years. Some of these children are briefly detained, beaten or otherwise maltreated, and then released. Isma'il, who confessed to throwing stones after he was tortured for several hours, spent seven months in a military prison. Others, like Rami, may spend years there.

As of June 2003 Israeli forces had arrested over 1,900 Palestinian children since September 2000, the beginning of the current Palestinian uprising. At various points over the last three years Palestinian children have constituted 10 per cent of all Palestinian detainees. At the beginning of 2003 Israeli detention centres or prisons held approximately 350 Palestinian children, four times the number prior to September 2000.

This book defines children as individuals under the age of 18, following the internationally accepted definition codified in the United Nations Convention on the Rights of the Child (CRC). While this age group overlaps with the initial stages of youth or adolescence, international law affords them special rights, recognising their vulnerability and dependency on adults. Israel signed and ratified the CRC in November 1991, and applies this definition to Israeli citizens.

We define as child political prisoners all children arrested by the Israeli authorities and either accused of offences against the occupation or detained during arbitrary mass arrests of Palestinian males.[3] In the vast majority of cases, these children are accused of throwing stones at soldiers or at Israelis who have illegally settled in the West Bank, East Jerusalem and Gaza Strip.

In 2002 around one-fifth of child prisoner cases handled by Defence for Children International/Palestine Section (DCI/PS) involved children aged 13 and 14 years with the remainder between 15 and 17 years. Historically, the Israeli military and police have targeted children aged between 12 and 17, although at times children as young as nine are arrested.

Since the Israeli occupation of the West Bank and Gaza Strip in 1967, there have been two major population uprisings, the first beginning in 1987 and ending in 1993, the second beginning in September 2000, and still ongoing in mid-2003. *Intifada*, an Arabic word literally meaning 'shaking off', is the popular term for these uprisings.

The arrest and detention of Palestinian children is not a new phenomenon. It is estimated that at the beginning of the first Intifada in 1987, Israel arrested more than 2 per cent of all Palestinian children between the ages of 9 and 17 and held them for varying periods of time.[4] The last four years have seen a sharp increase in arrests, in tandem with a general increase in violations of Palestinian children's rights.

Israel's policy of arresting Palestinian children entered a new phase in March/April 2002, when Israeli forces launched an invasion of all Palestinian towns in the West Bank, dubbed 'Operation Defensive

Shield' by the Israeli military. Israeli forces placed prolonged curfews on Palestinian cities and carried out mass arrest campaigns. During these curfews, Israeli troops drove through Palestinian towns and villages ordering from loudspeakers that all Palestinian males aged 14–60 leave their houses and gather in nearby locations such as schoolyards and football fields.[5] The majority of those detained were released within a few days, but many were to spend prolonged periods of time in detention.

The year 2002 also saw the first death in custody of a Palestinian child in many years. Seventeen-year-old Murad 'Awaisa died from gunshot wounds while Israeli soldiers held him in detention on 31 March 2002. Murad's death occurred after the soldiers raided his family's apartment and detained Murad in another apartment in the building. Murad was seriously ill and had undergone three operations for hydrocephalus (water on the brain). His naked body was found dumped outside the apartment building the morning following his death. Hospital workers could not reach cemeteries because of the Israeli-imposed curfew. Murad was buried in the car park of the Ramallah hospital on 3 April 2002, along with others whom the Israelis killed during the invasion. While Murad was buried, his father and brothers were being held in detention in a nearby Israeli military camp.[6]

CHILD PRISONERS: A MAP THROUGH THE SYSTEM

Most arrests of Palestinian children are made at checkpoints, on the street, or at their homes by heavily armed Israeli soldiers in the middle of the night. The soldiers take them to detention centres in Israeli settlements or military camps. Often neither they nor their families know where they have been taken, and they are denied lawyer and family visits.

In the detention centre, the children are interrogated. This almost always involves some form of torture or abuse, including sleep and food deprivation, threatening language, beatings with heavy batons, being punched and kicked, as well as being tied in painful and contorted positions for long periods of time (known as 'position abuse' or in Arabic, *shabeh*).

Following interrogation, the Israeli authorities bring the children before a military court. These courts, generally located in Israeli settlements, do not operate according to Israeli civil law but under a set of Israeli military orders designed to provide a legal framework for the occupation. Contrary to international guidelines, there are no juvenile courts, no specifically trained juvenile judges, no probation officers, and no special police officers to deal with the interrogation and detention of children.

Military personnel, who may not possess legal training,[7] preside over these courts. Israel employs two distinct bodies of law, one for Palestinian children from the West Bank and Gaza Strip, and another for Israeli children. Israeli children are afforded a much greater degree of rights, generally in line with international law. Discrimination is an entrenched part of the Israeli legal system.

After sentencing, the Israeli authorities incarcerate most Palestinian children in prisons inside Israel itself. Children are sent to two types of prisons. Male children under 16, and all girls, are sent to those under the jurisdiction of the Ministry of Public Security, administered by the Israel Prison Service. Males aged 16 and 17 go to prisons run by the Ministry of Defence. This distinction is pursuant to Israeli Military Order No. 132, which treats Palestinian children aged 16 and 17 as adults. This military order – as with all others – is applied only to *Palestinian* residents of the West Bank and Gaza Strip, not to Israeli settlers who live in these areas. The prison in which children are placed is determined by their age at the time of arrest.

In 2000 the Israel Prison Service reinstated a policy of locking some Palestinian children up with Israeli juvenile prisoners.[8] This practice often exposes Palestinian children to danger at the hands of Israeli prisoners, in which the prison authorities typically refuse to intervene. Palestinian child detainees have described many serious violations, including attempted rape, physical abuse and the theft of personal possessions by Israeli prisoners.

Child prisoners are regularly denied visits from lawyers and from family members. Owing to the permanent 'closure' that has been imposed on the Gaza Strip since 1989 and on the West Bank since 1993, Palestinian residents of the occupied territories must obtain permits in order to enter Israel. Many Palestinians are denied permits and, during periods of heightened political tension, permits that have been issued are often revoked. Since October 2000 family visits to imprisoned Palestinian children from the West Bank and Gaza Strip have been almost impossible.

When a Palestinian child is imprisoned, their entire family and community are affected. The fabric of family life is torn apart. In addition to the psychological toll, there is also a heavy physical and financial burden. Lives revolve around court appearances and attempts to secure family visits. Families spend many hours trying to obtain the required permit and, if they succeed, need many more hours for the bureaucratic procedures involved in the brief 30-minute visit.

The arrested children generally come from large, poor families, and many of them live in isolated villages or refugee camps.[9] Their families, already strapped for funds, find it difficult to pay legal fees and court fines, and to provide extra money to their imprisoned child. For friends and colleagues of the child and their family, plans must be put on hold or worked around. The life of everyone who knows the child is affected in some way.

Child rights organisations, counsellors and psychologists have documented the impact of prison on children after their release. Those working with child detainees have observed the widespread presence of severe Post-Traumatic Stress Disorder (PTSD). The psychological effects of torture and imprisonment are compounded by the practical obstacles the children face after release from prison. These include gaps in education, chronic unemployment and difficulties obtaining the permits for travel and movement that are so integral to Palestinian life under occupation.

CHILD DETENTION: CONTEXT AND LOGIC

Prison is a central feature of Palestinian life. Since 1967 over 600,000 Palestinians have spent time in prison. At various periods the number of Palestinian political prisoners per capita held by Israel has been among the highest in the world. Almost every family has a male member who has been arrested at some point. Every year, the Israeli army or police arrest and detain hundreds of Palestinian children.[10]

Consequently, the prison experience is a cornerstone of the Palestinian national narrative. Palestinians have written thousands of songs, poems and stories about it. Prisoners play a leading role in the Palestinian political process, and leaders outside of the prison regularly consult them. As political negotiations between the Palestinians and Israel resumed in May 2003, the issue of prisoners was high on the agenda.

Yet the approach to this issue, particularly from international bodies, tends to concentrate on humanitarian aspects. Conditions inside prisons, the use of torture, and the practice of 'administrative detention' without trial or charge, figure prominently on the agenda of human rights organisations. They rarely place imprisonment in a political context. They seldom explore the underlying reasons for this high rate of imprisonment, the strategy driving the way detainees are treated, and the role that imprisonment plays in the occupation.

For most outsiders, their image of Palestinian life in the West Bank and Gaza Strip is shaped by the pictures that have filled television screens around the world since the beginning of the current uprising. These images – often in stark contrast to the verbal commentaries that accompany them – show Israel's vast military machine in action against the Palestinian civilian population. Tanks, helicopters and the ubiquitous checkpoints reinforce a notion that Israel's 36-year-long occupation is, above all, a soldier with a gun. The occupation is generally equated with the Israeli army.

As this book examines Palestinian child political prisoners and Israeli incarceration policies in the OPT, it will show that the Israeli occupation is much more than the Israeli army. The overarching argument is that the occupation is a *system of control*, permeating every aspect of Palestinian life. It is a system backed by legal, political, economic, cultural and psychological structures, and designed to keep more than 3 million people under submission. Although the role of the Israeli army is critical in enforcing this control, the system runs much deeper than the young man from Tel Aviv whose gun appears as the public face of occupation.

Prison is a critical part of this system of control. This book focuses on Israel's practices as a form of state-backed institutionalised violence encompassing all stages of the incarceration process. It is a conscious policy aimed at demoralising and defeating the population, and is supported by a series of structures ranging from a discriminatory legal system to psychological strategies aimed at inculcating fear. It is designed not only to punish but also to intimidate. It is intended to convey the message that resistance is fruitless in the face of these overwhelming control structures. Above all, it is designed to render the population passive: the Israeli army, secret service (the Shabak) and police will reach out and target anyone – including the weakest and most vulnerable sectors of Palestinian society.

This analysis places the physical and psychological treatment of Palestinian child detainees within the context of what has been termed *state torture*. As knowledge regarding the practice of torture has developed over the past 20 years, so too has an understanding of the purpose of torture. Human rights defenders and mental health professionals across the globe now emphasise a purpose of torture beyond simply making a prisoner 'talk'. Torture is seen as a tool used by the state to undermine the identity and self-confidence of the individual and the community. It targets the fabric of national identity within society as a whole. As the Denmark-based International Rehabilitation Council for Torture Victims (IRCT) notes

> Torture is used to obtain information, or a confession, to punish, or to take revenge, or to create terror and fear within a population. The aim of torture is not to kill the victim, but to break down the victim's personality.[11]

Approaching the issue of child detention from this perspective clarifies the underlying reasons for arrest and abusive treatment. Palestinian prisoners, including children, can be seen not only as victims. They regain their position as political actors who are treated the way they are because of their actual or potential resistance to occupation, often simply because they are Palestinian. The various myths that Israel uses to justify these practices can be analysed, and shown to be part of the ideological edifice maintaining the occupation.

One major argument the Israeli government uses to justify its repressive policies and discriminatory legal system is that these measures are necessary because of the special threat of 'terrorism', or 'for security reasons'. As we shall see throughout this book, Israel has been largely successful in shaping the discourse about its practices in the occupied territories around this theme. Israel justifies its practices by arguing that the 'security' of Israeli civilians requires measures ranging from closure and curfew to imprisonment, home demolition and land confiscation. Tackling this myth is one of the central aims of this book. Israel's treatment of Palestinian child detainees, the vast majority of whom are accused mainly of stone-throwing, will demonstrate clearly that the security justification is used as a smokescreen to obscure deliberate policies of collective punishment against a civilian population.

As we examine the legal system Israel uses to govern the Palestinian population in the OPT, we will understand occupation as a system of control extending beyond military force. Law is very rarely neutral. Legal theorists and practitioners too often treat law as an abstraction, divorced from an understanding of power. The Israeli system of laws, military orders, courts and prisons is a maze of bureaucratic and administrative procedures created to offer a legal veneer to occupation. We will show that the Israeli legal system in the OPT is a complex structure designed to enforce discrimination, treating Palestinian residents of these areas under a different – and much harsher – body of laws than Israeli settlers living in the same area.

The problem with seeing law as neutral is equally true of humanitarian law and international human rights. All legal frameworks need mechanisms of enforcement, raising the issue of power. Those who control that power – whether an occupying force or countries that govern the global political order – decide if, when and how to wield that power. If we treat human rights abstractly, without also challenging these structures of power, we risk consenting to a system based on legalised injustice.

The importance of this issue of political context could be seen clearly in the discussions of Israeli 'goodwill measures' prior to the resumed political negotiations in May 2003. Israel promised to release several hundred Palestinian detainees. While their families and friends will certainly greet their release with joy, Israel has consistently used detainees as a bargaining chip in previous negotiations. In the broad context of occupation, experience suggests that prisoner releases may well be temporary, and new rounds of arrests will occur whenever Israel wants to increase pressure on the Palestinian population.

The book is divided into three main parts. Part I (Chapters 1–4), introduces the major issues, and proposes a framework for understanding Israel's policy towards Palestinian detainees, particularly children. In Chapter 2 we look at the system of control Israel has established over the West Bank and Gaza Strip, from the perspective of Israel's attempt to control the land, resources and economy. As their incarceration policies are an integral part of their efforts to suppress Palestinian uprisings against the occupation, we also explore the roots of the September 2000 Intifada. In Chapter 3, we expand our understanding of the system of control by examining the military order system, and the practice of recruiting collaborators and informants. Chapter 4 sets forth the international standards related to imprisonment and the treatment of child detainees.

In Part II (Chapters 5–7), with a focus on data about children arrested in the West Bank we discuss the actual experience of children from the moment of arrest until their release from prison. The final section of the book, Part III, (Chapters 8–11) analyses in detail the reasons underlying Israel's incarceration of children and the impact on Palestinian society.

For many readers, the stories, testimonies and case studies contained here will be shocking and perhaps difficult to comprehend. This book attempts to explore the reasons for these practices by placing them within the logic of occupation. Furthermore, it tries to explain why they have been permitted to continue and, most important, to suggest what actions should be taken to bring them to an end.

2
The Political Context

On the surface, Palestinian life during the early weeks of September 2000 appeared routine in every sense of the word. Political negotiations between Palestinians and Israelis were in their perpetual state of crisis and deadlock. Life continued as normal for most Palestinians – the usual intolerable litany of daily frustrations, military checkpoints, and the familiar sight of burgeoning Israeli settlements surrounding and choking off Palestinian towns.

On 29 September 2000 a large-scale Palestinian uprising gripped the world's attention and shattered this 'normality' in a few short days. The 'second Intifada', as this uprising was quickly dubbed, had begun. Israeli troops shot dead seven Palestinian demonstrators at Jerusalem's Al Aqsa mosque that Friday. Clashes erupted all over the West Bank and the Gaza Strip. Within three weeks, Israeli forces had killed over 100 Palestinians and wounded more than 4,000. Five Israeli soldiers were killed in the fighting.

In the months that followed, the common wisdom held that the uprising resulted from a contentious visit by Israeli Prime Minister Ariel Sharon to the grounds of the Al Aqsa mosque. Highly placed Israeli analysts argued that, although Sharon's visit had provoked the uprising, the Palestinian Authority then deliberately exploited it, orchestrating and encouraging the violence from behind the scenes to further their political cause. However, to claim that a cynical ploy by the PA somehow manipulated Palestinians into embarking on a 'path of violence' is either naive or disingenuous. These were sparks which fell in a tinder-box.

Undeniably, Sharon's provocative visit to one of Islam's holiest sites inflamed the Palestinians. Sharon had presided over the violent crushing of an uprising decades earlier in the Gaza Strip following Israel's occupation of Gaza and the West Bank in 1967. A leader of the right-wing Likud Party, he had served as Minister of Defence during the Israeli invasion of Lebanon. In 1983 an Israeli government inquiry held him partly responsible for an earlier massacre in the Palestinian refugee camps of Sabra and Shatila in Lebanon. The International Red Cross initially reported that 1,500 Palestinians died in the massacre; a subsequent international inquiry estimated 2,750.[1] Palestinians in the OPT had long seen Sharon as a principal architect of the settler movement – the 1977 'Sharon Plan' for settlement construction has served as a blueprint for successive Israeli governments.

Nevertheless, attempts to explain the Intifada through one specific event reveal a misreading of Palestinian history together with a shallow understanding. The real explanation for the September 2000 Intifada runs much deeper than an individual Israeli leader, even one as detested as Sharon, entering an Islamic holy site. The causes of every Palestinian uprising, including the most recent Intifada, can be found in the basic facts of occupation and Palestinian dispossession. This ongoing history of dispossession lies at the roots of every Palestinian uprising, beginning when the Israeli state was established in 1948, and followed by the 1967 occupation of the West Bank and Gaza Strip and the illegal annexation of East Jerusalem in 1980.[2]

Adopting an inappropriate binary model of peace/violence, Israeli government spokespeople have told us that Palestinians rejected peace and chose the path of violence. Others professing sympathy for the Palestinian cause criticise Israel for moving away from the path of peace chosen by Yitzhak Rabin and Shimon Peres and towards the violent methods of Ariel Sharon. Both viewpoints are based on a mistaken assumption – that the round of negotiations which began in 1993 was an effort made in good faith to bring about a just and peaceful solution. This assumption is not supported by the evidence.

Instead, a careful examination of recent history will show that the system of control characterising the occupation has evolved into ever-more-sophisticated forms while retaining the same basic premise. Israel's strategy towards the OPT forms a continuum from 1967 to the present day. The essential goal has always been to control the land, the economy, and the resources without assuming direct responsibility for the resident Palestinian population.

This chapter examines in detail how that system of control has evolved through various phases since 1967, from direct military occupation towards a form of 'remote' control, the essence of the Oslo Agreements: a self-governing Palestinian authority takes responsibility for the day-to-day lives of Palestinians, but in reality remains completely dependent upon the Israeli government.

PHASES OF CONTROL

Just prior to the beginning of the first Intifada in 1987, Raja Shehadeh proposed a useful analysis of Israel's occupation strategy. Shehadeh is a well-known Palestinian lawyer and human rights activist who founded Al Haq, one of the first Palestinian human rights organisations. He saw Israeli control over the OPT evolving through four phases since 1967.

The first phase, which lasted from 1967 until 1971, was primarily concerned with developing and putting into place a system to control individual movement, to expropriate land and natural resources, and to regulate all the administrative bodies in direct contact with the Palestinian population in the occupied territories.[3] These powers were set out in a system of military orders, providing a 'legal' basis for Israel's actions. These military orders are promulgated by the Israeli military commander in the OPT, and immediately become binding on all Palestinian residents. To illustrate the draconian nature of these orders: in 1967 Israel passed Military Order No. 58, defining as an 'absentee' anyone who was not in the West Bank at the time of the 1967 war. That order applied to the deed-holder of the property, not their family, and authorised the Israeli government to take over the property of any absentee, even if the family of the owner had been physically present during the war. Israel confiscated large areas of land this way – land later used to construct Israeli settlements. By 1978, 40 per cent of Israeli settlement land in the Jordan Valley was classified as absentee property.[4]

Similarly, Israeli authorities issued a series of three military orders in 1967–68, giving the military administration full control of West Bank water resource exploitation and administration.[5]

Raja Shehadeh's second phase, from 1971 to 1979, saw the beginning of Israeli settlement in the West Bank, with Israeli citizens encouraged to relocate on confiscated Palestinian land. The settlements not only had military significance, but also destroyed the contiguity of Palestinian population centres. Military orders formed the legal basis for these encroachments.

The third phase ran from 1979 to 1981. Another series of military orders placed the Palestinians under a newly formed Israeli civil administration. In fact, the Israeli military appointed these 'civil' bodies and retained ultimate control.[6] Meanwhile, Israeli settlers in the occupied territories enjoyed the full protection of Israel's own legal code, creating a dual system of laws to legitimise the discrimination which was already the reality on the ground.[7]

The fourth phase Shehadeh described began in 1981 and saw the consolidation of Israeli control over most of the West Bank. Israel concentrated on regulating the Palestinian economy and its relationship with Israel. It established a complicated system of tax and revenue collection which prevented real economic development in the occupied areas, making the Palestinian economy totally dependent on its larger and more powerful neighbour.

To Shehadeh's four phases we can add a fifth, which began with the first Oslo Accord in 1993 and lasted until the second Intifada erupted in 2000. It was the logical sequel to Israel's earlier rule. Israel ostensibly gave up direct responsibility for the Palestinian population in the OPT, but retained absolute control through a military, economic, political and legal framework that left Israel as the final arbiter. Israel redeployed its military from areas of concentrated Palestinian population. This created an illusion of sovereignty in the major Palestinian cities, but the actual occupation as experienced by the local population intensified.

HISTORY FORETOLD[8]

A series of plans drawn up by various Israeli leaders since 1967 lay behind these five phases. Together, they brought the OPT under Israeli control by forcing Palestinians into isolated population centres, divided from one another by Israeli settlements and 'bypass roads'. These plans envisioned giving Palestinians, directly or through an Arab government such as Jordan, a form of self-rule in these areas. With the Palestinian population living in isolated enclaves and having no control over their natural resources, their borders, or their economy, Israel would remain in complete control without having to maintain an expensive, direct, military occupation force.

Immediately following the 1967 war, Israeli General and Deputy Prime Minister Yigal Allon put forward his 'Allon Plan'. It called for annexing a third of the West Bank, along the Jordan River and the Dead Sea. Israel would construct settlements running along the north–south axis of the Jordan valley on the eastern side of the West Bank. The plan called for a second line of settlements on the highlands overlooking the valley, with a road connecting the two blocs. At the same time, Israel would build a ring of settlements around the city of Jerusalem. The 110,000 Palestinians then living in the eastern part of the city would be encircled, unable to expand into the neighbouring West Bank. The final version of the plan recommended establishing some form of Arab or Palestinian 'entity' in about 50 per cent of the West Bank, while Israel annexed East Jerusalem, the Jordan Valley, the Hebron Hills in the south of the West Bank, and the southern part of the Gaza Strip. The Labor Party followed the Allon Plan faithfully from 1967 to 1977.

The Likud Party came to power in 1977 and added three new plans, all aimed at controlling the land but avoiding direct responsibility for the population. First came the Sharon Plan, calling for a new belt of Israeli settlements on the western side of the West Bank, extending from Jenin in the north to Bethlehem in the south. Ariel Sharon, who would become Israeli Prime Minister two decades later, was then Minister for Agriculture and Settlements. He envisioned confiscating land on the western side of the West Bank for a settlement belt that would act as another buffer between Israel and the Palestinian population. His plan called for major highways running east–west across the West Bank, connecting the new settlements with those in the Jordan Valley.

Then, in October 1978, the World Zionist Organisation put forward a comprehensive 5-year settlement plan. It involved constructing further settlements around and between the major Palestinian population areas in the West Bank. Over the past two decades, both Labor and Likud governments have followed this plan. It has divided the West Bank into three separate areas: the northern West Bank towns of Jenin, Tulkarem, Qalqilya and Nablus; the central area of Ramallah and outlying areas of Jerusalem; and the southern part of the West Bank around Bethlehem and Hebron. In a now-familiar pattern, the WZO strategy built Israeli settlements between the Palestinian cities in each area to further fragment the Palestinians.

The new Likud government in 1977 also put forward a third plan, focused on the 'entity' they would establish in the Palestinian areas. The Begin Plan, named after Likud leader and then Israeli Prime Minister Menachem Begin, called for 'autonomy' for the Palestinian population in the occupied territories. Begin put forward a detailed plan involving an administrative council elected by Palestinians, and sitting either in Ramallah or in Bethlehem. It would take responsibility for internal Palestinian matters, while the Israeli government retained full control over foreign policy, borders and the economy. Begin's plan translated into politics on the ground by establishing village leagues, beginning with Hebron in 1978 and extending to other West Bank towns during the 1980s. The Israeli government backed these leagues in order to foster a local Palestinian leadership, collaborators who would mediate Israel's relationship with the Palestinian inhabitants. A new series of military orders issued during the early 1980s authorised these bodies to arrest and detain political activists and establish armed militias, as well as perform more innocuous tasks such as issuing drivers' licences and other permits. The Begin Plan complemented the 1978 Camp David Accords between Israel and Egypt, which talked of a 'self-governing authority' in the West Bank and Gaza Strip.

SETTING THE SCENE – SEVEN YEARS OF 'REMOTE' CONTROL

The Oslo period, which began in 1993, simply continued this earlier strategy under the banner of a new era of peace. While negotiations continued through the years following the signing of the first Oslo Accords (Oslo I), successive Israeli governments drove forward with a massive acceleration in settlement growth. Israel concentrated these settlements in several major blocs that protrude into the West Bank, dividing Palestinian population centres, preventing movement between them and restricting their natural growth. Between 1994 and the beginning of 2000, the number of Israeli settlers in the occupied territories doubled.[9]

A new feature of Oslo, large highways called 'bypass roads', connected the Israeli settlements with each other and with Israeli cities. They were Israeli Prime Minister Yitzhak Rabin's brainchild, and are designed as Israeli-only roads. Differently coloured number plates identify Palestinian residents and make it easy to keep them off these roads. The Oslo II agreement made Palestinian construction within 50 metres on either side of these roads illegal.[10] The Israelis demolished hundreds of Palestinian houses, and built over 400km of bypass roads on confiscated land.[11]

Yitzhak Rabin and the Israeli Labor Party also introduced the 'closure' policy in the months before the Oslo Accords. From March 1993 Palestinians required a permit issued by the Israeli military authorities for travel from the West Bank to Jerusalem or into Israel. This quickly intensified to include 'internal closures': Israeli checkpoints and soldiers restricted movement between Palestinian towns and villages, which the Oslo process had designated as Areas A, B and C.[12] By 2003, over 3 million Palestinians depend upon permits to travel between cities, and the West Bank consists of 64 separate enclaves divided from one another by checkpoints, settlements and bypass roads. For over a decade, Israel has prohibited almost all travel between the Gaza Strip and the West Bank.

Closure and the system of checkpoints have had tragic humanitarian consequences. In addition, the restrictions on moving people and goods, both externally and internally, has effectively destroyed the Palestinian economy. Roughly 75 per cent of all OPT imports originate in Israel, and 95 per cent of Palestinian exports go to Israel.[13] Meaningful Palestinian trade relations with a third country are impossible. This control is intentional and quite overt, and in fact was formalised in Oslo process economic agreements, particularly the 1994 Paris Economic Protocols.[14]

Money is another key lever. Between 1995 and 2000, 60 per cent of PA revenue came from the indirect taxes the Israeli government collected on goods imported from abroad for the OPT. According to a process outlined in the Paris Protocols, Israel collects this money and, in principle, transfers it to the PA each month. If the Israeli government chooses to withhold payment, the PA faces a major fiscal crisis. This was the case for over two years following the beginning of the September 2000 Intifada.

Throughout this entire period, Israel continued to control key services such as electricity, telephone, and even Palestinian internet access.[15] The Israeli government has confiscated more than 80 per cent of Palestinian groundwater, thereby supplying 25 per cent of Israel's water consumption. Israel consumes four times more water per capita than the Palestinians living in the OPT.[16]

All this naturally led to a massive decline in Palestinian living standards. Between 1994 and 2000 unemployment tripled and GDP declined by 21 per cent.[17] By 2000, more than 20 per cent of Palestinians were living on less than US$2 per day, the official UN poverty threshold.

This is the world the Palestinians lived in from day to day under the Oslo Accords. They progressively lost control over every basic element of their lives, while Israel no longer bore the burden of direct military occupation. There are countless practical examples of this degrading daily experience. We can find one in Annex 1 of the 1995 Interim Agreement (Oslo II), describing at length the security procedures for border crossings. Palestinians returning to the West Bank and Gaza Strip pass through a 'Palestinian wing' of the border terminal, replete with Palestinian flags and Palestinian policemen. This demonstration of Palestinian 'independence' occurs under the final authority of an Israeli officer with ultimate responsibility for the terminal. Annex 1 stipulates: 'Passengers will pass via a Palestinian counter, where their documents and identity will be checked. Their documents will be checked by an Israeli officer who will also check their identity indirectly in an invisible manner.'

THE SEPTEMBER 2000 INTIFADA

The Oslo period had used the rhetoric of 'peace', but occupation was the lived reality, and Palestinian conditions grew steadily worse. Negotiations continued for seven years. The Israeli military had 'redeployed', but the Palestinian daily experience was that Israel continued to seize their land, and settlements multiplied around their towns and villages. The uprising was not a choice of violence over peace, but a reaction to the continuing institutionalised violence of the Israeli occupation.

Local and world media reported regularly on how Israeli policies were affecting the Palestinian civilian population, painting vivid pictures of the living situation in the OPT. The Israeli government was fully aware of what it was doing, and of its consequences. These were not unintended by-products, but the results of a deliberate strategy of *collective punishment.*

Israeli government officials continue to state publicly that their policies aim to inflict severe damage on the population as a whole. Prime Minister Ariel Sharon summed it up in an address to the Israeli Knesset on 4 March 2002: '[Palestinians] have to be hit hard, and it has to hurt them...Israel must cause them losses, victims, so that they will feel it.'[18]

This policy of collective punishment takes many forms. Military force is the most obvious. Since the Intifada began, the Israeli military has repeatedly used excessive and arbitrary force against demonstrations and against civilian residential areas. In the first two and a half years of the Intifada, Israeli troops or settlers killed over 2,300 Palestinians.[19] Palestinian children accounted for more than 450 of those deaths.

The Israeli government has claimed that many of these child deaths came when Israeli troops were fired on by 'armed Palestinian gunmen' hiding behind Palestinian children as 'human shields'. An official Israeli government publication from the Ministry of Foreign Affairs says:

The PA even provided transportation, bussing children to violent flashpoints far from their own neighbourhoods. Armed Palestinian policemen and members of the Fatah militia, the Tanzim, often stood just behind this human shield of juvenile 'martyrs' and directed gunfire at Israeli soldiers, knowing they can exploit the children's wounds for their propaganda purposes, should Israeli soldiers have to defend themselves.[20]

The facts indicate otherwise. For example, in 2002, 85 per cent of Palestinian child deaths occurred in situations where these children were not involved in clashes or demonstrations.[21] Where children have been killed in demonstrations, the evidence overwhelmingly shows that these deaths generally occurred in situations where no exchange of fire had occurred. Defence for Children International/ Palestine Section (DCI/PS) studied 27 cases of child death during demonstrations in the first three months of the Intifada. They compared the official description of the demonstrations from three different sources: the Israeli army; *The Jerusalem Post*, one of Israel's leading English language newspapers; and the eyewitness reports of observers. The study found that all three sources – including the official Israeli military reports – concurred: there had absolutely been no exchange of fire at the time when Israeli troops shot these children.[22]

The Israeli army also undertakes military assaults on Palestinian residential areas. Many child deaths have occurred when Israeli tanks and helicopters repeatedly and indiscriminately shelled civilian areas. The Israeli army has adopted the practice of demolishing large swathes of residential areas with military bulldozers, backed by tanks, helicopters and troops. This terrifying practice caused the deaths of at least seven children in 2002 and 2003 – children trapped inside the buildings at the time of demolition and crushed to death as their homes collapsed on top of them.

These physical attacks and assaults are the most dramatic side of Israel's collective punishment of the Palestinians. The other side takes the form of a series of long curfews in the majority of Palestinian towns and villages, and hundreds of checkpoints navigable only with Israeli-issued permits. Hundreds of thousands of people spent most of 2002 and 2003 forcibly confined to their homes by army-imposed curfews. For example, Nablus, a city of 126,000 people, was under curfew for three-quarters of the time over an eight-month period following 21 June 2002. Palestinians living in the West Bank actually spent more time under curfew than free of it in the last six months of 2002.[23]

An outsider can scarcely imagine what these checkpoints and closures mean for Palestinian daily life. The simplest tasks become impossible as Israel prevents virtually the entire population from leaving their cities and small villages. Children and teachers are unable to reach their schools; the sick cannot get to hospitals; labourers spend hours trying to circumnavigate the checkpoints to reach work. The Israeli journalist Gideon Levy, pleading for the Israeli public to try to comprehend the effects of the checkpoints on Palestinian life, once described what he had witnessed:

> The sick, the elderly, children and women in labor – is there still a need to repeat the facts? – were cruelly and aggressively driven away. More than a few lost their lives: children who had thrown rocks at soldiers and were shot, drivers who tried to find alternate routes and were shot from a distance, and sick people whose strength failed them. Recently the Israeli Arab writer Salman Natoor described in a chilling way how he was once delayed for a long time at the Qalandiyah checkpoint while an ambulance siren wailed until it suddenly stopped. Natoor went to investigate and was told that the patient in the ambulance had died.[24]

This policy of collective punishment has caused an unprecedented humanitarian disaster. By the end of 2002, 75 per cent of the population was now living below the official US$2 per day UN poverty line.

These policies have had a devastating effect on health in the occupied territories. A January 2003 study by CARE International reported a 17.5 per cent rate of chronic malnutrition among children aged 6–59 months in the Gaza Strip, and 7.9 per cent in the West Bank. Chronic malnutrition ('stunting'), indicated by a child's height-for-age ratio, indicates past growth failure and can lead to serious, irreversible growth and developmental delays.[25] The CARE study attributed the increase in malnutrition rates to Israel's restriction on Palestinian freedom of movement.

The collapse of the Palestinian economy and of their health care system has hit Palestinian children hardest. Children constitute 53 per cent of the Palestinian population. Because they depend on adults for their survival and wellbeing, the children suffer when a parent is unemployed or unable to reach their place of work. The areas having the highest rates of poverty and most affected by closure and house demolition, such as Hebron, Khan Younis and Gaza City, for example, are the areas with the highest number of children (both absolute and relative).[26]

There is one more – potentially very dangerous – element of Israel's current collective punishment policies. In 2002 Israel began constructing a massive concrete wall, eight metres high, which looks like the outer wall of a prison, on confiscated Palestinian land. According to projections from Israeli and Palestinian organisations, it will completely surround each of the Palestinian 'enclaves'. The wall is formalising the prison-like essence of Palestinian life. It is cutting off entire communities from their main source of livelihood: their agricultural lands and their water resources. Permits will control all movement in and out. The final contours of the wall coincide almost exactly with the various Israeli settlement plans put forward since 1967.

All these are not simply emergency measures. They are institutionalised policies, implemented to varying degrees since the occupation began in 1967. Palestinian society has felt their effect for decades. This is the context for the detention of children. Israel's policies of arresting and imprisoning Palestinian minors is embedded in a broader web of repression and intimidation aimed at sustaining occupation. They are simply elements of collective punishment, as Israel steadily divides the West Bank and Gaza Strip into a series of isolated Palestinian cantons separated by concrete walls, bypass roads and Israeli settlements.[27]

3
Israel's System of Control

On 7 June 1967 the new Israeli occupying forces in the West Bank issued Military Proclamation No. 1. It justified itself with the words 'in the interests of security and public order'. Since that time, the Israeli authorities have issued over 2,500 such military orders, with enormous impact on Palestinian life.

These orders serve as justification every time the Israeli authorities arrest a Palestinian child in the occupied territories. Issued by the Israeli Military Commander in the OPT, they provide the 'legal' basis for charging Palestinians with political offences and for bringing them before the Israeli military courts, which enforce these decrees and punish offenders with imprisonment and fines.

This chapter explores how Israel's system of control operates in the West Bank and Gaza Strip, focusing on the role of these military orders and military courts which are specifically designed to provide the legal framework for the Israeli occupation. We shall look at the structure of the court system, and also how the courts function in practice. We shall see how the system relies heavily on information gathered from detainees themselves, and is partly aimed at coercing Palestinians to work with the Israeli authorities against their own communities.

MILITARY ORDERS

The Israeli military command issues military orders as decrees which immediately become law, binding on all Palestinians in the occupied areas.[1] After the Oslo Accords were signed, the military order system continued to apply to all Palestinians in the West Bank or Gaza Strip, even those living in areas defined as under Palestinian Authority control. They do not apply to Israeli settlers living in the West Bank and Gaza Strip, who are governed by Israeli civil law. Palestinians are often unaware that new military orders have been issued because they have not been made public or translated into Arabic.[2] They are frequently revised, almost impossible to challenge, and can apply retroactively.

Israel rationalises military orders as necessary for 'security'. In practice, security is defined so broadly that virtually any restriction of Palestinian freedom can be covered. For example, in 1980, the Military Commander of the West Bank issued a military order that effectively placed all West Bank universities under military control.[3] Hiring and firing university staff, creating new departments and facilities, the curriculum itself, and even the books held in university libraries came under the control of the Israeli military. During the first Intifada, a number of military orders closed universities for long periods – Birzeit University, near the West Bank town of Ramallah, has been ordered closed 15 times, including a 51-month period immediately after the first Intifada began.

Many other military orders restricted freedom of speech and organisation. Military Orders No. 50 and No. 51, for example, authorised the Israeli military to confiscate newspapers or other materials published without licence. Israeli military censors approved all printed material and were free to edit or delete articles, or to refuse permission for publication. The Israeli Censor banned thousands of books from publication and distribution in the OPT.

Israel also used these orders to expropriate and confiscate Palestinian land for settlement construction, typically claiming 'security' requirements. Military Orders Nos 59, 108, 321 and 378 authorised the Israeli military to confiscate any land for 'security reasons', prevented anyone whose land had been expropriated from appealing to a local court, and abolished the requirement that the authorities publish their intention to expropriate. The victim can only appeal to the Israeli High Court, which clearly stated it would not dispute any military decision where 'security' was a justification.[4] Israel has confiscated thousands of acres of land this way for military reasons, and then turned it over for settlement construction.

As we discussed in Chapter 2, a new phase of Israeli control over the OPT began in 1981 when Israeli policy took aim at the Palestinian economy, implementing a policy of deliberate de-development and fostering complete dependency on Israel. The military order system was one of the major tools to this end. Military orders required Palestinians to submit all industrial proposals to an office headed by an Israeli military representative. Only this office could authorise investment projects, dictating the 'administration of the industrial project and the way in which capital is invested'.[5] Other military orders empowered the Israeli military to transfer money 'found in a bank or credit institution to the Bank of Israel', and made it illegal to take any commodity into or out of the West Bank or Gaza Strip without a permit – issued by the Israeli military.[6] Military orders even regulated growing decorative flowers.[7]

In summary, military orders primarily aim at controlling the Palestinian population, facilitating the confiscation of land, preventing any independent growth of the Palestinian economy, and undermining Palestinian social and cultural life. They have served as the legal underpinning for Israel's progressive domination of the West Bank and Gaza Strip. The enforcement of these orders takes place in another arm of the Israeli military, the military courts.

Palestinians in the OPT charged with political offences are arrested, prosecuted, tried and imprisoned entirely within the Israeli military system, which also appoints and administers the bodies which hear any appeals, except those made to the Israeli High Court.

THE MILITARY COURT SYSTEM

In the post-Oslo period two sets of courts have operated in the West Bank and Gaza Strip. Civil courts operated by the Palestinian Authority handle matters internal to Palestinian society such as inter-Palestinian crime, while Israeli military courts deal with anything defined as relevant to Israel's 'security'.[8]

One judge and two magistrates preside over the military courts. These three individuals as well as the prosecutor are all military personnel. While the judge is a legal professional, the two magistrates do not necessarily hold any legal qualifications. The judges are often settlers who bring their own prejudiced view of Palestinians to the court.

Lawyers face extreme difficulties defending Palestinians before these military courts. Accessing case files is laborious. Many obstacles can prevent lawyers from visiting their clients before a court session, so they are rarely able to explain the whole process to them or set out options before the hearing. Moreover, children regularly face extreme forms of physical and psychological abuse during interrogation without any access to legal representation. They often sign confessions before the trial takes place, whether or not they understand the document they are signing.

Accessing case files and visiting detainees

Lawyers spend countless frustrating hours trying to obtain case information. Case files are handwritten in Hebrew and held at the court so lawyers have to arrange to copy the files on the court premises. As one Palestinian lawyer described the process:

> In order to get information about the file, I have to ring the court and arrange a date to come and copy the file. When I get to the court I have to wait for soldiers to stand with me while the file is photocopied. Often I might wait an hour or two until soldiers make themselves free for this. I have to pay a few cents for every page and so have to be sure I have small change with me. My file photocopying days are difficult and I dread them. After I have photocopied the files I then have to get them translated and typed up as they are handwritten in Hebrew. We can't afford to pay the fees of a legal translator so the quality of the translation is often poor. But the story doesn't stop there. Often on the day of the hearing the prosecutor will come to court and say, 'I want to make some changes because I have received new information.' Prosecutors have the right to change the information on which their case is based on the day of the hearing. Then I have to go through the whole process of copying this new information which means more delay.[9]

One of any lawyer's major professional responsibilities is to meet with the client to explain the court process, the charges brought by the prosecutor and the various options open for defence. International standards hold that the time spent between lawyer and client is a basic necessity in building a defence, and this communication must be confidential. In the case of Palestinian children in the military court system, none of these basic rights exist.

Palestinian child detainees have no guaranteed and automatic right to legal representation – lawyers must seek permission from Israeli military or prison authorities to visit their clients. Procedures can be impossibly bureaucratic. The authorities often refuse access, or revoke permission at whim. When visits are granted, they take place at considerable personal risk to the lawyer, and prison guards and soldiers create delays and harassment. Interviews are neither comfortable nor confidential – children are often handcuffed during the meeting or behind an iron mesh, and prison guards or soldiers are almost always present.[10]

Because of this systematic obstruction and harassment, most children do not see a lawyer until they reach the court, and are brought to trial with no clear idea of court procedures, the charges they face, and the possible sentence they may receive.

The trial

The environment of a typical military court session is antagonistic to detainees and their families. Children are usually handcuffed during the trial and flanked by heavily armed soldiers. Families generally have not seen their children since their arrest, and the experience is especially traumatic because they are denied any private or physical contact with their children. The Jurist Birgitta Elfstrom from the Swedish Section of the International Commission of Jurists, who observed a trial in the Beit El Military Court on 8 July 2001, reported a typical experience. Said, a 15-year-old boy accused of stone throwing, had spent four months in prison before his trial:

> Said was taken into the courtroom by armed soldiers. He was handcuffed and looked very pale and shy. Neither his mother nor I were allowed to shake hands with him or sit on the public bench next to him. I was not even allowed to offer him a piece of chocolate in the break. Instead, M-16-armed soldiers with bullet-proof waistcoats pushed us back in the court room.
>
> ...I asked the prosecutor if the Military Court knew anything about the UN Convention on the Rights of the Child and if ten months of imprisonment would benefit Said or be 'the best for him'. I also asked if they have a rehabilitation program and 'why they haven't got a juvenile court system'. He answered that Said was not a child. The court's definition of a child is a person who hasn't yet reached the age of 14. A child between 14 and 16 'is a big child' and if more than 16, an adult.
>
> ...Later, the judge reduced Said's sentence to eight months of imprisonment and 1500 'shekel' [fine] which is a part of the punishment. Said's mother hoped that they would find people to help them to collect that amount of money so he could be released very soon. If not, he would have to remain in prison for two [extra] months.[11]

Palestinian lawyers and child detainees face language barriers which further disadvantage them during court sessions. All court proceedings are conducted and recorded in Hebrew, which Palestinian lawyers often do not speak fluently. The court does not employ professional translators, but relies on Israeli soldiers who happen to speak Arabic. Lawyers estimate that only 60 per cent of the translation is accurate, and the accused children often cannot understand what is occurring during their trial.

Court regulations allow only immediate family members to attend the trials. These family members must hold an ID card that is only issued to Palestinians aged 16 years and over. The Israeli military says this regulation exists because children under 16 are too young and may disrupt the court proceedings.[12] In other words, a child of 14 has reached an age where he may be arrested by heavily armed Israeli soldiers in the middle of the night, face torture, be brought before a military court, and sentenced to many months in prison for the alleged offence of throwing stones, yet his 15-year-old brother isn't considered mature enough to attend his trial.

Court neutrality

Trials before military courts are seriously flawed. Judges and prosecutors are officers serving in the IDF or the reserves. Judges are appointed by the IDF Regional Commander upon the recommendation of the Military Advocate General who is advised by a special committee. They are promoted almost exclusively from the ranks of prosecutors. Once appointed, judges have no right of tenure and can be removed by the Regional Commander. As a result of this lack of tenure and the close links between military judges and prosecutors, serious doubts have been expressed about their impartiality.[13]

This report by Amnesty International identifies a key problem with the military court system – there is no neutral and separate judicial apparatus. Judges and prosecutors are appointed by the Israeli military, the same body that arrests, detains and interrogates the children. The military's primary role in the OPT is maintaining the occupation, and children brought to court are by definition accused of opposing this occupation.

The lack of court neutrality is compounded by the role of the notorious Israel Security Agency (the Shabak), a secret intelligence force reporting directly to the Israeli Prime Minister, and not under the authority of any government ministry. The Shabak plays a central role in the occupation, including undercover surveillance of Palestinian society, recruiting and following up Palestinian collaborators, and interrogating and torturing detainees in the four interrogation centres directly under its control. The Shabak has a central but covert role in the military court system. In practice, it has ultimate authority over court decisions and often instructs judges to pass particular decisions on the basis of 'secret evidence'. This is particularly evident in administrative detention cases, in which judges will decide to hold someone without charge or trial on instructions from the Shabak. The Shabak's role also extends to non-administrative detention cases, including those of children. Court judgements may be determined by the Shabak before the trial begins. One of the authors of this book witnessed a parole hearing at Megiddo Prison during which the judge dismissed three out of four reduction-in-sentence cases on the basis of such 'secret' decisions – that is, before the hearing the Shabak had instructed him not to release the children.

Court Sentencing

Examining how children have been sentenced provides more evidence of the lack of neutrality in military courts. In periods of widespread resistance to the occupation children receive longer sentences, even though their alleged offences are the same. For example, military courts have imposed increasingly long sentences on Palestinian children since 1999, particularly after the beginning of the current Intifada in September 2000.

Perhaps the clearest comparison is between the years 1999, prior to the current Intifada, and 2000, which marked its onset. In both years, DCI/PS estimates that approximately 95 per cent of arrested children faced the same charge: throwing stones. In 1999, 43 per cent of these children were sentenced to less than one month of prison, while 19 per cent received sentences between six months and a year. In 2000, the proportion of children receiving sentences of less than one month had decreased to 35 per cent, while the proportion of sentences between six months and a year doubled, reaching 40 per cent. This suggests that the courts sentence Palestinian children on the basis of the political atmosphere in the OPT at the time of sentencing rather than on any objective legal standard.

Military courts thus serve as a tool of the military order system, offering a façade of justice to the process of detention and sentencing, while really serving as a key linchpin of the occupation. Lawyers who represent Palestinians before the military courts are well aware of this dilemma. While doing their best to defend detainees, lawyers readily admit that they are participating in a system actually designed to support the occupation. Many lawyers believe their most important role is to offer detainees human contact and psychological support rather than legal counsel.

INFORMATION GATHERING, COLLABORATORS AND INFORMANTS

The military court system relies heavily on information gathered from detained children in order to arrest and convict others. The courts commonly judge a child guilty solely on the testimony of another detainee, with no corroborating evidence.

Box 3.1   What Lawyers Say About the Military Court System

One of the most difficult things for me as a lawyer is living with the double injustice: the detention and the use of the courts as a tool of oppression...Objectively I am colluding with the system. They [the Israeli military] need lawyers to provide the appearance of legality...The occupying judiciary and the lawyers and accused have differing concepts about what is happening in court. The 'judiciary' has some illusion that they are administering justice. The accused and their lawyers don't experience this as justice but as another kind of shooting. It's not a court for everyone.[14]

In the majority of cases my role is really to show the child that someone Palestinian is around in a very hostile environment. It is human contact. That is what all the lawyers think...Often prisoners are beaten in the court and I feel like a captain of the occupation. My hands are totally tied, I have no real role.[15]

I find myself fighting a system I don't know or understand. I can't see the evidence against my clients...Ultimately our role is more psychological, to give detainees the feeling that they are not forgotten...It is difficult for lawyers to have confidence in a system where most evidence is provided by soldiers – and a judge who is part of that military system and process has to choose between the evidence of soldiers and children...The whole system is a military one and often the judges are settlers so lawyers have to suffer their personal and political prejudices.[16]

Palestinian minors are treated as suspects from the moment they enter the military court system. There is no parole office. There is no possibility of providing the court with a social report as no attention is paid to such issues...Our role is purely damage limitation. Basically it is very frustrating and a waste of time, but I try to make their life as difficult as possible by raising as many issues as I can and demanding to see things like the outcome of an interrogation.[17]

We are seen as a necessity, they want to make it seem like a court.[18]

This practice does not necessarily require ongoing substantial contact with the Israeli authorities, but may involve releasing the prisoner in exchange for information. This is particularly repugnant when very young children are placed in terrifying situations and told they will not be released until they provide some information. DCI/PS handled a typical case in 1999: a 13-year-old boy from Jalazon refugee camp was arrested in the middle of the night, pulled from his bed, deliberately not informed about where he was going, and interrogated late into the night:

At 2 am the soldiers came and entered the house and dragged K. from his bed, tied his hands behind him, blindfolded him and took him from the house. They placed him in a jeep and for two hours he was driven around so he didn't know where they were taking him. Finally, they took him to Beit El detention centre which is only 2km from his house. K. had no idea where he was and they refused to tell him. K. was taken to interrogation the following day at approximately 10 pm. They continued interrogating him until midnight for throwing stones. K. was very tired, but he was prevented from sleeping. He began to cry and asked to be allowed to sleep but they replied, 'only if you confess. Then we will let you sleep. We want to sleep too.' He signed a piece of paper in Hebrew which he didn't understand. After signing the paper (at this point it was beyond midnight) they didn't let him sleep but took him back to the camp where they showed him pictures of other boys and asked him to tell them where they lived. K. did not know why they wanted these boys but he showed them their houses. Later on, it turned out that the confession which he had signed said that he had been throwing stones with these boys. He was eventually released with a 2000 NIS fine.[19]

Campaigns of arbitrary arrest against children are aimed at exactly this type of information gathering, as a Shabak officer admitted to one Palestinian lawyer during a military court session in late 2000. When asked why so many children were arrested, the Shabak officer said the aim was to gather as much information as possible, explaining, 'We shake the tree, whatever falls from it we take – whatever doesn't, stays.'[20]

In addition to one-off information gathering, Israel's arrest of Palestinians is partly aimed at the recruitment of longer-term collaborators and informants. Collaborators are a critical element to Israel's system of control in the OPT and this practice is particularly pernicious when it involves children. Indeed, the Coalition to Stop the Use of Child Soldiers discussed this practice in a recent report on Israel.[21]

Throughout history, collaborators have been a major issue in societies under occupation.[22] Israeli military commanders have acknowledged that recruiting Palestinian collaborators has played an important role in maintaining the occupation. The Palestinian resistance movement has long debated how to deal with this issue.[23]

The nature of Israel's rule in the OPT facilitates recruiting collaborators, and in turn, the recruitment of collaborators reinforces Israeli control. Palestinians are forced to depend on Israel's military establishment to fulfil the most basic life tasks, seeking permission from the Israeli authorities at all points. The most obvious is movement from one area to another. International travel, and all movement between areas in the West Bank and Gaza, is totally regulated by Israeli-issued permits. In order to travel only a few kilometres from one city to another in the West Bank, Palestinians must apply to the Israeli authorities for permits which will only be issued after the Israeli secret police have approved the application. Without them movement is almost impossible.

This system of permits, closure and checkpoints became much more apparent following the Oslo Accords than it was before 1993. For example, Palestinian passports exist but, in fact, all passports must be approved by the Israeli military after passing through the Palestinian bureaucracy. All births and deaths must be registered with the Israeli military, and life is impossible without an Israeli-issued ID card that must be carried at all times.

In this way, Israel maintains a carrot-and-stick approach to occupation. The Israeli army forces every Palestinian to submit and follow their procedures or be dealt with extremely harshly. As Moshe Dayan, then Israeli Defence Minister, stated a few months following the beginning of occupation in 1967:

> Let the individual know that he has something to lose. His home can be blown up, his bus license can be taken away, he can be deported from the region; or the contrary: he can exist with dignity, make money, exploit other Arabs, and travel in [his] bus.[24]

Of course, complying with military orders is not as simple as Moshe Dayan states. Permit-seekers face a torturous process navigating bureaucracy and military officialdom. The Shabak are intimately involved in the process, and permits may be revoked at any time. This total dependence deliberately encourages active collaboration with the secret police to obtain favours or move applications along. The Israeli authorities may grant favours to certain individuals who become known in their communities for their ability to speed up a permit, authorisation, or otherwise prohibitively slow process. B'Tselem quotes a 34-year-old collaborator who was eventually granted residency in Israel:

> I was young. I was attracted by the idea of having power and status and earning fast, easy money. I liked walking around with a concealed weapon, getting through Israeli army roadblocks with no problems, dispensing favours, especially permits, to whoever I wanted.[25]

Of course, most people who apply for or receive a permit are not collaborators. Other factors also influence an individual's ability to obtain permits: class background is important, as are links with the Palestinian Authority or employment in an international organisation.[26] Israel has deliberately established a system that enforces dependency and thereby facilitates recruiting collaborators.

This pressure to collaborate and inform is even more acute once a Palestinian is arrested. Violent forms of torture during interrogation are often coupled with promises of respite or release if the prisoner agrees to work with the Israeli authorities. Detainees can be offered the alternative of long punishment and violence towards their families, or quick release if they agree to provide information on an ongoing basis. This is an even more insidious practice when applied to Palestinian children. One child described his experience of torture in 1998, linked with attempts to recruit him as a collaborator:

> The interrogators would say, 'If you work with us we'll give you money and let you go otherwise you'll be given a very long sentence.' When I refused they tied me to a small chair with 15cm legs (kindergarten chair) and tied my hands behind my back and my feet to the chair. They put a filthy sack (with no ventilation) on my head. I was placed in this position for 6–12 hours. Other times I was placed in solitary confinement.[27]

Reports from countless ex-detainees confirm this pattern. The Jerusalem weekly *Kol Ha'ir* carried an interview with a collaborator B., who stated that he had personally met more than 300 Palestinians whose sentences were reduced or dropped in return for collaborating.[28]

The overall system of Israeli military control is characterised by minute regulation of Palestinian life. This context is necessary not only to understand the actual experience that arrested Palestinian children face in interrogation centres, military courts and prison, but also to comprehend the underlying logic that drives the arrest of children and their treatment. The system is multi-faceted and highly legalistic. It relies not only on brute force, but on a codified set of orders and procedures that attempt to 'legalise' discrimination and obfuscate the actual practices of soldiers, police and settlers. This system is supported through the attempted recruitment of child collaborators, helped by the very dependency to which Palestinians are driven under Israeli military orders.

4
International Law
and Child Detention

Over the past 50 years, the international community has developed a complex system of human rights instruments. They identify specific rights held by all human beings, and appropriate mechanisms to protect those rights. In addition, the past 20 years have seen growing attention to the concept of *children's rights* and to measures for protecting children, recognising that they are uniquely vulnerable to rights violations.

Out of this new legal framework, detailed and well-established international *standards* have emerged which define the minimum acceptable treatment of children. These include detained children, who fall under the additional category of individuals 'deprived of their liberty'. A country's human rights record is based on the extent to which it adheres to these international standards, so these standards play a central role in assessing how Israel treats Palestinian child prisoners, and in understanding how Israel systematically violates their rights.

This chapter outlines the main provisions of international humanitarian and human rights law as they apply to the situation of Palestinian child prisoners. It aims to condense a broad body of law and legal discourse into a brief, user-friendly guide against which the following chapters should be read. Box 4.1 and Table 4.1 define key terms in the field and cite the main legal references for the rights and principles discussed here and used throughout the rest of the book. The chapter focuses on the more recent UN Convention on the Rights of the Child (CRC), which specifies a wide range of rights and protection measures for children, and is the most widely ratified human rights treaty ever. It ends by examining the international prohibition on torture, and issues concerning its definition.

Table 4.1   Overview of Rights and Principles

Right/Principle	Human Rights Instrument and Article
General Principles	
'Best interests' principle	CRC, art. 3.1
'Last resort' principle	CRC, art. 37b
Principle of non-discrimination	ICCPR, art. 2.1; CRC, art. 2; Standard Minimum Rules, 6.1
Right to be presumed innocent until proven guilty	UDHR, art. 11; CRC art. 40.2 b.i; Standard Minimum Rules, 84.2
The aim of punitive measures is rehabilitation and reformation.	ICCPR, art. 10.3; CRC, art. 40.1
Children shall be accorded treatment appropriate to their age and legal status.	ICCPR, art. 10.3; CRC, art. 37c
Child-specific laws, procedures, authorities and institutions should be established.	CRC, art. 40.3
Special measures shall be available to ensure that children are dealt with in a manner appropriate to their wellbeing and proportionate both to their circumstances and the offence. Examples of 'special measures' include: care, guidance and supervision orders; counselling; probation; foster care; education and vocational training programmes and other alternatives to institutional care.	CRC, art. 40.4
Right to maintain communication with wider community, including family and legal counsel	CRC, art. 37c; Beijing Rules, 26.5; UN Rules for the Protection of Juveniles Deprived of their Liberty, 59–62
Rights Regarding Treatment	
Right to be free from torture, cruel, inhuman, and degrading treatment or punishment	UDHR, art. 5; ICCPR, art. 7; CRC, art. 37a; CAT
Right to be treated with humanity and respect for the inherent dignity of the human person	ICCPR, art. 10.1; CRC, art. 37c
Carrying and use of weapons by personnel should be prohibited in any facility where juveniles are detained.	UN Rules for the Protection of Juveniles Deprived of their Liberty, 65
Disciplinary measures constituting cruel, inhuman or degrading treatment shall be strictly prohibited, including corporal punishment, placement in a dark cell, closed or solitary confinement or any other punishment that may compromise the physical or mental health of the juvenile concerned.	UN Rules for the Protection of Juveniles Deprived of their Liberty, 67

Rights Regarding Arrest Procedures

Prohibition on arbitrary arrest or detention	UDHR, art.9; ICCPR, art. 9.1; CRC, art. 37b
Right to be promptly brought to court to see if detention is lawful	ICCPR, art. 9.4; CRC, art. 37d
Right to be informed of reasons for arrest	ICCPR, art. 9.2
Right to know of any charges	ICCPR, art. 9.2; CRC art. 40.2b.ii
Right to a defence and legal counsel	UDHR, art. 11(1); CRC, art. 37d; Beijing Rules, 15.1
Right not to be compelled to confess	CRC, art. 40.2b.iv

Rights Regarding Judicial Proceedings

Non-judicial proceedings should be used whenever possible when dealing with children.	CRC, art. 40.3b
Right to fair trial by impartial legal body	UDHR, art. 10; CRC, art. 40.1b.iii
Right to have case adjudicated as quickly as possible	ICCPR, art. 10.2b; CRC, art. 40.2b.iii
Right to appeal	CRC, art. 40.2b.v

Rights Regarding Pre-Trial and Post-Trial Detention

No detention with convicted persons while pending trial	ICCPR, art. 10.2a; Standard Minimum Rules, 8b
No detention with adults while pending trial	ICCPR, art. 10.2b; CRC, art. 37c; Standard Minimum Rules, 8d
No detention with adults after sentencing	ICCPR, art. 10.3; CRC, art. 37c; Standard Minimum Rules, 8d
Detention with same category of prisoners	Standard Minimum Rules, 8
Conditions of detention shall be hygienic.	Standard Minimum Rules, 12–13
Right to medical care	UN Rules for the Protection of Juveniles Deprived of their Liberty, 49–55; Beijing Rules 26.2
Detainees shall be provided food sufficient for maintaining good health. Food should be of good quality and well prepared.	Standard Minimum Rules, 20.1
Right to practice religion while detained	Standard Minimum Rules, art. 41–42
Right to pursue education while detained	UN Rules for the Protection of Juveniles Deprived of their Liberty, 38; Beijing Rules, 26.2; Standard Minimum Rules, 77
Right to pursue vocational training	UN Rules for the Protection of Juveniles Deprived of their Liberty, 42
Right to recreation and daily exercise in open air, where possible	UN Rules for the Protection of Juveniles Deprived of their Liberty Rules, 47

Notes: This list is not intended to be a comprehensive listing, but rather to offer an overview of the main provisions relevant to the situation of Palestinian child political prisoners and cite support for these provisions in existing human rights documents. See page 42 for definitions of the various human rights instruments.

Box 4.1 Key Terms Related to Human Rights and Humanitarian Law

International human rights law defines and protects rights held by every individual. These rights are inherent, meaning they are bestowed by nature of one's status as a human being, and applicable to everyone, regardless of distinguishing characteristics such as race, sex, nationality, religion, ethnic origin, and others.

International humanitarian law (IHL) specifically deals with war, armed conflict and occupation. It seeks to control the conduct of armed conflict, limit its effects, and to protect persons not taking part, or no longer taking part, in hostilities.

Treaties are legally binding agreements between States. In the UN system, various nations develop a treaty. Individual States may make 'reservations' on particular articles, noting that they do not intend to abide by that provision, or clarifying exactly what they understand it to mean. The State is then bound to uphold that particular article according to its specified definition. Certain articles are 'non-derogable', meaning that States cannot make reservations to them – they are considered to be integral to the spirit of the document, and if States were allowed to make reservations to them, they would in essence contradict the spirit of the treaty. The text of the treaty often specifically identifies these articles. Examples of such non-derogable articles are Article 6 of the Convention on the Rights of the Child, which outlines children's right to life, or Article 7 of the ICCPR, prohibiting torture.

UN Declarations and Rules set forth the general agreement of the international community about a particular issue. They are developed by the international community and adopted by the vote of a UN body, usually the General Assembly. In contrast with treaties, they are not subject to signature and ratification, and are not legally binding on States. However, they form an important part of the human rights framework as they further develop and clarify aspects of human rights treaties, and many of their provisions have subsequently been incorporated into binding treaties.

Customary International Law (CIL) is composed of rules that have been applied in such a way by the international community that they are considered binding on all countries, regardless of whether a country has signed and ratified a particular treaty containing the provision.[1] Customary law is not written, but has developed through practice. There is some debate over which principles form part of customary international law, but the international community has reached consensus on others, such as the prohibition on torture and the Hague Regulations. Some of the principles of CIL, referred to as *jus cogens,* cannot be rejected, changed or ignored in any way except by the creation of another such 'overriding' principle. The prohibition on torture is an important example.

Enforcement – The extent to which treaties are enforced varies. Ideally, since a State is legally bound to uphold the treaties it has signed, its national legislation will comply with the treaty provisions, and the State's domestic legal system will provide a means of enforcement. When there is no domestic means of enforcement, or when the domestic system fails to ensure compliance, there are enforcement mechanisms within the UN system. However, to make this work, political will is necessary. States must be willing to take action to ensure compliance with human rights and humanitarian treaties, and enforcement is frequently a political rather than a legal issue.

THE LEGAL INSTRUMENTS

Two bodies of international law govern the situation of Palestinian child prisoners:

- International humanitarian law (IHL), which deals with war, armed conflict and occupation;
- International human rights law, which defines and protects universal rights held by every human being.

These two bodies of law are designed to complement one another. Many internationally accepted provisions, such as the prohibition on torture, are part of both human rights and humanitarian law.

Also relevant is 'customary international law' (CIL) as well as the numerous United Nations (UN) guidelines and rules relevant to prisoners. Although not legally binding on UN member states, these guidelines represent the general consensus of the international community on the proper treatment of persons deprived of their liberty, including children. Palestinian children are entitled to special consideration as 'protected persons', defined in the Fourth Geneva Convention of 1949, and as 'children'.

As international human rights and humanitarian law have evolved, provisions designed to protect civilians, detainees and children have become increasingly specific. For example, while children were not mentioned as a distinct group in the Hague Regulations of 1907, the Convention on the Rights of the Child (CRC) was adopted in 1989, recognising that children are the most vulnerable to rights violations.

International humanitarian law

International humanitarian law seeks to limit the effects of armed conflict and is intended to protect persons not taking part, or no longer taking part, in hostilities. The main IHL instruments pertinent to Palestinian child political prisoners are:

- The 1907 Hague Convention (IV) Respecting the Laws and Customs of War on Land, and its annex, Regulations Concerning the Laws and Customs of War on Land (The Hague Regulations);
- The Geneva Conventions of 1949.

The Hague Regulations are widely considered to be customary international law and are thus binding on all countries, as are the majority of the provisions of the Geneva Conventions.[2]

The Hague Regulations do not contain specific protection measures addressing children, but Article 46 concerning territory occupied by the army of a hostile State stipulates that 'family honour and rights, the lives of persons, and private property, as well as religious convictions and practice, must be respected'. These broad protections are applicable to both adults and children.

The Geneva Conventions of 1949 and their subsequent Additional Protocols are a cornerstone of international humanitarian law. Article 1, common to all four Conventions, requires all High Contracting Parties to 'undertake to respect and to ensure respect for the present Convention in all circumstances'. The Fourth Geneva Convention relative to the Protection of Civilian Persons in Time of War specifically addresses situations of occupation. It sets out the protections to be provided to 'protected persons', those individuals 'who, at a given moment and in any manner whatsoever, find themselves, in case of a conflict or occupation, in the hands of a Party to the conflict or Occupying Power of which they are not nationals'.[3] Article 27 states:

> Protected persons are entitled, in all circumstances, to respect for their persons, their honour, their family rights, their religious convictions and practices, and their manners and customs. They shall at all times be humanely treated, and shall be protected especially against all acts of violence or threats thereof and against insults and public curiosity.

The Geneva Conventions and their Additional Protocols are specifically designed to offer protection for vulnerable populations during armed conflict and occupation, and apply to both children and adults. They include approximately 25 articles emphasising special protection for children, particularly Articles 77 and 78 of Protocol I. Article 77.1 states that: 'Children shall be the object of special respect and shall be protected against any form of indecent assault. The Parties to the conflict shall provide them with the care and aid they require, whether because of their age or for any other reason.'

The Geneva Conventions and their Additional Protocols also specify rights of prisoners of war, internees, and protected persons who are imprisoned.[4] Under the Fourth Geneva Convention, protected persons who are detained by the occupying power have the right to:

- freedom from torture (Articles 31, 32, and 147);
- prompt information on the charges against them (Art. 71);
- defence and legal counsel (Art. 72);
- an interpreter during interrogation and hearings in court (Art. 72);
- submit an appeal (Art. 73);
- detention inside the occupied territory (Art. 76);
- conditions of food and hygiene sufficient to maintain good health (Art. 76);
- spiritual assistance (Art. 76);
- visits by the International Committee of the Red Cross (Art. 76).

Article 76 specifically states, 'Proper regard shall be paid to the special treatment due to minors', and Article 31 says, 'No physical or moral coercion shall be exercised against protected persons, in particular to obtain information from them or from third parties.'

International human rights law

In 1948, the Universal Declaration of Human Rights laid the foundation of the United Nation's system of international human rights law. Later human rights instruments became increasingly specific and dealt with either a particular group of rights (such as civil and political, or economic, social and cultural) or with a specific group of people (for example, women or children). Many general provisions were then incorporated into more specific treaties such as the 1984 Convention Against Torture. The UN also standardised some provisions in declarations, not binding on State Parties, but reflecting generally accepted principles and practices which the international community agrees upon.[5]

Children's rights emerged as a distinct category of human rights out of this broader framework of human rights law. Particular documents and treaties had contained occasional references to children, but it had become clear that without a specific child focus they failed to acknowledge the unique status of children and led to situations where children fell through the cracks and remained insufficiently protected.

Ten years after the Universal Declaration of Human Rights, the UN General Assembly adopted the Declaration of the Rights of the Child in 1959, providing the first detailed measures of protection specifically addressing children on a global level. Thirty years later, the international community in 1989 adopted the UN Convention on the Rights of the Child. This binding document reflected three major shifts in the international approach to children, recognising that:

- children's *status* is distinct from that of adults, on whom they largely depend;
- children, as a distinct group of people, have specific *rights* (in contrast to the traditional approach, which focused on protection of minors but failed to acknowledge children as holders of rights);
- children have special *needs* and require additional protection due to their vulnerable status.

There is greater consensus about the CRC than about any other human rights treaty – only two countries, Somalia and the United States, have failed to ratify it – and its principles are accepted almost uniformly by the international community. It far exceeds any other international legal instrument in the number of protections it provides for children, and represents an important and positive step forward. Yet, it also leaves gaps, which the international community attempts to fill through additional protocols, case law, and the commentary of relevant UN committees. The most recent stages of this development are two optional protocols to the CRC: the Protocol on the Sale of Children, Child Prostitution and Child Pornography and the Protocol on the Involvement of Children in Armed Conflicts.[6]

Several human rights instruments provide specific protection pertinent to *detained* children. These include:

- Universal Declaration on Human Rights (UDHR,1948);
- International Covenant on Civil and Political Rights (ICCPR, 1966);
- Convention against Torture and Other Cruel, Inhuman or Degrading Treatment or Punishment (CAT, 1984);
- Convention on the Rights of the Child (CRC,1989);
- Standard Minimum Rules for the Treatment of Prisoners (1955);
- Minimum Rules for the Administration of Juvenile Justice (*Beijing Rules*,1985);
- Body of Principles for the Protection of All Persons under Any form of Detention or Imprisonment (1988);

- Basic Principles for the Treatment of Prisoners (1990);
- Guidelines for the Prevention of Juvenile Delinquency (*Riyadh Guidelines*,1990);
- Rules for the Protection of Juveniles Deprived of their Liberty (1990).

A set of detailed principles and protections for child prisoners has emerged from these many instruments. Many of them are also embedded in international humanitarian law. Table 4.1 summarises the main rights and principles from international human rights law that are applicable to the situation of Palestinian child political prisoners, and provides specific article references.

Certain protections, such as the principle of non-discrimination, are found in each of the instruments listed, while other protections may be included in one or more instrument but not in all. For example, the UN Rules for the Protection of Juveniles Deprived of their Liberty contains detailed protections for juvenile detainees that are not included in the International Covenant on Civil and Political Rights.

A fundamental principle concerning persons deprived of their liberty is that the aim of punitive measures should be reformation and rehabilitation. They are to be afforded key protections including the right:

- to be presumed innocent until proven guilty;
- to legal counsel;
- to be informed of charges;
- to challenge the legality of the detention, the charges, and the sentence;
- to a fair trial;
- to maintain communication with the outside world, particularly family members, while detained.

In terms of treatment, detained persons have the right:

- to be free from torture;
- to be free from cruel, inhuman, and degrading treatment or punishment;
- to be treated with humanity and respect for the inherent dignity of the human person;
- to be held in hygienic conditions of detention;

- to medical care;
- to practice their religion while detained.

Detention facilities are required to segregate prisoners according to category, both before and after trial. For example:

- Those held pending trial are not to be detained with convicted persons.
- Female prisoners should be separated from males.
- Political prisoners should be separate from those held for criminal offences.
- Child prisoners are not to be detained with adults.

There are specific rights and principles to be followed in the case of children deprived of their liberty. In particular, two principles are critical to any discussion of Palestinian child political prisoners:

- The 'Best Interests' principle, set forth in Article 3.1 of the CRC: In 'all actions concerning children, whether undertaken by public or private social welfare institutions, courts of law, administrative authorities or legislative bodies, the best interests of the child shall be a primary consideration'.
- The 'Last Resort' principle, in CRC, Art. 37b: 'The arrest or imprisonment of a child shall be in conformity with the law and shall be used only as a measure of last resort and for the shortest appropriate period of time.'[7]

Accordingly, when a State detains children it should:

- treat them appropriately to their age and status;
- ensure their wellbeing;
- use non-judicial proceedings whenever possible;
- establish child-specific laws, procedures, and institutions;
- utilise special measures such as counselling and probation where possible;
- allow them to pursue their education;
- allow them recreation and daily exercise in the open air, where possible.

International standards strictly prohibit any disciplinary measure that may compromise the physical or mental health of the child, such as placement in a dark cell or solitary confinement.

DEFINITIONS OF TORTURE

The international prohibition on torture is absolute and is codified in international humanitarian law, regional and international human rights treaties, and UN guidelines.[8] No circumstances whatsoever can justify its use. It is an indictable war crime and crime against humanity, pursuant to articles 7 and 8 of the Rome Statute of the International Criminal Court.[9] The prohibition of torture forms part of customary international law and thus is binding on all countries.

Legally, torture is a concept distinct from cruel, inhuman, or degrading treatment or punishment, for which international law provides no further definition. Yet, the question remains: Where does cruel, inhuman, or degrading treatment or punishment end and torture legally begin? Article 1 of the UN Convention Against Torture sets forth the definition of torture as:

> any act by which severe pain or suffering, whether physical or mental, is intentionally inflicted on a person for such purposes as obtaining from him or a third person information or a confession, punishing him for an act he or a third person has committed or is suspected of having committed, or intimidating or coercing him or a third person, or for any reason based on discrimination of any kind, when such pain or suffering is inflicted by or at the instigation of or with the consent or acquiescence of a public official or other person acting in an official capacity. It does not include pain or suffering arising only from, inherent in or incidental to lawful sanctions.

Thus, in order to constitute torture according to the CAT definition, four criteria must be met:

- The act must cause *severe* pain or suffering (mental or physical).
- The act must be *intentionally* inflicted to achieve a specific end (i.e. extracting information, punishment, coercion, intimidation, or for any other reason based on discrimination).
- The act must be *committed by a state functionary*, as defined above.

- It does not involve pain or suffering arising only from, inherent in, or incidental to *lawful sanctions*.

While establishing an agreed definition was a positive step in the movement against torture, the CAT definition remains vague and open to interpretation. What constitutes *severe* pain or suffering? How does one prove *intent*? In addition, the CAT definition excludes 'pain or suffering arising only from, inherent in or incidental to lawful sanctions', which leaves grey areas in which states can manoeuvre. Furthermore, who will decide when treatment qualifies as torture based on the accepted definition?

Although the CAT definition of torture is widely invoked as the ultimate standard, other international documents use different definitions. For example, the Rome Statute of the International Criminal Court defines torture as a crime against humanity 'when committed as part of a widespread or systematic attack directed against any civilian population, with knowledge of the attack'. It elaborates in Article 7.2e that:

> Torture means the intentional infliction of severe pain or suffering, whether physical or mental, upon a person in the custody or under the control of the accused; except that torture shall not include pain or suffering arising only from, inherent in or incidental to, lawful sanctions.

This definition differs from that of the CAT in not requiring that the act must be intended to achieve a particular goal. Numerous human rights treaties and international humanitarian law documents, including the CRC, the ICCPR, the Fourth Geneva Convention, and many regional human rights conventions, do not include any definition of torture at all.

Different interpretations of torture range from the position that *private* actors can be perpetrators of torture to the view that *patterns* of abusive treatment can constitute torture,[10] even though any one individual act within that pattern may not.[11] From a child rights perspective, it is absolutely essential to consider children's unique status when determining whether or not a particular act constitutes torture. The assessment must take into account such criteria as the age, physical stature, and level of maturity of the child, as well as the nature of the mistreatment, its physical and psychological effects, the context in which it was applied, and the duration.

International attempts to clarify what constitutes torture are an important part of the effort to offer the widest protections possible to the most likely victims of torture. Sadly, however, perpetrators routinely manipulate both the definition and the discourse in order to deny that their practices are indeed torture.

As we assess Israel's treatment of Palestinian child prisoners in the following chapters, we will frequently refer to the standards outlined here. There is a vast gulf separating Israel's treatment of Palestinian children from the very detailed and well-established international standards developed over the past 50 years to protect children, including those deprived of their liberty. Given this pattern, the following chapters will carefully examine why Israel has failed to adhere to these standards, and how it has managed to do so with relative impunity.

Part II
Arrest through Incarceration

5
Arrest and Transfer

Around 30 soldiers invaded my home at 2:30 a.m. on 17 August 2001. They searched the home and messed up our belongings, breaking the windows and confiscating our telephone agenda. They took me to the roof of the house for two hours and asked me about people they wanted. After that they took me to the street, blindfolded me and tied my hands with plastic ties behind my back. After that they forced me to walk quickly for around 1km. If I slowed down they pushed me. When we reached the jeep they pushed me inside and I hit my head on the roof. My brother Abed was inside the jeep. They forced us both to sit on the floor of the jeep...There were four soldiers who beat us while the jeep drove for about half an hour. They swore and insulted us throughout the journey and threatened to sexually assault us. After that we reached the military camp where they took us to the clinic. Then they put us in a yard where we were tied and blindfolded. We spent the whole night outside without food or drink.

Mohammed Al Jaberi, 17 years old[1]

Mohammed Al Jaberi is one of hundreds of Palestinian children arrested and imprisoned each year by the Israeli military for alleged 'security' offences. When Mohammed was arrested for the first time in December 2000 for stone-throwing, he was sentenced to eight and a half months in Megiddo Military Prison. This time, he was released after eight days of interrogation without ever being charged.

Like Mohammed, most imprisoned Palestinian children are charged with throwing stones at Israeli military personnel and military installations or at Israeli settlers. More serious charges might include stabbing or attempting to stab Israeli soldiers or settlers, throwing 'Molotov cocktails', or membership in a political group. Before 2002 Palestinian children were rarely involved in very serious offences such as planning violent attacks on civilians inside Israel, but since then such charges have increased.[2]

The Israeli military makes most of the arrests, although Military Order No. 898 authorises Israeli settlers to arrest any Palestinian, with no warrant required. These arrests take place in a number of contexts: at a child's home; on the street and at checkpoints; at the scene of an offence, real or alleged. In addition, since 2002 Israel has arbitrarily detained, and later released, hundreds of male Palestinian children during mass arrests.

Drawing on a wide range of compelling testimony, this chapter examines in detail the first stages in the process of child imprisonment – arrest and transfer to a detention facility.

HOW ISRAEL ARRESTS CHILDREN

Arrest at home

The Israeli army frequently arrests Palestinian children in their homes, in the middle of the night. In a typical scenario, a large number of Israeli soldiers will surround the child's residence, forcibly enter it and remove the child, all without any warrant. Usually the soldiers search the home, damaging or destroying the family's property, and are physically and verbally violent towards the suspected children and their families. The violence includes curses, offensive or threatening language, sexual harassment and physical beatings.

The following are typical excerpts from sworn affidavits:

On Sunday, 5 November 2000, around 12:30 at night, I was awakened by pounding on the door of our house. My parents, brothers, and sister also woke up. A voice from outside told us in Arabic to open the door, saying they were from the Israeli army. Before my father could open the door, they kicked the door, breaking the handle and lock. Other soldiers broke two window panes and called out to us to open the door.

As soon as the door opened, more than fifteen soldiers came into the living room. They included soldiers, who had blackened their faces, and two policemen. As they entered, they aimed their weapons at my family and me. A soldier asked me who I was. I told him that my name was Nadir and that I was ten years old. They asked me where my brother Muhammad was. My father answered, telling them that he was upstairs, in the empty room. Soldiers went upstairs and came back down with him. He was in handcuffs and his eyes blindfolded. In the meantime, several soldiers conducted a quick search of the bedrooms. They turned over the carpets and chairs and made a mess of the clothes.

When they were finished, the soldiers left with Muhammad, but returned two minutes later. The door was still open. They came over to me. The policeman said that I was a liar, and that my name was Sultan I told him that he was right. They told me to come with them. I said that I didn't have my shoes, and that I wanted to get them. One of the soldiers went to the bedroom with me. I took my shoes and put them on. Then the soldiers cuffed my hands behind me and blindfolded me.

Two soldiers held me by my shoulders and pushed me into the jeep, which was parked on the main road, one hundred meters from my house.[3]

Sultan Mahdi, 15 years old
from Al-Arroub Refugee Camp, Hebron District

At 12:40am on 15 December 2000, my family and I were asleep at home. We heard a very loud knock on the door of the house that woke the whole family. After five minutes my father went to the door and we discovered that Israeli soldiers had broken the glass in the door. Fifteen soldiers entered the house, three of them were masked and wearing civilian clothes. There were also two members of the Israeli intelligence dressed in civilian clothes. One of the masked soldiers asked me my name and for my ID card. I went to my room in order to bring the ID and one of the soldiers followed me. When I lent over to get the key for my drawer he kicked me on my back six times, pushing me to the ground. After that I got my ID and gave it to the soldier. The soldier saw a ticket I had from a trip to Canada that I made in September for study purposes. The soldier said I went there to learn how to throw stones. He searched my drawer, then grabbed me by my neck and took me back to the main room where I found the soldier had upturned our furniture.

The masked soldier whispered in my ear, 'We'll rape you one by one.'[4]

Murad Abu Judeh, 17 years old
from Al-Arroub Refugee Camp, Hebron District

On Monday, 25 December 2000, around 1:00 a.m., I was asleep in bed and awoke to the sound of violent pounding on the door of the house. My father opened the door and ten soldiers came in. Some of them wore [were] in masks and others, among them their commander 'Rami,' had black lines drawn on their faces. Within a few seconds, four soldiers came into my bedroom. They demanded that I get dressed and told me that I was under arrest for throwing stones. They took me outside.[5]

> *Muhammad Za'ul, 14 years old*
> *from Husan, Bethlehem District*

On Saturday, 6 January 2001, around 2:30 a.m., I awoke to the sound of an Israeli soldier who ordered me to get up. I opened my eyes and thought that I was dreaming that a soldier was waking me, but there were in fact five masked soldiers standing over me. Their appearance frightened me a lot. I got dressed and they took me outside.[6]

> *Hamzeh Za'ul, 15 years old*
> *from Husan, Bethlehem District*

Arrest itself can be traumatic, so international standards include detailed provisions to give as much protection as possible to children deprived of their liberty. Israeli arrest procedures like these are in clear contravention of all international standards, and blatantly violate the fundamental 'best interests' principle.

Arrest on the street and at checkpoints

The Israeli army commonly arrests Palestinian children on the street; they may be at a demonstration, or simply out in public. A soldier may 'remember' the face or clothes of a child they believe threw stones or participated in a demonstration. These children generally are not informed of the reason for their arrest or allowed to contact a lawyer or relative. Often they are forced to wait for long periods in handcuffs, without food, drink or shelter, sometimes in the direct sun, or in the freezing cold and rain.

Here is one of the many case reports of this type:

On 2 April 1999, 17-year-old A.Z. was arrested on his way to work. The soldiers made him wait on the side of the road for four hours before another soldier came and accused him of throwing stones. A.Z. spent two weeks in prison before being released on bail of 5000 NIS. During the court hearing a year later, the soldier who had accused A.Z. of stone throwing admitted that he had seen youths throwing stones for only one minute. He finished his shift immediately afterwards, returned to his home in a settlement, and was recalled to his post at 6 p.m. where he identified A.Z. The

DCI/PS attorney asked the soldier how he had recognized A.Z. and he had replied, 'because of his clothes'. When the attorney suggested that perhaps there were other people dressed like A.Z., wearing jeans and a tee shirt at the time, the soldier replied in the negative. Court proceedings continued until late 2000, when the court decided to dismiss the case.[7]

Israel issues special ID cards to all Palestinian residents 16 and over – they must carry them at all times. Their ID numbers are recorded in a central database along with information about place of residence, political affiliation, and prior arrests. Palestinians who pass through Israeli checkpoints and border crossings must present these cards. Israeli soldiers there often carry lists of ID numbers of individuals they want to detain. If a child's card number appears on a 'wanted' list, he or she is subject to immediate arrest. There is no way for the children to know if their names will appear on these lists, since new versions are issued frequently. If arrested, the children are not informed of the reason and are often forced to stand or kneel blindfolded with their hands tied behind them as they wait for transportation to an interrogation centre.

Arrest at scene of offence

Palestinian children are sometimes arrested while committing, or suspected of committing, the offence with which they are later charged. This happens only rarely. In these cases, too, children are systematically denied the protections they are entitled to under international human rights and humanitarian law, and are often exposed to extremely violent mistreatment.

In December 1998, 15-year-old Su'ad Ghazal was arrested after stabbing an Israeli settler in the northern West Bank. In the period immediately following the stabbing and throughout her interrogation, Su'ad was exposed to serious abuse, including being beaten, spat on, and dragged on the ground. She describes this period in the following extract from a sworn affidavit provided to DCI/PS:

On the morning of Sunday, 13 December 1998, I was arrested at the entrance of Tsvi Shemron settlement. When I tried to leave the place, two settlers in civilian clothes got out of two cars which cornered me there, assaulted me and took off my head-cover.[8] They beat me all over my body with their hands and feet. They held me by the hands and pulled me for about 10 metres, until they placed me inside the settlement. There, a crowd of settlers and soldiers started to beat me with rifle butts and boots, as well as with their hands and feet, and all this was accompanied with swearing and spitting. This lasted for about 15 minutes.[9]

On 20 February 2003, 15-year-old Riham Musa was shot several times by Israeli soldiers who accused her of trying to stab one of them with a knife. On 27 March 2003, Riham gave the following sworn affidavit to a DCI/PS attorney about the shooting:

When the soldiers saw me, they opened fire on me and I was hit in the stomach, although I didn't fall to the ground. I kept standing in the same spot, not moving, so that they would stop shooting. However, another soldier shot me in the leg and then I fell to the ground. Many soldiers appeared and started to cordon off the area, but none of them came near me. They asked me – from a distance – to take all my clothes off except my underwear, so that they could examine them. I said not unless they brought me a cover, so they did that and I took my clothes off under the cover, and put them on one side. They took them, even though I was wounded and bleeding.[10]

Riham was later taken to a hospital for surgery. Afterwards, she was shackled to her hospital bed, a procedure that generated widespread criticism. Physicians for Human Rights Israel intervened, noting that:

It is unreasonable to think that a 15-year-old girl, who was hit in the kidney, had part of her intestine surgically removed, is attached to an intravenous solution, and two bullets are still in her body, will escape from the hospital by overcoming the IDF guards – or that she poses any danger to the doctors or the other patients.[11]

Nevertheless, 20 days after her arrest, she remained handcuffed to the bed.[12]

Mass arrests

Since the Israeli army's invasion of Palestinian towns and villages in 2002, soldiers have subjected hundreds of Palestinian children to mass detention. There have been house-to-house searches of Palestinian neighbourhoods, round-ups on the street, and public announcements by the army that Palestinian males in a specified age range (which might be anywhere from 14 to 60 years) must come out of their houses and gather in a nearby school or other facility.

On 5 April 2002 Israel's military commander for the West Bank issued Military Order No. 1500, empowering the army to detain any Palestinian in the West Bank for up to 18 days, even if he or she is not suspected of any offence. During these 18 days, the detainee is generally not allowed to meet with a lawyer and does not appear before a court. This order, covering children as well as adults, was retroactive to 29 March 2002. According to Amnesty International, some 8,500 Palestinians from the West Bank were arrested in two phases between 27 February and 20 May 2002.[13] Human rights advocates estimate that some 5 to 10 per cent of these were children.[14]

These mass arrests left no area of the West Bank unaffected. In a May 2002 report, Amnesty International quoted Israeli military statistics regarding arrests that had taken place by 11 March 2002, including 800 from Tulkarem, 600 from Dheisheh refugee camp in Bethlehem, 600 from Qalqilya, and 200 from Al-Amari refugee camp in Ramallah. Of the 2,500 held during the first phase of mass detentions, from 27 February to 18 March 2002, all but 135 were subsequently released. During the second phase of arrests, beginning 29 March 2002, over 6,000 Palestinians were arbitrarily detained. Of those, 2,350 remained in custody as of 5 May 2002, most without charge or trial.[15]

Heavily armed Israeli troops carry out these types of arrest, treating children exactly the same as adults. The children are blindfolded and handcuffed. In some areas, they are taken to a temporary detention facility set up in a Palestinian school or some other large facility and then are transferred to a military installation within an Israeli settlement. In other locations they are transported directly to the chosen military camp.

The testimonies of these detainees leave no doubt that all, including children, are subject to systematic abuse and severe mistreatment, often amounting to torture.[16] During the 2002 arrests this abuse included:

- being handcuffed and blindfolded for extended periods of time;
- receiving little or no food;
- being denied access to medical treatment;
- being forced to sleep outside with insufficient or no bedding;
- being held in extremely overcrowded, unhygienic facilities;
- repeated physical and psychological abuse.

Detainees were often forced to strip to the waist upon arrest.[17] In May 2002 Amnesty International reported: 'Detainees were not allowed to notify their families, and the IDF and the GSS [Israel Security Agency] frequently appeared to lose track of individuals among the thousands of Palestinians they had detained.'[18]

Palestinians arrested and then freed during the Israeli military invasions that began on 29 March 2002 faced further danger on their release, because most of the West Bank was under direct re-occupation, and the population under total curfew. In many cases prisoners were released onto the streets in areas several hours' drive away from their homes. They were forced to seek shelter during the curfews, when anyone leaving their homes risked being shot by Israeli soldiers. The military did not give discharged prisoners documents showing that they had been released, and failed to return many confiscated ID cards. Consequently, these released detainees risked not only being shot, but also being re-arrested if Israeli soldiers stopped them. Most had to take refuge in nearby homes, empty buildings, and community centres.

The following statement by 17-year-old Samih Sameeh Atta Judeh from the Ramallah area is typical of the abuse faced by thousands of Palestinians, including hundreds of children, during the mass arrests in 2002:

On 30 March at 2:30 a.m. a group of Israeli soldiers came to my house. Five of them entered the house and others surrounded it. While the soldiers were in the house, they damaged our belongings and furniture. They were very aggressive towards my family and I. They began beating me while I was in the house, using their hands and rifle butts. After that, they transferred my brother and I in an armoured personnel carrier to the Al-Mughtarabeen school in Al-Bireh. We were placed in the outside yard of the school, handcuffed and blindfolded, and left there for two days in the rain and cold without blankets. The treatment there was very bad. The soldiers beat us and shouted at us.

After two days we were transferred to Ofer military camp. There we spent three days in an outside yard next to the office of the interrogators. We were still handcuffed and blindfolded and were left there in the rain and cold without blankets for three days. During these three days, we were given no food whatsoever. After the three days, I entered interrogation, which lasted for approximately 15 minutes. The interrogators asked me general questions, such as who my friends are and who visits me. I was beaten and threatened during the interrogation.

After the interrogation, they placed me in a small tent with around 60 other prisoners. Shortly after, they brought another small tent and we divided ourselves among the two. There were a few blankets available, but not enough for everyone and they were wet. Moreover, the tent was leaking. I spent two days in the tent. Afterwards, I was transferred to the barracks, where I spent another two and a half days. Finally, we were transported to Qalandia camp where they released us. As we were disembarking from the bus, we were again beaten. During the time we were detained at the school and after interrogation we were given very small portions of food. In one instance, one apple was given to be divided among four persons, one yogurt container was to be divided among ten persons, and we were each provided one and a half pieces of bread per day.[19]

The mass arrests and maltreatment of Palestinians in the winter and spring of 2002 prompted Amnesty International to call upon the Israeli government to establish an independent commission of inquiry to 'investigate the arbitrary arrests and the cruel, inhuman or degrading treatment immediately after detention of Palestinians arrested after 27 February 2002'.[20] However, despite international condemnation, mass detentions continued.

In April 2003 the Israeli military was widely criticised for its behaviour during the mass round-up and expulsion of Palestinian males from Tulkarem refugee camp.[21] The Israeli military invaded Tulkarem refugee camp on 2 April 2003 with the stated objective of searching for 'wanted' militants and weapons.[22] The soldiers used loud-hailers to order all Palestinian males between the ages of 15 and 40 to report to the courtyard of the UNRWA (United Nations Relief and Works Agency) girls' school, or face punishment.[23] Those who refused the order were detained during the house-to-house searches of the camp. Between 1,000 and 2,000 Palestinians were rounded up.[24]

The army initially held detainees at the UNRWA school they had requisitioned for use as a detention centre, and later expelled them, driving some to the nearby Nur Shams refugee camp, forcing others to walk there. They ordered the detainees not to return home until the Israeli military completed its operation in the refugee camp. Those expelled spent about three days in Nur al-Shams camp before being allowed to return home.[25] At the end of the operation, the

Israeli military announced that, out of the thousands of Palestinians arbitrarily detained for three days during the invasion of Tulkarem refugee camp, it had arrested 21.[26]

This April 2003 invasion was quite reminiscent of the events of the year before when, in March 2002, over 800 Palestinians from Tulkarem refugee camp had been arbitrarily detained.[27] However, the tactic of expelling detainees was a new practice and exacted a severe psychological toll. These expulsions rekindled widespread fears that detainees would suffer the same fate as Palestinian refugees from 1948 and 1967 who have never been allowed to return to their homes. There were also fears that the expulsions marked the start of a campaign of ethnic cleansing. Many Palestinians and outside commentators believed this could happen under the cover of the March 2003 war on Iraq.[28] Others predicted that such practices would continue and become increasingly severe.[29]

One of the detainees, 17-year-old camp resident Samer Omar, described in detail the experience during his three-day expulsion in April 2003:

> When the soldiers came they threatened to arrest, beat or shoot us if we did not come outside immediately. So, as we were ordered to, thousands of male residents went to the grounds of the UN school. Tulkarem camp is home to about 18,000 people, so as you can imagine there were a lot of us who left our homes. This was at around 6 a.m. Once we got there, the soldiers split us into groups, forcing the guys who were between 15 and 20 years old into one corner, separated from the rest. Some of the younger ones were too young to have ID, but the soldiers did not care. They then moved us into one of the school rooms. We were in the room together and the commander started to ask us if we wanted to work for the Israelis, saying he would give us money if we did. When the commander left one of the soldiers made us rip up pictures of martyrs and spit on them – for no reason except that he had the gun. Then he took a Quran and threw it on the floor and demanded that one of the guys stood on it, but he refused so the soldier then tried to force him by pointing his gun at his head. But the commander came back then so the soldier stopped it.
>
> At this point we were blindfolded and our hands were tied and we were put into one of the big military trucks and were driven to Nur Shams refugee camp eight kilometres away. It was 10 a.m. at this time I think. The soldiers took off our blindfolds, untied

our hands and let us go, saying we could go anywhere as long as it was not back to our homes in the Tulkarem camp. As far as I was concerned this was the most terrifying part of the whole ordeal. I knew I would find somewhere to stay in Nur Shams as I had friends there and everyone would try to help us. But what scared me most was that I might never be able to go back home again, nor see my family or my brother who is ten years old. Everyone believes the Israelis want to use the opportunity of war in Iraq to force all Palestinians from the land – and I thought I was one of the first in their latest attempt; first in 1948, then in 1967 and now me in 2003.

I spent the night at my friend's place, until Friday when we were told that the curfew had been lifted and we were allowed to go home. I can't tell you how relieved I felt when I went home, despite the fact that a lot of the camp had been attacked, including my home. I thought I would never see the place again so it was great.[30]

The experiences of these children highlight one of the most alarming aspects of the campaign of arbitrary mass arrests that terrorised and abused hundreds of Palestinian children simply for being male and Palestinian. When they are arrested they are not charged with any particular crime, and they have no legal recourse. Israel isolates the prisoners from the outside world, and there is no way to monitor what Israel is doing inside the detention centres.

The nature and scale of the mass arrests that began in 2002 is new, but the general strategy is not. As early as 1999, the Israeli army launched a campaign of 'group' arrests of Palestinian children accused of stone-throwing. They targeted and arrested groups of children from several locations. In 1999, DCI/PS handled over a hundred such cases of children aged from 12 to 17. They included 20 children from Deir Abu Mashal, a village in the Ramallah area; 21 from Al-Arroub refugee camp outside Hebron; and 16 from Beitounia and Al Jalazon refugee camps, both in the Ramallah area. Most of these children were arrested in the middle of the night from their homes.[31]

While group arrests were a new trend and prompted serious concerns from human rights organisations, the scale and nature of the 2002 mass arrests marked a radical change from the previous group arrests of relatively small numbers of Palestinian children. Additionally, the children arrested in 1999 were accused of a specific offence, unlike the hundreds arbitrarily detained in 2002, and the number of children involved in the 2002 mass arrests far exceeded those made earlier.

TRANSFER TO DETENTION AND INTERROGATION FACILITIES

When the Israeli army arrests Palestinian children, they often immediately confiscate their ID cards. In most cases they handcuff and blindfold detainees, and force them to sit on the floor of military vehicles while they transport them to an interrogation centre. These children usually have no idea where they are being taken or why they have been arrested, and they are not allowed to contact their families or a lawyer.

The following are excerpts from the many related case reports:

> The soldiers took me outside, covered my eyes with a kerchief and tied my hands and feet. We walked for about three hundred metres to their jeep. They put me inside, with my head next to the speaker of a tape recorder that they played at high volume for a few minutes. One of the soldiers hit me in the head. We drove for twenty minutes before getting to Etzion. They left me lying on the ground in a summer shirt in the freezing cold for around twenty minutes.[32]
>
> *Mufid Hamamreh, 15 years old*
> *from Husan, Bethlehem District*

> They handcuffed us behind our backs, covered our eyes with our clothes and made us sit on the ground for one hour...A vehicle came and took us to Al Fawwar area. During the trip, they kicked us and swore at us. They then took us to Majnouna Detention Centre and again made us sit on the ground until the afternoon. Then another vehicle came and took us to Etzion Detention Centre. They forbade us to move or speak during this transfer and all the time they were beating us and swearing at us. The driver drove slowly and took a long time to reach Etzion in order to prolong our suffering.[33]
>
> *Tareq Al Ribai', 17 years old*
> *from Dura, Hebron District*

Travel time to a detention facility depends on the place of arrest, of course, but many children report that the transit period far exceeds the amount of time required to go from the place of arrest to the interrogation centre. These consistent reports suggest that the trip is deliberately extended, either to disorient the child, to prolong the period of abuse, or both:

> Thirteen-year-old S.K. was arrested from his home in Al Jalazon refugee camp on 24 December 1999. Immediately after being taken into custody, S.K. was placed in a military jeep that drove around for two hours. He was then taken to Beit El Detention Centre, only 2km from his house.
> Because of the long period of transport, S.K. was completely disoriented and when he asked the soldiers where he was, they refused to tell him.[34]
>
> *K.S., 13 years old*
> *from Al Jalazon Refugee Camp*

Families are rarely told where their children are being detained and finding them can be complicated. Human rights organisations that specialise in locating detained Palestinians report that the process generally takes one to five days, sometimes longer.[35] Since many detained children are under 16 and have not yet received their ID cards, they often are not properly registered in the military's files.[36]

Once the arrested child is located, the military still denies their families any contact, and in most cases refuses access to their lawyers, too. One lawyer representing Palestinian children estimates that Israel allows him to visit only 10 per cent of the children he represents prior to their first court appearance.[37] In most cases, the first time families see their children is during that same court appearance.

Lawyers are often the only link between a detained Palestinian child and the outside world, so denying them access is particularly serious. Effectively, Israeli soldiers have total licence in the way they treat the children, with no external monitoring or observation. In some cases, Palestinian detainees have died shortly after Israel took them into custody.

Murad 'Awaisa was killed while in Israeli custody in March 2002, as described earlier in this book.[38] He was 17. In December 2002, an 18-year-old Palestinian man was found dead 20 minutes after being detained by Israeli Border Police operating in the southern West Bank city of Hebron.[39] The Border Police initially denied having taken the man into custody, but further investigation and pressure from human rights organisations resulted in the arrest of four Border Police accused of murdering the 18-year-old in revenge for the earlier killing of a friend of theirs by Palestinian militants.[40] Those involved reportedly videotaped the fatal beating.[41]

An initial investigation conducted by the Israel Ministry of Justice uncovered a 'series of cases of severe abuse of Palestinians and a conspiracy of silence'.[42] Not only did the investigation produce evidence about the young man's murder, but it raised 'suspicions that almost the entire company was involved in systematic abuse, harassment, and violence against Palestinians'.[43] The inquiry revealed that, despite denials, the Border Police were well aware of the murder. It also led to the arrest of eight other Border Police.[44]

Violent treatment of Palestinian children, including physical and psychological abuse, characterises the entire process of their arrest and transfer to detention facilities. The arrest usually happens without warning. The shock of the sudden arrest creates feelings of instability and disorientation and the transfer process exacerbates these feelings. Home arrests take place in the middle of the night, targeting children and their families when they are asleep and most vulnerable, violating their homes, the places they should feel most secure.

These children have grown up under Israeli military occupation. Israeli soldiers make most of the arrests, but Israeli settlers are also empowered to arrest any Palestinian, with no warrant required. The authorities arresting the children are either armed soldiers who have a history of conflict with the children's larger community, or those most aggressively involved in the occupation.

The clear conclusion to be drawn from the countless testimonies of children following their arrest is that the types of abuse to which they are exposed are not arbitrary or accidental. The fact that the same types of abuses are recounted by almost every single child arrested by Israeli soldiers indicates the deliberate and conscious nature of the arrest process.

6
Interrogation and Detention

A case study, recorded in May 2001 by the Israeli human rights organisation B'Tselem, illustrates how a typical child detainee faces a systematic barrage of abuse from the moment of arrest until release.[1]

At midnight on 9 November 2000 the soldiers took me outside, covered my eyes with a kerchief and tied my hands and feet [that is, shackled to impede the ability to take large steps or to run]. We walked for about three hundred metres to their jeep. They put me inside, with my head next to the speaker of a tape recorder that they played at high volume for a few minutes. One of the soldiers hit me in the head. We drove for twenty minutes before getting to Etzion [Detention Centre]. They left me lying on the ground in a summer shirt in the freezing cold for around twenty minutes.

Two soldiers came and took me to the clinic. I remained blindfolded. At the entrance to the clinic, they told me to walk straight and I bumped into the door. Then I was taken to the interrogation room. The interrogators beat me and trampled heavily on my legs.

The beating lasted for around an hour. Then they stood me up in the middle of the room. The interrogators stood on opposite sides of the room. They turned me into some kind of ball, throwing me from one to the other for about fifteen minutes. They took a water sprayer filled with very cold water and sprayed the water on me, mostly into my ears and mouth and on my chest.

Then they brought three iron steps, tied me to them, and told me to lift them up, but I fell and couldn't do it. My shoulder hurt a lot when I fell. I still have a scar from the steps. One of them stood me up and punched me with great force. I fell to the floor and my nose started to bleed. The interrogators brought a bottle of water. I thought that they would try to stop the bleeding, but they poured it [the water] on my back. They took me to the doctor, who treated me and gave me medication. After a few minutes, my nose stopped bleeding. Among the things that they did to me during the interrogation were to extinguish cigarettes on my body and to beat me with a metal ruler.

Two interrogators took me to the courtyard. Because of the nosebleed, the blindfold had been removed, and I could see the two soldiers. They were in civilian clothes and their faces were covered. I remained in the outer courtyard. They put an empty pail on my head and, for half an hour, splashed water on the upper part of my body. They brought pieces of ice and forced me to swallow a piece and rubbed another piece along my chest. Then they took me to the bathroom, and for about five minutes flushed the toilet and splashed water on my face.

Then they took me to the Police offices. There were two people there. One of them was Alex, who was around forty years old and was wearing a police uniform. He limped and was bald. The other fellow was nicknamed 'Captain John'. He was around thirty, tall, and had white hair. The two of them kicked me and asked me how many times I threw stones. I told them that I never did.

... [During another period of interrogation] There were three interrogators in the room. My brother Hasnin was also there. He had turned himself in the day after I was arrested. Right in front of me, the three interrogators beat my brother, kicking him in the abdomen and legs. One of them burned my brother with a cigarette and told Hasnin that he would shoot me if he didn't confess to everything.

Mufid Hussein Muhammad Hamamreh,
15 years old from Husan, Bethlehem district

In the previous chapter we followed Palestinian children as they went through the trauma of arrest and transport – bound, blindfolded and beaten – to an unknown destination. The systematic regularity of this process, confirmed by thousands of testimonies from released detainees, indicates that the type of abuse experienced during arrest is not arbitrary or an expression of the individual soldier's whim. Rather, it can only be understood as a deliberate and institutionalised attempt to frighten, intimidate and disorient the detainee in preparation for the next stage of the arrest process, detention and interrogation.

Once arrested, children are brought to Israeli detention centres, where they are kept in very poor conditions and prevented from contact with families and lawyers. These detention centres are in military camps or police stations in Israeli settlements. All are in areas barred to Palestinians – some may be on land that has been expropriated from the child's own village or town.

Most of the Palestinian child detainees will be interrogated by Israeli police or military in an interrogation centre located in or near the detention centre (see Table 6.1). Children suspected of more serious offences will likely be taken directly to an interrogation centre run by the Shabak (Israel Security Agency) and may be kept incommunicado for long periods. There are four Shabak centres in Israel outside the West Bank, and one in the Israeli settlement Beit El, near Ramallah (see Table 6.2). The Shabak centres are renowned for using particularly violent methods of torture in interrogations.

In the detention centres, children find themselves uprooted from any familiar setting, in an alien environment and surrounded by the armed, hostile soldiers of an occupying force. Children are highly vulnerable to pressure during this initial period of detention, preceded by their sudden arrest and physical abuse during transportation. It is precisely at this stage that the Israeli state apparatus uses its full weight, bearing down on children to frighten and intimidate them into giving confessions. Given the climate of fear and exposure to physical mistreatment and intimidation, most children tend to confess relatively quickly, even if they are innocent.

DETENTION CENTRES

Israel holds Palestinian children in one of eight detention centres in settlements or military camps throughout the West Bank, and one at the entrance to the Gaza Strip. In addition, the Ofer Detention Centre located in an Israeli military camp near Ramallah was recently re-opened. Interrogation takes place in separate sections in these centres, in separate facilities nearby, or in one of the Shabak centres in Israel or Beit El.

Ofer Detention Centre/Military Camp

At the end of the first Intifada Israel closed the Ofer Detention Centre, but it was reopened in the wake of the mass arrests in April 2002, and quickly became the major detention centre in the West Bank. The military arrested adults and children alike, took them to detention centres near their homes for a few days, and then transferred them to Ofer. Soon Ofer was holding nearly a thousand detainees in overcrowded and dirty tents – conditions widely

Table 6.1 Detention and Interrogation Centres

West Bank and Gaza Strip Detention Centres

Name of Facility	Location	Approximate No. of Palestinian Detainees (May 2003)	Approximate No. of Palestinian Child Detainees (May 2003)	Description
Huwwara	West Bank – Near Nablus	85	15	Military camp with cells used for detention.
Salem	West Bank – Near Jenin	16	10	Military camp with cells used for detention.
Addoriym (Al Majnouna)	West Bank – Near Hebron	closed	closed	Closed in October 2002, Military camp with three cells. Previously a military court.
Etzion	West Bank – Near Bethlehem	70	12	Located in an Israeli military camp in the Israeli settlement of Gush Etzion.
Kiryat Arba	West Bank – Near Hebron	N.A.	N.A.	Police station in Israeli settlement with cells for detention.
Kadumim	West Bank – Between Nablus and Qalqilya	75	12	Police station in Israeli settlement with cells for detention.
Beit El	West Bank – Near Ramallah	48	9	Israeli settlement and military camp. Used for detention and interrogation. Also the central command for the Israeli military in the West Bank and military court. There are six rooms measuring 2.5m x 2.5m with up to ten people in each room.
Maale Adumim	West Bank – Near Jerusalem	N.A.	N.A.	Police station in Israeli settlement. Detainees are usually kept here for only a few hours or at most a few days.
Erez	Gaza Strip	N.A.	N.A.	Military camp with cells for detainees from the Gaza Strip.

Note: N.A. = information not available

Table 6.2   Shabak Interrogation Centres

Petah Tikva	Israel – near Haifa
Moscobiyya (Russian Compound)	West Jerusalem
Askelan	Israel – Askelan
Beit El + Detention Centre	West Bank, near Ramallah
Kishon (Al Jalame)	Israel – near Jenin

Note: In April 2003, Palestinian prisoners reported that a new Shabak interrogation centre had been opened and was being used for interrogation characterised by particularly violent forms of torture. Its location is unknown as prisoners are taken there blindfolded and not informed of their whereabouts (*Al Quds* newspaper, 24 April 2003, p. 4 (Arabic)).

condemned at the time by international, Israeli, and Palestinian human rights organisations.

A lawyer who visited Ofer Detention Centre on 15 May 2002 gave the following description after meeting with several child detainees:

The detention centre consists of nine sections each with four tents that house the prisoners. The sections are separated by barbed wire covered by heavy cloth that prevents communication between each section. The prison contains over 900 detainees, including 40 to 50 children. These detainees are distributed between the nine sections with each tent holding between 25 and 35 prisoners. The tents are in poor condition and are erected over an asphalt surface. The tents are filled with dust and insects. Each tent contains wooden pallets with a thin sponge on which the detainees sleep. Each detainee is given four dirty blankets to use as bedding. There are no pillows provided. There is no electricity in the tents.

The detainees are completely isolated from the outside world. They are forbidden family visits and have no radios, TV, newspapers or books. There is nothing to do inside the tents except sit and talk. There is no canteen and clothes are not provided by the Ofer administration.

The food provided for the detainees is unfit for human consumption and provided in very small quantities. Until 13 May, the detainees were not provided with any hot meals or beverages. Instead, the detainees were given frozen schnitzels, which they had to place in the sun to defrost. They are provided with powdered coffee and tea bags and told to take hot water from the bathroom in order to make drinks. A couple of cucumbers and pieces of fruit are provided for every ten detainees. A small container of yogurt is also given to every ten prisoners. Detainees

1   Telmond Compound (Hasharon and Ofek)
2   Megiddo Military Prison
3   Salem Detention Centre
4   Kishon (Al Jalame) Interrogation Centre
5   Kadumim Detention Centre
6   Huwwara Detention Centre
7   Petah Tikva Interrogation Centre
8   Ramle (Neve Tertze) Women's Prison
9   Beit El Detention and Interrogation Centre
10 Ofer Military Camp
11 Moscobiyya Interrogation Centre
12 Ma'ale Adumin Police Station
13 Etzion Detention and Interrogation Centre
14 Kiryat Arba Police Station
15 Addoriym (Al Majnouna) Detention Centre
16 Askelan Interrogation Centre
17 Erez Detention Centre
18 Ketziot (Ansar III) Military Camp

West Bank and Gaza

⊙ Major Population Centres

● Prisons, Detention and Interrogation Centres

20   0   20   40   60 km

Based on map from
The Applied Research Institute - Jerusalem

Figure 6.1   Detention and Interrogation Facilities Imprisoning Palestinian Children

who suffer from chronic diseases such as diabetes and blood pressure problems are not given any special food, so other detainees give them their food portions in order to ensure an adequate diet for these sick detainees. The detainees are not given plates and instead every eight prisoners are forced to eat collectively from a large bowl.

There is a shortage of cleaning supplies and thus it is impossible to keep the tents clean. In two sections, open sewage runs from the pipes into the tents.

After nightfall, movement between the tents in each section is forbidden. At night, soldiers harass the detainees by firing bullets in the air, throwing gravel at the tents and yelling at the prisoners.[2]

In December 2002 the Chief Justice of the Israeli Supreme Court admitted that the Ofer detention conditions were sub-standard but nevertheless dismissed a petition brought by several human rights organisations condemning conditions there. A few months later the Supreme Court also ruled that the mass arrests which led to the large numbers of detainees in Ofer was lawful, as each arrest was an 'individual case'.[3] Detainees continued to be denied appropriate medical care, given poor-quality food and held in overcrowded tents. On 3 January 2003 Israeli soldiers used tear gas and stun grenades against prisoners who were protesting against the poor conditions. Also in January 2003, all Palestinian political prisoners launched an open-ended strike, refusing to attend Israeli court sessions, in response to widespread reports of mistreatment during transfer of Palestinian prisoners at Ofer Detention Centre.[4] By May 2003 Ofer had been transformed into a permanent prison resembling Megiddo Prison, holding around 800 prisoners, many of whom were administrative detainees.

Other detention centres

Detainees held in other detention centres in the West Bank also face severe overcrowding and very harsh conditions.

Huwwara Detention Centre – based in a military camp near Nablus. Prisoners stay in overcrowded cells. They cannot go to the toilet when they want – guards give them empty bottles to urinate in.[5] Sanitary conditions are very poor and many prisoners contract skin infections from sleeping on the floor or on dirty mattresses. Each cell contains on average six to nine detainees, but at meal times they are only given enough food for two people. The detention centre does not give detainees hot water, soap or shampoo. Dr 'Abd al-Fatah Labadeh who was arrested by the Israeli army on 11 March 2003 and detained without charge, described the conditions in Huwwara as follows:

> There are about nine cells in the prison. The one I was placed in measured approximately 3m by 3m, had no lights, no toilet and contained six other men. We had small, thin mattresses which were wet as the cell was very damp. There was no heating, and the cell was very cold. There were insufficient blankets to keep us all warm. The only form of daylight was through a window which measured no more than 50cm by 50cm. Whilst I was there, we were taken out of the cell three times, for about 10 or 15 minutes each. We were forced to urinate into bottles as there was no toilet, and the only source of water was a small bottle which was filled at meal times...The sanitary conditions were very poor. We were unable to clean the room, there were no drinking glasses and no water to wash with. Most of the men had stomach problems such as constipation, stomach cramps and stomach acid.[6]

On 1 May 2003 detainees in Huwwara set fire to their mattresses in protest. Conditions did not improve.

Beit El Detention Centre – testimonies reveal a similar pattern of overcrowding, lack of bedding and restrictions on leaving the cells. A 14-year-old boy arrested in early 2003 describes the conditions in Beit El:

> The detention circumstances are very hard. We are with eleven detainees in this very small room of a bit more than five metres square. There are two adults being held with us. We sleep on four mattresses and share four blankets. We are allowed to use the bathroom three times a day only and we can take a shower once a week. We are given a recess once a week of 15 to 30 minutes. The administration does not provide any goods, or clothes. We do not have anything to spend our time with, just we sit and talk. Sometimes we are given Hebrew newspapers, but we cannot read Hebrew.[7]
>
> *Munir Zahran, 14 years old*

Gush Etzion – one of the most notorious detention centres, located in a police station in the Israeli settlement bloc near Bethlehem. It holds Palestinian children and adults and is infamous for cases of severe torture and ill-treatment. Detainees live in small, cold cells (known as 'fridges') and do not have proper bedding. In some cases, detainees have to sleep on concrete floors without mattresses.

As with other detention centres, the food in Etzion is sub-standard in quality and quantity. Children can only go to the toilet three times a day, and have been forced to defecate in their clothes or in makeshift containers.[8] Detainees can only leave their cells for a 40-minute recreation once every 13 days.

The Israeli military used Etzion as a holding centre for thousands of the Palestinians detained during the April 2002 mass arrests. Some of the children taken to Etzion at that time lived outside in tents rather than in cells.

Addoriym Detention Centre – near Hebron. A report from early 2002 notes that 14 prisoners (including three children) were being held in one small room.[9] Prisoners have mounted many hunger strikes over the poor quality and lack of food.

Salem Detention Centre – a military camp near Jenin. At the end of June 2003, 52 of the detainees including seven children in Salem fell ill with food poisoning and diarrhoea because they were given rotten food. The administration of the camp refused to give them medical attention and continued to restrict use of the toilet to only three times daily.[10] As a result, many of the detainees were forced to defecate in their cells.

As these reports suggest, detention conditions which violate relevant international standards are the rule, not the exception. All the detention centres are severely overcrowded with many prisoners crammed into small cells or tents. Cells are dirty and often infested with rats and insects. Detainees are forced to sleep on the floor or to share filthy mattresses. Food is insufficient and often stale or not nutritious. Detainees can rarely leave their cells and may have to urinate into bottles as they are denied access to the toilet. Children are kept completely isolated from the outside world, as family and legal visits are generally prohibited.

INTERROGATION AND DETENTION TESTIMONIES

On Friday, the 20th of July I was taken with my friend J. to a small isolation room [in Beit El Interrogation Centre] which measured one meter by one meter and a half. The walls were very rough. There was no toilet, but one bed and three blankets, without pillows. There were no windows, just a small slit in the door. It was locked. There was a light bulb, but it was turned off from outside. After two hours, they took J. and I stayed there in this room alone. I was very afraid. Especially since there was no light. I remember that during these days they were intentionally waking me up from sleep during the night, hitting the door or turning on loud music. It was music I did not understand. I also heard the sound of screaming women, and the sound of people screaming in pain.[11]

M.R., 15 years old
from Kissara Region, Hebron

17-year-old M.E was arrested on 25 February 1998 from Hebron and taken to Majnouna Detention Centre where he was held for eight days without being questioned and then taken to Askelan Interrogation Centre. He was taken directly to interrogation and interrogated by two Shabak agents. The interrogators demanded he confess and promised they would then give him fruit and juice. He refused. Finally he confessed to throwing stones and a Molotov cocktail. After he had confessed, they took him to the collaborator room where he thought he was in a cell with normal prisoners. He made the same admission of throwing stones and a Molotov to the collaborators. The collaborators attempted to trick him into confessing to throwing a grenade but he repeated what he had said to the interrogators. He was returned to the Shabak. They tied him to a kindergarten chair and placed a filthy sack on his head. One of the interrogators grabbed him by his chest and began to shake him violently for a long period of time until he began to lose consciousness. He screamed for them to stop. After that they took him to a small isolation cell where he was kept for 1 month.[12]

Concerning M.E., 17 years old
from Hebron

Israeli troops arrested B.N. in the middle of the night on 24 March 2003, the day after his 14th birthday. He was taken from his bed to the Etzion detention centre, where he was immediately inter-rogated, without any legal representation. B.N. told his lawyer that he was very frightened during the interrogation and, when the interrogators accused him of something, he confessed. When they had finished, they asked him to sign a document in Hebrew (a language he does not understand), so that he could be released, adding that he was too young to be charged. He signed the document, which turned out to be a confession to nine charges involving stone-throwing and setting fire to a telegraph pole. He was eventually sentenced to three months imprisonment, with an additional nine-month suspended sentence for three years, and a 2,000 NIS fine [approx. US$425].[14]

Concerning B.N., 14 years old
from the Bethlehem area

The soldiers took me to a room and sat me down on a chair. One of them took off the handcuffs and tied my hands and feet to the chair's legs. My eyes remained covered. About a half an hour later, they removed the blindfold. I saw five or six people in civilian clothes. They asked me questions about my involvement in clashes with soldiers. They asked if I threw stones at army vehicles on the main road. At first, I denied that I did. But two or three of them started to beat me in the face and head. The interrogation lasted for around five hours. I was very tired from sitting all the time on the chair and from the beatings. At the end, they took me to the bathroom near the interrogation room. One of the interrogators grabbed me by the hair and put my head in the toilet. I was frightened. When they took me back to the interrogation room, I decided to confess. I told them that I threw five stones at a settler's vehicle. They wrote up a detailed testimony and forced me to sign it.[15]

S.M., 15 years old
from the Hebron area

During his two-day detention in Etzion, Y. was beaten severely on his arms and face. When a lawyer saw him his nose appeared broken. After two days in Etzion, he was taken to Ofer in a military jeep for interrogation. With his hands and legs tied, he continued to be beaten on the road to Ofer. When he arrived at Ofer he was given only a painkiller for his nose. During interrogation his head was smashed on a table. He was taken to a temporary court at Ofer, but he did not understand what happened in the court session.[16]

Concerning Y, 17 years old
from Al-Aroub Refugee Camp, near Hebron

ACCESS TO LEGAL ASSISTANCE

In further violation of international standards, lawyers' ability to visit children is highly restricted. The regulations covering lawyers' visits to prisons and detainees before their trials are changed constantly, so that lawyers cannot rely on a consistent set of procedures. As the following case illustrates, the system seems designed to obstruct the right to legal representation and make life for lawyers as difficult as possible.

On 14 May 2002, a lawyer from DCI/PS contacted Ofer and said he wanted to visit 16 child prisoners. As instructed, he faxed a list of those prisoners to the detention camp. The following day, the person in charge of Ofer rang the lawyer and told him he had to visit in half an hour or otherwise he would have to wait several weeks and that he would only be able to see seven detainees, as the other nine were not allowed to receive visits. When the lawyer questioned this, he was told that only detainees who had received administrative detention orders could be visited.

The lawyer took his own car to the checkpoint at the edge of Ramallah where he had to leave it and walk several kilometers through garbage and mud to reach Ofer, which is in an Israeli military camp. On his arrival at around 9.30 a.m. he found three other lawyers waiting, who said they had been waiting for over an hour and described a similar experience in trying to get permission to visit. One said he had rung Ofer several times and that the soldiers had told him on separate occasions that he had rung a pizza shop, a butcher and a supermarket.

After waiting for about an hour the DCI/PS lawyer was ordered to enter the camp. His mobile phone was confiscated and he was led into a tent. The detainees were brought to meet him in handcuffs and three soldiers remained in the visiting tent throughout the meeting. The soldiers refused to untie the prisoners' hands even when they were signing affidavits. When the lawyer complained that the soldiers' presence violated lawyer–client confidentiality he was told: 'You either do the visit under these conditions or leave.'[17]

THE SYSTEMATIC VIOLATION OF CHILDREN'S RIGHTS

In the course of detaining and interrogating Palestinian children, Israel systematically commits clear and inexcusable violations of established international standards of human rights. Three main bodies carry out interrogation of Palestinian child detainees:

- **Shabak (ISA):** The Shabak is a quasi-independent body within the Israeli state apparatus and reports directly to Israel's Prime Minister. The Shabak generally supervise interrogations undertaken by other agencies, but will conduct interrogations directly for more serious offences, or for those who are particularly active politically. The Shabak regularly practices torture, including psychological methods and painful physical torture. When the children confess, the Shabak send them to the police to repeat their confessions and, if they refuse, bring them back for more interrogation.
- **Police:** The Israeli Police, who come under the authority of the Ministry of Internal Security, deal with the vast majority of child detainees, accused of minor offences. Although police carry out the interrogation, Shabak agents often supervise the process. Abuse is widespread in these situations.
- **Military intelligence:** The Israeli Military Intelligence, under the authority of the Ministry of Defence, is renowned for using highly physical forms of torture, such as severe beatings, burning with cigarette butts and other painful physical abuse. Once again, Shabak agents are often present. If they extract a confession, they send the child to the police station to repeat it. This gives a veneer of legality to the interrogation – the courts only accept confessions signed in the presence of police officers. If a child refuses to repeat the same confession in the presence of the police, they are brought back to Military Intelligence for further interrogation.

Almost without exception they subject these children to one or more of the following well-documented forms of abuse (see Figure 6.2):

- **Beating:** From the moment of arrest until entering prison, Israeli military personnel and police subject children to beating all over the body, in particular the head and genitals. This beating may take place with fists, batons, guns, cables or pieces of furniture. Beating most often occurs during transportation to and from detention centres and as part of the interrogation process. Detainees are often blindfolded while being beaten. Prior to a 1999 Israeli High Court ruling that restricted some forms of torture, adult prisoners were usually hooded with a heavy canvas sack wrapped tightly over the entire head. The hoods were often covered in sweat, vomit, urine or faeces, and some adult prisoners told of soldiers who threw their hoods to the wet and dirty ground of the toilet before making them wear it.[18] In many cases Israel has done the same to child prisoners. Following the 1999 ruling most detainees are now blindfolded with a piece of cloth or goggles that cause discomfort because they are tied very tightly around the head.[19]

- **Collective interrogation**: Sometimes more than one interrogator participates in interrogation, making the child feel as though they are being 'ganged-up' upon by armed soldiers or police.
- **Denial of family visits**: By preventing any family contact, Israel subjects the child to psychological pressure and increases the sense of isolation.
- **Denial of legal counsel**: This not only contributes to the child's psychological isolation, but prevents any external witness from directly witnessing the abusive treatment and its results.
- **Deprival of food and drink**: Detainees may be given little or nothing to eat or drink, or served inedible, unidentifiable food.
- **Exposure to extreme temperatures**: Often detainees are placed outside for long periods, sometimes after they have been partially stripped. This practice was particularly common during the mass arrests of 2002, many of which took place when the weather was very cold and wet, and is often combined with other forms of abuse such as being denied food or access to the toilet. In 1992 35-year-old Mustafa Akawi froze to death after being placed in an exposed area while it was snowing. He had previously been severely beaten, hooded and prevented from sleeping.[20] A related form of abuse involves repeatedly dousing children with extremely hot and/or cold water during interrogation.[21] Cold water is generally used in winter, hot water in summer.

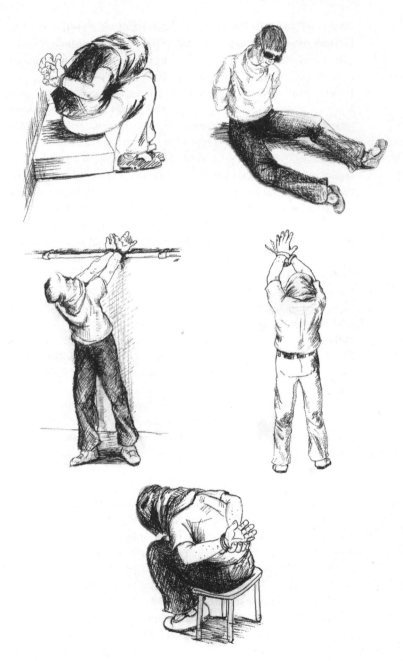

Figure 6.2 Israeli Position Abuse

- **Exposure to humiliation and degrading situations**: Typical scenarios include spitting on child prisoners, overstressing them physically, making them undress, or forcing them to curse God or their relatives.
- **Forced signing of confessions**: In the face of severe abuse and an environment of fear, children are forced to sign confessions written in Hebrew, a language they do not understand. Often the authorities mislead them about what the confession is, or deceive them into signing by telling them they will be released.
- **Isolation**: Children are often placed for long periods in isolation cells approximately 2m by 2m in size, with a small window or vent. An open toilet fills the cell with an overwhelming stench. Once inside, the child cannot communicate with anyone. At times the floor of the cell is wet, or open sewage may flow through it. The cell may either be completely dark, or brightly lit all the time.
- **No access to toilet facilities**: Frequently, detainees are not allowed to use the toilet and are forced to relieve themselves while fully clothed in the presence of others, or are only allowed to use the toilet at very limited times. These restrictions reinforce a feeling of powerlessness where even control over bodily functions is in the hands of the Israeli police or military.
- **Position abuse (*shabeh*)**: This particularly violent form of torture involves forcing detainees into contorted positions for very long periods. It may involve them being handcuffed to a chair or pipe in a painful position, being forced to stand on the tips of their toes for extended periods of time, or standing against a wall for hours. There is no escape from this severe pain and discomfort.[22] For the torturer, *shabeh* has the great advantage of leaving little visible physical mark on the prisoner.
- **Pressure to collaborate with the Israeli security services**: In order to get children to collaborate, the Israeli authorities often threaten them with other punitive measures, or place them in cells with those who are already collaborators, and who then exert pressure on the child to do the same.
- **Shaking**: This practice involves vigorously shaking the children until they lose consciousness. This particularly dangerous form of torture can cause death. It was supposedly outlawed by the September 1999 High Court ruling, but there is evidence that

it continues to be used against some adult detainees, and in the past it has been used against children.[23]

- **Sleep deprivation:** Soldiers or police will often prevent children from sleeping during interrogation by continually waking them up, blasting loud music through their cells, or leaving a bright light on in the cell. This type of abuse is physically and psychologically exhausting.
- **Threats:** The captor threatens the child with long prison terms, imprisonment of family members, demolition of their family home, rape or the rape of female members of the family.

In a series of interviews undertaken by a DCI/PS staff member with 50 Palestinian child ex-detainees who had been arrested during 1999–2000, all claimed they had been exposed to some form of physical or psychological abuse during their arrest.[24] Half of them had scars or physical marks, or reported bruising from torture during interrogation. Nearly all were blindfolded and handcuffed during their arrest and interrogation. These figures are confirmed by other studies. A few years prior to the Intifada, B'Tselem estimated that 85 per cent of all Palestinian detainees had been tortured during their incarceration.[25] A detailed series of interviews in 1994 with 60 released prisoners from the Bethlehem area found that 85 per cent had faced physical torture during their interrogation.[26]

This kind of abuse is designed to frighten and intimidate the child into confessing to offences they may never have committed. The children are alone during the entire process, denied any outside contact and interrogated by heavily armed Israeli soldiers, police or Shabak agents in a foreign environment. The methods used against them play on their vulnerabilities and are calculated to exhaust them physically and induce fear and terror.

The pattern of abuse carried out by different branches of the Israeli state is strikingly consistent in virtually all of the testimonies gathered by international, Israeli and Palestinian human rights organisations. It is characterised by violent methods of torture combined with tactics designed to induce psychological pressure and stress in the detainee. Each individual act is a complementary part of a process designed to induce fear and terror. Taken individually, particular acts may alone not constitute torture. Considered in its entirety, however, the combined abuse, which succeeds in physically and psychologically exhausting the child, constitutes torture.

As outlined throughout this book, the type of torture experienced by Palestinian children should be conceived in the framework of *state torture*. It is a conscious decision of the Israeli state to employ these techniques, as part of an overall strategy aimed at weakening any actual or potential resistance to occupation. It is not aimed solely at the individual, but at the entirety of Palestinian society. In the following chapter, we trace the continuity of this strategy through the experience of children in prison.

7
Imprisonment

Since the occupation began, Israel has imprisoned Palestinians in a variety of facilities, some of which remain open, others are now closed. Prison conditions depend on the place of detention and the period. After September 2000 the situation on the ground deteriorated, the number of prisoners increased, and new procedures were implemented. However, despite differences in time and place of detention, and the age of prisoners, there are clear threads of continuity in Israel's treatment of Palestinian political prisoners.

Imprisonment is an active state, and Palestinian prisoners are engaged in two struggles. Inside the prisons, they organise collectively to demand humane conditions of detention for themselves and for Palestinians detained elsewhere. Externally, they remain active in the larger Palestinian struggle for freedom.[1] The prison population is a powerful political force.

This chapter deals with the experience of Palestinian children in Israeli jails. The prison experience is unique for each individual, influenced both by their own personality and specific prison conditions. Their experience mirrors that of adult detainees. In a number of prisons Palestinian children are detained with adults – in some facilities, they are detained *as* adults. However, their age, level of emotional maturity, physical stature, and other factors leave them particularly vulnerable to abuse and less prepared for the trauma of prison. Imprisonment often represents the first time they have been away from home. The experience may constitute the end of childhood and the beginning of their lives as adults.

The chapter looks first at sentencing trends, focusing on sentences imposed on Palestinian children in 2002. It then describes the prisons the children are sent to, and their fellow inmates, who include Israeli and Palestinian adults and Israeli juvenile offenders. It also provides an overview of conditions in each facility, demonstrating recurring patterns of treatment, highlighting the critical issues and focusing on the facilities with the most children and the worst conditions.

The chapter also examines the difficulties lawyers encounter in visiting detained children, the resistance strategies that Palestinian prisoners including juveniles use, and efforts made to liaise with the Israeli prison administrations. Finally, it compares the experience of recent child detainees with those of the first Intifada and the Oslo years.

TRENDS IN SENTENCING

Chapter 3 showed how Israeli military courts issue prison sentences to Palestinian children based not on objective legal standards but on Israeli policy objectives, which are influenced by the current political situation. Over the past four years, particularly since the second Intifada began, Israeli military courts have issued increasingly severe sentences to Palestinian children, though the majority have been tried on the same charge: throwing stones. Table 7.1 summarises this pattern, on the basis of cases handled by DCI/PS from 1999 to 2002.

Table 7.1   Breakdown of Sentence Lengths, 1999–2002

Duration of Sentence	1999 %	2000 %	2001 %	2002 %
Less than one month	57/43	22/35	19/20	15/10
1–6 months	40/31	9/15	14/15	43/29
6 months–1 year	25/19	25/40	46/49	46/31
1–3 years	9/7	6/10	15/16	28/19
Three years and more	–	–	–	17/11
TOTAL	131/100	62/100	94/100	149/100

While more children have been charged with serious offences in 2002, stone-throwing sentences themselves have become increasingly severe. In 2002, 10 per cent of DCI/PS cases resulted in sentences of less than one month, compared with 44 per cent in 1999. Examples of 2002 sentences include:

- a 17-year-old boy convicted of throwing stones, sentenced to 20 months in prison plus 24 months if he should commit the offence again, and a 4,000 NIS fine;[2]
- a 14-year-old boy convicted of throwing stones, sentenced to six and a half months in prison and 2,000 NIS fine;[3]
- a 16-year-old boy convicted of throwing stones, sentenced to 18 months in prison and a 2,000 NIS fine.[4]

The courts also imposed harsh sentences on children charged with somewhat more serious acts:

- A 16-year-old boy convicted of making – not throwing – a Molotov cocktail was sentenced to 53 months in prison plus 18 months should he commit the same offence within the next 5 years.[5]
- A 17-year-old boy who threw stones and a Molotov cocktail was sentenced to six years imprisonment.[6]

Administrative detention orders have also increased significantly. In 1999 and 2000, DCI/PS shows no cases receiving administrative detention; in 2001 it dealt with two cases; in 2002 the number dramatically increased to 32. This parallels the overall increase in administrative detention orders for Palestinians: in late 2001, there were 32 Palestinians in administrative detention; by May 2002, over 700.[7] As of April 2003, there were more than 1,000.

SETTING THE SCENE: THE PRISONS

When it has finished interrogating them, Israel imprisons Palestinian children in five facilities. Megiddo Military Prison and Ketziot Military Camp are controlled by the Ministry of Defense and administered by the army. Telmond compound and Ramle (Neve Tertze) Women's Prison are administered by the Israel Prison Service, under the Ministry of Public Security.[8] All these facilities are located outside the occupied territories, which violates international humanitarian law and makes family visits extremely difficult.[9] These facilities detain Palestinian children pending trial, as well as those who have been sentenced. Children may also be detained after interrogation in Ofer Military Camp in the West Bank. However, since Ofer now serves as the main initial detention and holding centre in the West Bank, it has been fully discussed in Chapter 6.

Male children 16 and older at the time of arrest are imprisoned in Megiddo and Keziot. Prior to April 2002, they were all held in Megiddo, an outdoor tent prison, opened in 1982 during Israel's invasion of Lebanon. Ketziot, also known as Ansar III, is a notorious outdoor tent prison that housed thousands of Palestinian political prisoners during the first Intifada. The facility was closed in 1995 and re-opened in April 2002, an act which was widely acknowledged as signalling Israel's intention to continue the policy of mass arrests launched at that time.[10] There are no Israelis detained in either prison.

Male children 15 and under at the time of arrest are imprisoned in Hasharon and Ofek, two facilities in the Telmond compound, which dates back to the 1920s. Hasharon is a prison for both Palestinian children and Israeli adults. Ofek was opened in 2000 and designed to hold Israeli juvenile detainees.[11] Because of overcrowding in Hasharon, Ofek currently also holds a number of Palestinian child political prisoners. There is no criterion to determine whether a Palestinian child political prisoner will be detained in Hasharon or Ofek.

Female children are imprisoned in Ramle (Neve Tertze) Women's Prison. Ramle is a maximum security prison holding both Israeli and Palestinian adult female prisoners held for criminal offences, and Palestinian female political prisoners.

There is no distinction made between adult and child prisoners detained in Megiddo or Ketziot, because they are operated by the Ministry of Defense and follow military orders. The children are imprisoned *as* adults because they meet the age criteria for 'adult' set forth in Military Order No. 132. While there is a technical distinction afforded to minors detained in Ramle Prison, in practice children are treated the same as adults.

CONDITIONS OF DETENTION

Prison conditions for Palestinian children are often as abusive as the arrest and interrogation process and have dramatically worsened since 2000. After the second Intifada began, a massive increase in Palestinian arrests led to overcrowded conditions, and treatment grew harsher. Without regular visits by family and lawyers, monitoring the conditions of detention has grown increasingly difficult.

Since 2002 thousands of new detainees have arrived during waves of mass arrests, with a radical impact on conditions of detention. When military operations end and new detainees decrease, there is often a slight improvement in conditions in some facilities – then, as the next phase of mass arrests is launched, conditions again deteriorate. Nevertheless, the treatment received by Palestinian political prisoners, including children, consistently violates international standards. Table 7.3 provides an overview of the main problems facing Palestinian child political detainees in each of the four prisons.

Table 7.2 Characteristics of Prisons

Name of Prison	Administering Authority	Physical Characteristics	Category of Prisoners	Other Notes
Megiddo Military Prison	Ministry of Defense	Tent prison	Male prisoners; Palestinian child and adult political prisoners	Male Palestinian children aged 16 and 17 at the time of arrest
Ketziot Military Camp	Ministry of Defense	Tent prison, re-opened in April 2002	Male prisoners; Palestinian child and adult political prisoners	Male Palestinian children aged 16 and 17 at the time of arrest, including those given administrative detention[12]
Telmond Compound	Israel Prison Service, under the Ministry of Public Security	Contains two facilities that detain Palestinian children: Hasharon and Ofek.	Male prisoners: Palestinian child prisoners and adult Israeli prisoners in Hasharon; Palestinian child prisoners and male Israeli juvenile prisoners in Ofek	Male Palestinian children aged under 16 at time of arrest
Raule (Neve Tertze) Women's Prison	Israel Prison Service, under the Ministry of Public Security		Female prisoners; Palestinian child and adult political prisoners; adult Israeli and Palestinian criminal prisoners	All female Palestinian child prisoners are imprisoned in Ramle.

Table 7.3 Main Problems by Prison

Main Problems in Each Prison

| | | | Telmond | |
Megiddo	Ketziot	Ramle	Hasharon	Ofek
Lack of family visits	Lack of family visits	Lack of family visits	Lack of family visits	Lack of family visits
Outdoor location makes conditions harsh	Overcrowding	Repeated attacks by prison staff and Israeli criminal prisoners and lack of follow-up by prison administration	Overcrowding	Attacks by Israeli juvenile prisoners
Leaky tents	Inedible food and inadequate portions	Harsh punitive measures	Lack of sanitary toilet facilities	Inadequate provision of supplies
Children pressured to collaborate	Harsh punitive measures	Inedible food and inadequate portions	Repeated attacks by prison staff and lack of follow-up by prison administration	Lack of outdoor recreation time
Lack of adequate provisions, particularly blankets, warm clothes, and underwear	Lack of supplies by prison, including no clothes	Inadequate provision of supplies	Harsh punitive measures	Educational instruction in Hebrew, a language Palestinian children do not understand
Surprise raids and body searches	Treatment by prison personnel, including attacks and theft by prison guards	Lack of outdoor recreation time	Inadequate provision of supplies	
No child-specific procedures	Lack of adequate medical care	Lack of adequate medical care	Lack of outdoor recreation time	
Lack of formal education and educational material	Outdoor location makes weather conditions harsh	Failure to acknowledge or cooperate with prisoners' representative	Failure to acknowledge or cooperate with prisoners' representative	
	No child-specific procedures	No child-specific procedures	Surprise raids and body searches	
	Lack of formal education and educational material	Lack of formal education and educational material	Inedible food	
	Presence of rodents		Lack of adequate medical care	
			Lack of educational material	
			Leaking in some cells causes permanently wet mattresses and belongings	

Since Israel denies detaining children in some facilities, and fails to provide information about others, it is difficult to obtain exact figures regarding the numbers of children in each facility. Both Megiddo and Ketziot can and do deny holding any children because the military defines children 16 and over as adults. While Telmond and Ramle acknowledge detaining children, lawyers and human rights organisations frequently encounter difficulty obtaining lists from the prison administrations. Ramle, with few child prisoners, does not pose a major problem.

In practice, professionals needing to determine how many children are incarcerated must frequently rely on information provided by the prisoners themselves. The numbers continuously change with new arrests and releases, so maintaining an accurate count is a constant struggle, and estimates are frequently used throughout this chapter.

Megiddo Military Prison

Most Megiddo prisoners, and all children, are housed in tents; there are five rooms reserved for those convicted of particularly serious offences. In February 2003, of approximately 1,000 prisoners in Megiddo, between 70 and 100 were children.

In Megiddo, Palestinian children are detained with adult Palestinian political prisoners. As Chapter 4 noted, international law requires the separation of prisoners according to category – children should not be detained with adult prisoners. However, article 3.1 of the CRC sets forth the 'best interests' principle, stipulating that, '(i)n all actions concerning children...the best interests of the child shall be a primary consideration'.

Child rights defenders and adult and child detainees themselves believe it is in the best interests of Palestinian children to be detained with adult Palestinian political prisoners, considering their physical and emotional vulnerability and their status as members of an occupied population detained in the prison of the occupying power. Detention with adult Palestinian political prisoners provides a means of support for children who have been separated from their families, and offers a degree of protection from physical and psychological abuse.

As Megiddo is an outdoor tent prison, inmates are constantly subjected to the elements, which is particularly difficult in the cold, rainy winter months. The tents leak and prison authorities do not provide adequate bedding and clothing to keep prisoners warm and dry. Families cannot visit to supplement the provisions as they could in the past, nor has the International Committee of the Red Cross been able to provide additional supplies. Despite requests for a heater during the extreme winter cold, the prison administration has refused, citing 'security' reasons.[13] In 2003, repeated and invasive body searches and raids of prisoners' tents have become a major problem. Prisoners' personal possessions are often confiscated, damaged, or destroyed during the raids.

Since children in Megiddo are treated as adults, they fail to receive the special treatment outlined by international human rights law for children deprived of their liberty. Israel has consistently denied Palestinian child detainees access to education. In a 1997 court ruling, the Tel Aviv Central Court ruled that detained Palestinian children do have the right to education and that the education should follow the Palestinian curriculum.[14] As of May 2003, however, Palestinian children receive educational instruction only in Telmond. In Megiddo, Ramle, and Ketziot prisons, Palestinian children receive no formal education whatsoever.

Although children are detained *as adults*, both detainees and human rights attorneys agree that they are singled out *because they are children*, and face intense pressure to collaborate with the Israeli authorities. During a May 2002 visit by DCI/PS, the prisoners' representative reported that Israeli intelligence officers attempt to recruit children to collaborate with the Israeli army in return for reduced periods of imprisonment. He argued that this policy often lies behind the harsh treatment of child detainees, both during interrogation and afterwards.[15]

Ketziot Military Camp

Prisoners referred to Ketziot as the 'Camp of the Slow Death' during the first Intifada.[16] Leaky tents provide little protection against the Negev desert's harsh weather, with stifling heat by day and freezing temperatures at night. In winter, with frequent rain, prisoners battle constantly to keep themselves, their belongings, and their environs clean and dry. Insufficient bedding and clothing make it impossible to stay warm. The prison is filthy and unsanitary: overcrowding, insufficient bathroom facilities and cleaning supplies, and infestations of rodents and insects all render the camp unsuitable for human habitation. Prison authorities fail to provide sufficient food to meet prisoners' nutritional needs, particularly those of children.

Ketziot is divided into four sections of four units each, with an additional half section opened in October 2002. In March 2003, between 30 and 60 boys were among over 1,000 Palestinian political prisoners detained in Ketziot, most of them administrative detainees.[17] Again, children are treated as adults and there is no formal education.

Each unit contains three tents designed to house 18 prisoners, but normally holding 20 to 22. The unit is surrounded by a wall five meters high. Beds consist of a wooden shipping pallet on the ground, covered by a thin sponge mattress. When new arrivals increase, as many as 70 detainees are held in one tent.[18]

Each unit, designed for around 60 prisoners, has one toilet facility with three toilets, one of which includes a shower. The 'toilet' is actually a dug-out channel in the ground. There are twelve taps outside the toilet area for washing hands and laundry. Little hot water is available even in the winter, and the toilet areas are extremely filthy and unsanitary.

The administration provides no clothing and, if families or outside organisations cannot provide supplementary clothes, prisoners remain for months in what they were wearing when first detained. The prison authority provides only one bar of soap for every ten detainees. Each prisoner is given three thin blankets; one is generally used as a pillow. A one-litre bottle of chlorine is distributed to each unit every 20 days for cleaning purposes.[19]

Relations between the detainees and the prison administration are poor, with daily searches, widespread reports of theft by prison staff, and repeated attacks by armed guards who fire sound bombs and tear-gas into prisoners' tents. In October 2002 Israeli soldiers attacked prisoners in Ketziot following a dispute. As Addameer Prisoners Support and Human Rights Association described it:

A large force of Israeli soldiers, armed with automatic rifles, tear-gas and sound grenades, surrounded the sections of the detention camp. Soldiers fired tear-gas and sound grenades into all the sections and, in particular, into Section D of the prison tents. Tents in the Section D/4 caught fire, burning down the tents themselves, detainees' mattresses, blankets and other items within the tents...All 60 detainees from Section D/4 were trapped in the fire, unable to flee from the force of the flames because of (surrounding) walls, whilst simultaneously being attacked with tear gas and sound grenades. The detainees were eventually able to force a hole through one of the walls separating the sections to escape the fire.[20]

Access to medical care is a serious problem in all these facilities. Prisoners' medical complaints are almost always treated with only a basic pain reliever such as paracetamol. The extent of the problem varies between facilities, but has been consistently severe in Ketziot. In October 2002, Addameer reported that 60 detainees required immediate medical care; some of them had been in need since their April 2002 arrests.[21] The failure to provide medical care extends to prisoners suffering severe ailments such as gunshot wounds.[22] Prisoners report rat infestations causing skin diseases.

Telmond Compound

Both facilities in Telmond feature dismal conditions. In Hasharon, children are confronted by overcrowded, unsanitary conditions, repeated attacks by prison guards, and little outside time. In Ofek, Palestinian children are repeatedly threatened and attacked by Israeli juvenile detainees. In neither facility are Palestinian children provided with adequate clothes and other basic supplies.

Additionally, the education provided in both fails to adhere to the 1997 Central Court ruling entitling Palestinian children to receive instruction according to the Palestinian curriculum. Palestinian child political prisoners in Ofek sit through the formal study given to Israeli children in Hebrew, a language they do not understand. In Hasharon, Palestinian children receive instruction in only three subjects, Hebrew, Arabic, and Maths, rather than the eight subjects featured in the Palestinian curriculum.

Hasharon

In the past, Hasharon used sections 7 and 8 for Palestinian child political prisoners. In early 2002 the administration transferred all prisoners from section 8, the better of the two, into section 7, in order to house Israeli adult prisoners in section 8.

Each of the 24 cells in the section is approximately 2.5m by 3m and should hold two prisoners. Each contains a bunk bed, an open toilet, and a small window. The rooms are too small to pray in, and the children have resorted to covering their faces when their cellmates use the toilet due to lack of privacy. In many of the cells, the shower is located over the toilet, so the children must stand over the toilet to shower.[23] Water leaks into many of the cells, so mattresses on the floor are perpetually wet. The windows are covered by iron – while air can pass through, the children cannot actually see outside.[24]

Moving the prisoners into one section exceeded the maximum capacity of 48 and created intolerable living conditions. In March 2003, the section held 72 prisoners – with only 48 beds, new prisoners sleep on the floor.

Prisoners get little outdoor time and insufficient food and basic supplies. The year 2003 brought a new policy of fines up to about US$50 for violations of prison policy such as disobeying orders or being late, so already scarce money normally used for canteen purchases is now being confiscated.

Relations between the administration and the children have continually deteriorated since September 2000, and child prisoners in Hasharon face repeated attacks by prison guards, harsh punitive measures, and humiliating and degrading treatment such as being shackled and/or strip-searched prior to court visits or while meeting with lawyers.[25] Problems between prisoners and the administration over slight deviations from prison protocol often result in prisoners being attacked and beaten or placed in isolation, or their personal possessions confiscated.

In December 2000, a child prisoner was placed in isolation for one week for failing to stand when the director of Hasharon entered his cell. In an affidavit taken by DCI/PS, he recounted:

On 21 December 2000 at around 11 a.m. I was laying in my cell and felt ill. The Director of the Prison was conducting a visit and as he entered my cell he asked me why I wasn't ready for his visit and wasn't standing and if it was because I was using drugs. I was angered by what he said and asked him not to speak to me like that. He told me we would discuss the matter outside and he took me to his office. There he told me that because I didn't stand when he entered the room I was to be placed in isolation. They took me to a small cell measuring 2m by 2m which had a toilet inside with no door. There was a putrid smell coming from this toilet. There was a mattress with no covers. I was only wearing pajama pants and a light t-shirt...My hands and feet were handcuffed to the bed from 1 p.m. on that day until 1 p.m. the next day, in other words 24 hours. At 9:30 a.m. on the second day I started shouting to let me go to the toilet, they untied me and let me go to the toilet and when I finished they tied me to the bed again...I stayed in this isolation cell until 28 December 2000. During this whole period I was not allowed out of my cell. I received my meal [to break the fast] half an hour late and they didn't allow me to smoke or give me any clothes. For this whole period I kept asking to be allowed out before the holiday on 26 December but they refused and kept me in this small cell until the 28 December.[26]

Nasser Zeid, 17 years old

When injured children are taken to a physician by prison staff following an attack, they generally receive little attention and inadequate medicine, and the medical record misrepresents their actual condition. On 26 June 2001, an attack by prison guards resulted in the injury of at least 11 children, four of whom were then placed in isolation. Separate affidavits provided to the DCI/PS attorney on 5 July 2001 by the four detainees in isolation reported consistent patterns of medical mistreatment:

A 17-year-old prisoner was beaten severely, passed out, and then regained consciousness while being beaten by three prison police. At that point, his hands were tied behind his back and his feet bound. He was then taken to the clinic. He reported that his clothes were torn and he was bleeding from his nose and other cuts on his face. According to the affidavit, the physician did not examine him or treat his injuries. His injuries were photographed and the doctor informed him he was fine. The marks of the beating were witnessed by the DCI/PS attorney during a visit ten days after the attack.

A 17-year-old prisoner, also beaten by a group of prison police while his hands and legs were bound, passed out after being struck with a gas canister. When he gained consciousness, he was taken to the clinic. At that time, he reports that he was bleeding from his mouth. Again, the physician photographed his injuries, but failed to treat him. The DCI/PS attorney witnessed marks of the beating on his back ten days after the attack.

A 17-year-old prisoner was beaten by a group of prison police. During the beating, one of the officers opened a canister of tear-gas directly in front of the prisoners face, causing him to pass out. He regained consciousness while two nurses were giving him oxygen. Shortly afterwards, he was moved to another room and beaten again by four prison police officers. After the second beating, he was taken to the clinic, where the physician photographed his injuries, but failed to treat him.

A 16-year-old prisoner was struck with batons and a gas canister, then beaten by more than seven police officers. His arms and legs were bound and he was transferred outside the area. Hours later he was taken to the clinic where the physician photographed his injuries, but did not treat him.[27]

As of early 2003, access to medical treatment in Hasharon had not significantly improved. The Palestinian human rights organisation LAW reported repeated instances where child prisoners were denied appropriate medical treatment, even gunshot wounds being treated with only a basic pain reliever.[28] F.J., a child prisoner with a broken leg, received medical treatment only after four days of protests by the prisoners.[29]

The denial of medical treatment for Palestinian prisoners is not simply a matter of neglect. Rather, it is used as a form of pressure against detainees. The prison administration will refuse or delay medical treatment in an attempt to pacify the prisoners and prevent collective action to improve conditions. Even more insidious is the use of medical treatment as a means of recruiting collaborators. In a series of interviews with 60 ex-prisoners from the Bethlehem area in 1994, 90 per cent of those interviewed claimed that the administration used the denial of medical treatment as a way of recruiting collaborators.[30] One ex-child prisoner stated that the use of prison hospitals to recruit collaborators was so well known amongst prisoners that they would refuse to ask for medical treatment for fear of being suspected as a collaborator.[31]

The desperate conditions in Hasharon have prompted widespread protest from prisoners, lawyers, human rights groups and others. In a report submitted to Israeli Public Security Minister Uzi Landau in September 2001, even before the two sections of Hasharon were combined, Zahava Gal-On, a member of the Israeli Knesset from the Meretz Party, stressed that Hasharon should be closed immediately on the grounds that living conditions were inhuman. Gal-On declared that: 'Conditions at the Hasharon detention centre are unfit for humans, infringe the detainees' human rights and violate the law.'[32]

Ofek

In 2001 an average of around 20 Palestinian child political prisoners were regularly detained in Ofek, which also holds Israeli juveniles. The situation is dangerous and frequently life-threatening for the Palestinians.

DCI/PS has documented many cases of Israeli juvenile prisoners attacking Palestinian children, including beatings, attacks with knives and razor blades, and at least one case of attempted rape. There are repeated reports of clothes and private property being stolen.

Ramle (Neve Tertze)

In Ramle (Neve Tertze) Women's Prison, Palestinian girls and adult political prisoners are detained in the same area as Israeli females held for criminal offences. The number of Palestinian children has increased over the past two years, from four in September 2001 to ten in March 2003.[33] Special treatment for minors is largely limited to housing them in the same room.

Israel provides no formal education to the child detainees. Adult Palestinian prisoners offer instruction to the minors, but the lack of adequate educational materials limits the effectiveness of these informal courses.[34] In March 2003, prisoners reported that the prison refused to allow them to apply to universities while detained.

Lack of sufficient outdoor time has long been a point of contention between the Palestinian prisoners and the administration of Ramle. Prison regulations stipulate that prisoners should have six hours per day outside their cells. However, because Ramle houses both Palestinian and Israeli prisoners, the allotted time outdoors has been reduced, with each group having only three hours per day. In 2003, internal disputes among Palestinian prisoners have resulted in dividing them into two groups, limiting the amount of their outdoor time to 1½ hours per day.[35]

Ramle also suffers from insufficient supplies. Prisoners must purchase items from the prison canteen or have families or outside organisations provide them. In April 2003 Adalah, The Legal Centre for Arab Minority Rights in Israel, sent a protest letter to the IPS director after prisoners were informed that the IPS would stop providing personal hygiene supplies (soap, toothpaste, toothbrushes, toilet paper, among others) to political prisoners, though prisoners incarcerated for criminal offences continued to receive such provisions. Prisoners had been informed that budget cuts had prompted the decision and that prisoners' families could supplement the lack of services.[36]

Since September 2000 there have been virtually no family visits, and lawyers and other organisations faced repeated obstacles to bringing in supplies. Female prisoners have been forced to barter their personal possessions for basic provisions such as sanitary napkins. As with Hasharon, the Ramle administration in 2003 implemented a policy of fining children for infractions of prison policy. The quality and quantity of food has been another consistent problem.

Since 2001, prison guards have brutally attacked female prisoners, using tear-gas and beating them in their cells. Prisoners have spent extended periods in isolation, have been tied to their beds, had personal belongings confiscated, have been financially penalised for infractions of prison rules, and subjected to degrading treatment including repeated strip-searches. In March 2002, 13 female Palestinian prisoners were forcibly stripped naked and searched while handcuffed, and then left in an open room in an area where male wardens were present.[37]

In June 2001, Palestinian female political detainees in Ramle launched a hunger strike: one of the major demands was access to adequate medical treatment. Prisoners reported that 'instead of being treated, we are beaten'.[38] In the ensuing attack, over 20 prison police used tear-gas and heavy batons to beat prisoners. 14-year-old Sanaa' Amer was beaten on her arms and legs. Her arms were tied behind her back and she was kicked repeatedly in the stomach, leaving her coughing up blood.[39] In September 2001, guards attacked when several women refused to stand up during roll call in protest about poor conditions. Six prisoners, including two children, were taken to isolation where they were beaten and tied to their beds overnight with their legs spread apart.[40]

In October 2001, three 14-year-old detainees were placed in isolation as a punitive measure following a hunger strike in the prison. Two of the children were held at least two weeks in isolation, the other at least one week.[41] In the same month, a 14-year-old had her limbs spread and cuffed to her bed throughout the night on two consecutive evenings.[42] The Palestinian political prisoners in Ramle have also repeatedly been harassed, threatened and attacked by Israeli prisoners.

FAMILY AND LAWYER VISITS

Since the beginning of the Intifada in September 2000, Israel has denied almost all family and lawyer visits to imprisoned Palestinian children. Families from the West Bank and Gaza Strip cannot usually obtain the necessary permits to enter Israel where all the prisons are located, or the additional prison permit needed to visit their children. Families from East Jerusalem are in a slightly better position since they do not need permission to enter Israel, but they are often turned away at the prison gate. Visits to some prisons have been completely banned at points, and the right to family visits is often revoked as a punitive measure.

When family members are able to visit, they face rigorous and often humiliating procedures. The mother of a prisoner arrested at the age of 16 recounted her ordeal:

> During visits I leave the house at 5 a.m. and go to the Red Cross bus in Al Bireh that takes us to the checkpoint in Qalandyia. We get out of the bus and then walk across the checkpoint to another bus on the other side. During the trip we are stopped and searched by Israeli soldiers – the bus, the driver and the representative of the Red Cross and, of course, the families. For the whole trip there is an army jeep in front of us and behind us. They place us in the sun for hours as they search us.
>
> When we reach the prison the police take the licence from the driver and tell him not to move from in front of the prison until we come back. When we enter the prison we are forced to wait for hours and they take our ID cards. Finally at around 3 p.m. the visit begins, with everything we have brought, clothes, etc., being searched. We enter a different section and are forced to wait again until they bring our sons. There is a wire grill between me and [her son] and a guard alongside both of us. This prevents us from speaking freely. After all this we spend only 45 minutes with our sons.
>
> After seeing our sons we wait for the rest of the families to finish their visits. During the return home we face the same procedures as our visit, depending on the checkpoints etc. I arrive home between 8 and 9 p.m. I am unable to sleep until the next day because of the pain from this trip. I am able to survive this journey just to see my son, but when I am forbidden from seeing him I just can't stand it and the rest of my family suffers from my stress. My last visit was on 20 August and I was forbidden from seeing him despite going through the whole procedure. I had really hoped he would be given parole but instead they increased his sentence by another six months.[43]

Israel introduced new guidelines in July 2001 sharply limiting Palestinian attorneys' visits to Palestinian children. They forbid all visits to those who have been sentenced, and stipulate that:

- Palestinian lawyers need Israeli military permits to travel into Israel – this permission must state that they are lawyers, but several lawyers who applied were told that no permits were issued with that classification.
- Israel only allows visits to those who have not yet been sentenced.
- Lawyers have to prove that they are representing a child in court, which requires the child to sign a form, normally written in Hebrew, so the lawyer has to fax it to the prison where the guards must have the prisoner sign it. The children do not understand the form, and guards have tricked children into signing a confession at the same time.[44]
- Lawyers must send their ID cards, proof of power of attorney, and a permit to visit Israel as a lawyer to the prison 48 hours before the visit, which makes it impossible to visit a prison quickly in case of an emergency.

Palestinian and Israeli human rights organisations appealed these procedures unsuccessfully in early 2002.[45]

In April 2002 a new set of procedures was introduced requiring a letter from the Office of Legal Affairs in the Israeli Civil Administration stating that the individual was a lawyer and allowed to visit Israeli prisons. The lawyer required a permit from the Israeli military to travel, and an identification card from the Palestinian Bar Association. If all of these requirements were met, visit approval would still almost always take more than one week's notice. Palestinian lawyers refused, and the Palestinian Bar Association decided to boycott the written-letter requirement, saying that they should have free access to the prisons as lawyers recognised by the Palestinian Bar Association.

Lawyers with Israeli citizenship or members of the Israel Bar Association can visit Palestinian children, but still face many obstacles and constant harassment. To visit children in Megiddo and Ketziot, they must send a list of the prisoners to be visited. The military authorities then set a date for the visit, usually not less than a week away. In Ketziot, child prisoners have their hands bound and legs cuffed and Israeli soldiers monitor the visit from out of hearing range.

Telmond and Ramle do not require appointments, but visiting time is only 8.30 a.m.–12.00 p.m. and 2–4 p.m. Frequently, lawyers will wait two to three hours before gaining entry, then guards take 30 or 40 minutes to bring the children from their cells to the visiting area. Lawyers can only meet with prisoners individually, so they can only see two or three prisoners per visit. In Telmond, the boy's hands and legs are cuffed; in Ramle, the girl's hands are bound. A guard will be often be present during the meeting.

COLLECTIVE ACTION IN PRISONS

When the political situation on the ground deteriorates, so do conditions inside prisons. This is partly because the mass influxes of Palestinian prisoners take a toll on prison services. In 2002 prison facilities were simply not equipped to absorb the thousands of Palestinians rounded up and detained by the Israeli army in March and April, leading to extreme overcrowding and grossly inadequate basic supplies such as food and bedding.

When the situation outside prison becomes volatile, as at the beginning of the Intifada, the internal prison environment becomes correspondingly tense. Likewise, negative detention conditions lead to increased tensions outside prisons. In May 2000 widespread demonstrations erupted throughout the West Bank in response to the terrible prison conditions facing Palestinian political prisoners.

Inside prisons, detainees use collective action to pressure the prison administrations for better conditions, refusing to cooperate with prison procedures such as standing up during counting, or launching strikes such as declining to take part in prison life and refusing food. Palestinian child political prisoners almost always choose to participate.

A protest may be localised to a specific prison in order to improve conditions there, or inmates may engage in collective action throughout the prison system to address larger issues affecting prisoners everywhere or as a solidarity measure in response to particularly harsh treatment of prisoners in another facility.

Palestinian political prisoners often select one prisoner to represent them. Finding strength in numbers, this enables them to maintain their group identity as prisoners and counter any 'divide and conquer' strategies. The prisoners' representative is responsible for resolving problems by negotiating with the administration, and is extremely important in building consensus among the prisoners and dealing effectively with the administration. Consequently, a strong, charismatic prisoner is chosen. The selected representative is often targeted for harsh treatment by prison guards and staff as a message to the other prisoners. Prison officials frequently refuse to acknowledge the representative's authority and attempt to deal with prisoners individually, or, if the chosen representative has been very successful at mobilising the inmates, the administrations may press for another prisoner as representative – prisoners have consistently rejected such efforts.

Prisoners typically launch their protests by registering complaints with their representative, who then tries to raise the concern with the prison administration and negotiate a solution. If the problem is not resolved, a new form of protest is added – for example, refusing to stand during counting, and prisoners take increasingly serious action – refusing to partake in outdoor time or to leave their rooms. Throughout, the representative continues to negotiate with the administration on the original issue.

Hunger strikes are generally the most serious form of action prisoners can take, when repeated efforts to improve conditions have failed. Frequently, harsh responses by prison authorities to collective protest lead to a drastic deterioration in the situation. Failure to stand while counting will result in attacks on prisoners, prompting a hunger strike which has as much to do with the prison's response as with the original issue.

Prison life is a near-constant series of collective actions. As soon as one issue is resolved, another equally difficult one arises. The influx of new prisoners, the release of others, and changes in administration staff or political events outside mean the situation is rarely stable, with the result that it is difficult to assess the extent to which collective action undertaken by prisoners is successful. It almost uniformly results in some punitive measure from the administration, but some actions have resulted in concrete changes in treatment. Regardless of individual successes, overall prison conditions for Palestinian political prisoners, including children, remain far below international standards, but the conditions would perhaps be far worse were it not for the ongoing pressure by prisoners, lawyers, and others to improve them.

For the Palestinian detainees, organising themselves is an important aspect of the prison experience. The effect of their collective efforts should also be measured by what these actions provide to the prisoners themselves. The sense of collective identity engendered during imprisonment and embodied in collective action is a key coping mechanism for dealing with the harsh realities of prison life, underpinning the resilience of the prisoners and their ongoing struggle to be treated humanely.

For child prisoners, this sense of being part of a collective whole can help alleviate the trauma of forced separation from one's family, creating an essential support structure during imprisonment. Relationships created during imprisonment are intense, and the bonds forged often last for years after detainees are released. For children the experience is particularly important, occurring at a time when they are coming of age, defining themselves and their values.

A HISTORY OF ABUSE: THE FIRST INTIFADA AND THE OSLO YEARS

The prison conditions Palestinian child political prisoners experience today parallel those faced by the previous generation, the children arrested and incarcerated by Israel during the first Intifada, and by children detained during the Oslo years. The same forms of abuse occur: unhygienic, overcrowded facilities; inedible and inadequate food; lack of medical care; abuse by prison staff; little or no education; and irregular family visits.

In early 2003, DCI/PS asked individuals from all areas of the West Bank who were child prisoners at the time of the first Intifada to recall their prison experiences by completing a questionnaire. It covered details of arrest, interrogation, and imprisonment as well as how the prison experience impacted their lives, highlighting the continuity in Israel's treatment of Palestinian child political prisoners.

A.J., arrested at the age of 16 in February 1989, was interrogated for ten days, convicted of throwing stones and given a one-and-a-half-year sentence.[46]...During interrogation, he was subjected to position abuse for several hours at a time and violently beaten. During interrogation, Israeli soldiers urinated on him. His family was not allowed to visit him during interrogation, and during imprisonment he saw them only once every two months. Neither his lawyer, nor the Red Cross visited him during his detention. He reported that the conditions in the interrogation centres were particularly difficult, as the number of prisoners detained in one tent reached as many as 70. The detainees slept on wooden pallets covered with thin mattresses and the quality and quantity of food was poor.

A.A., arrested at the age of 14 in September 1990, was convicted of throwing stones and participating in demonstrations.[47] He served seven months in three different prisons, one of which was Megiddo. His family paid a 1,500 NIS fine so that he would not be detained an additional three months. He reported being beaten and put in *shabeh* during interrogation and notes that the Israeli authorities pressured him to collaborate. He was able to see his lawyer once a month and was visited once by a representative of the International Committee of the Red Cross. A.A. noted one of the most difficult hardships was the lack of contact with the outside world. Educational books were not available and there were no newspapers. Additionally, the abusive treatment by the prison authorities and overcrowded conditions made life inside prison hard. At times, he was detained in rooms with 15 other prisoners and the quality and quantity of food they received was bad. Like numerous other prisoners, from both the first and second Intifada, he recalls that almost all illnesses were treated with a basic pain reliever.

With the signing of the Oslo Accord in 1993, the number of Palestinian political prisoners, including children, drastically decreased, but the same pattern of rights abuses continued unabated. 15-year-old A.B. from Khan Yunis was arrested on 3 January 1996 and held for months at an Israeli detention facility before being tried. During his pre-trial detention, a prisoner tried to escape from the facility. Shortly afterwards, A.B. and his cellmates were severely beaten by prison guards in an attack that can only be considered collective punishment, since neither A.B. nor his cellmates were in any way connected to the escape attempt. In 1996, A.B. recounted the abuse and described his present prison conditions in an affidavit provided to a DCI/PS attorney:

On 15 September, we were outside the room. At 4 p.m. [guards] searched the room and saw a loose tile in the cell. They removed the tile. I remember the tile – it was an old cell and this tile was loose for a long time. They asked everyone to return to their cells except for the prisoners in cell four. There were six of us in that cell. They asked us to go and bring our belongings from the room. [B.] was the first one and I remember him screaming as they started beating him. He came back to us in the yard and we refused to go into the cell because we were afraid we would be beaten. They closed the door and brought around 50 police carrying tear gas, guns and clubs and forced us to enter. They took us to another cell for punishment, at first we thought it would only be for one day but later we discovered it would be longer. That night they took us for interrogation one by one, where they beat us. [B.] was badly beaten in his eye with a club and kicked in his testicles. The interrogator told us he had been waiting for this opportunity. The interrogators asked us who had loosened the tile and we told them we didn't know, maybe the people who were in the room before us.

A few days later we were told to gather our clothes and to take them to the jeep. They accused me of swearing at them and they beat me badly. We were taken to Telmond where they confiscated everything we had including our books and pens. There are three of us in each room which is 4m by 4m with a tiny window. Two of us sleep on mattresses and the third on the floor. There is an open toilet located in the cell. We went on hunger strike for five days until they gave us access to the canteen. At 7 p.m. each night they allow us to go outside for one hour. Our hands and legs are cuffed during this time and we are also chained to each other.[48]

Also during the Oslo years, 14-year-old B.A. was arrested in September 1995 for carrying a knife as he passed by the Israeli Military Court in Nablus. After his arrest he was taken to the Israeli police station in Nablus where he was interrogated for nine days. During the interrogation he was badly beaten, forcing him to make a false confession that he was carrying a knife because he was planning to kill an Israeli soldier. He was transferred to four different prisons and was eventually placed in Hasharon in November 1995, in the same section as Israeli juvenile prisoners. The Israeli juveniles regularly attacked the Palestinian children, and on several occasions threw boiling water at them through the small window in their cell while they were sleeping. The Israeli prisoners would also push a stick through the window and beat them with it, and tie a newspaper around the end of the stick, set it on fire and throw it into the Palestinian children's cell. The Palestinian children were terrified of approaching the window. In December 1995, the Israeli juvenile prisoners cut B.A. and his cellmate with razors. The DCI/PS attorney saw the cuts on their arms.

A year after B.A.'s arrest, DCI/PS received the case. During the court hearing, the police witness claimed that B.A.'s confessions had been taken without force. However, the soldier whom the prosecution claimed had been the target of the killing said under oath that he had called B.A. over to him, which clearly indicated that he had not been carrying a knife with the intent of killing the soldier. The hearings continued until May 1997 when B.A. was released and the accusation dismissed. He had spent 19 months in prison.[49]

The information gathered through these questionnaires and case files document the continued pattern of harsh treatment to which Israel subjects Palestinian child prisoners. DCI/PS's experience representing these children shows that prison conditions have become worse in many ways. Family visits, though difficult and often irregular during the first Intifada, are even less frequent now.[50] Also, the support system among prisoners is less developed than during the first Intifada, when prisoners imposed an organisation on daily life including formal discussion sessions, study circles, and political meetings. On the other hand, detained children are now transferred less frequently from one facility to another.

In June 2003 Israel Prisons Service Director Orit Adato acknowledged the gross deterioration in conditions of detention for Palestinian prisoners during the current Intifada. She outlined a number of security measures she had implemented during her three-year position, including strip searches, prohibitions on receiving packages of food, and refusing to allow prisoners to hug their family members during visits. Overcrowding, she noted, was forcing around 200 Palestinian prisoners to sleep on the floor. Adato said those measures as well as overcrowding 'have set (prison conditions) back 20 years'.[51]

The historical record makes it patently clear that Israel's current treatment of child prisoners is part of a larger pattern of abuse going back decades. In studying the thousands of children arrested during the Israeli occupation, particularly those arrested from 1987 to the present, the same themes emerge of sub-standard prison conditions and prisoners' collective struggles to improve them. These are the threads that weave the Palestinian prison experience together.

Part III

Analysis and Conclusions

8
State Violence and Discrimination

As we saw in Chapter 4, the international community has developed and detailed international standards defining the minimum acceptable treatment of children, particularly children 'deprived of their liberty'. The cornerstone is the 1989 UN Convention on the Rights of the Child (CRC), which Israel, along with almost every country in the world, has ratified. The testimonies of Palestinian children detained by Israel, confirmed by Israeli, international and Palestinian human rights organisations, point to countless violations of international law.[1] For decades, Palestinian children have recounted a consistent story of detention. From the moment of their arrest and throughout their interrogation, trial and imprisonment, the state of Israel subjects these children to brutal, degrading and intimidating treatment.

These violations are partly enabled by Israel's use of two very different legal systems: Israeli civil law applied to Israeli citizens, and the framework of military orders applied to all Palestinians living in the West Bank and Gaza Strip. This dual system institutionalises discrimination. Israeli civil law not only contains a much broader array of rights largely in line with international standards, but also extends to settlers living in the OPT, who enjoy the benefits of Israeli citizenship. Two different groups living in the same area receive vastly different treatment based on their nationality, an inherently racist practice. This framework of institutionalised discrimination, confirmed by evidence from thousands of Palestinian prisoners including children, points not to random, isolated acts of mistreatment, but to a deliberate strategy of state-sanctioned violence.

INTERNATIONAL LAW AND
INSTITUTIONALISED DISCRIMINATION

The CRC states: 'In all actions concerning children...the best interests of the child shall be a primary consideration.' It also advises that the arrest and imprisonment of children should be a measure of last resort and for the shortest possible period of time. When arresting children is unavoidable, international legal instruments guarantee them a range of rights and provide detailed rules to protect them.

Blatantly violating these fundamental principles, Israel routinely and arbitrarily arrests Palestinian children as a matter of course, not as a last resort. Violations at the arrest stage include disregarding their right:

- to be treated as innocent until proven guilty;
- to be informed of the reason for arrest;
- not to be arbitrarily arrested;
- to have immediate access to an attorney;
- to be treated at all times with dignity and respect;
- for their families to be informed of the arrest and the place of detention.

The arrests, carried out by armed and often masked soldiers, conspicuously disregard several other important international standards: those detaining children should treat them in ways appropriate to their age and according to their needs as children; and they should use child-specific procedures.[2]

In particular, Point 10 of the UN Standard Minimum Rules for the Administration of Juvenile Justice stipulates that contact with the child should be 'managed in such a way as to respect the legal status of the juvenile, promote the wellbeing of the juvenile and avoid harm to him or her, with due regard to the circumstances of the case', and Rule 12 specifies that all law enforcement officials involved in administering juvenile justice should receive special training. The Commentary to these Rules takes careful account of the particular vulnerabilities of adolescence:

To 'avoid harm' admittedly is flexible wording and covers many features of possible interaction (for example the use of harsh language, physical violence or exposure to the environment). Involvement in juvenile justice processes in itself can be 'harmful' to juveniles; the term 'avoid harm' should be broadly interpreted, therefore, as doing the least harm possible to the juvenile in the first instance, as well as any additional or undue harm. This is especially important in the initial contact with law enforcement agencies, which might profoundly influence the juvenile's attitude towards the State and society...Compassion and kind firmness are important in these situations.[3]

Following arrest, the Israeli authorities subject Palestinian child prisoners to highly brutal treatment during detention and interrogation and later in prison, and to degrading physical conditions in all detention facilities. This treatment violates the human rights standards detailed in Chapter 4, and contrasts starkly with the international norms cited above of 'compassion and kind firmness'.

Israel's treatment of Palestinian detainees also exposes the racist basis of the discriminatory legal framework applied to all Palestinians. In July 1967, the Israeli army issued an emergency regulation placing Israeli settlers under Israeli civil law, rather than under the system of military orders applied to Palestinians.[4] From that point, the nationality of the accused determined which legal system would be applied in the same geographical area. Illegal Israeli settlers accused of a crime enjoy far greater rights than Palestinians in sentencing options, the period of detention, access to legal counsel, and protections during questioning and trial. In this regard Israel's system of control in the West Bank and Gaza Strip closely resembles another historical example of legalised racism: apartheid-era South Africa. The extent of this discrimination is sharply exposed by comparing how Israel's two legal systems treat children in conflict with the law, against the benchmark of international standards.

Definition of a 'child'

The definition of a child highlights one of the fundamental differences between Israeli civil law and Israeli military orders. Article 1 of the Convention on the Rights of the Child, to which Israel is a State Party, defines a 'child' as anyone under 18 years of age. Section 3 of the Israeli Guardianship and Legal Capacity Law (1962) follows this standard, stating that 'an individual who has not reached the age of 18 is a minor'.[5]

In contrast, Israeli military law defines Palestinian children from the OPT of 16 and over as adults. This is reflected in their trials, sentences and detention in prisons controlled by the Israeli military.

Detention of minors

The Israeli government, reporting in 2001 to the UN Committee on the Rights of the Child, noted that: 'Juvenile Court case law indicates that the courts regard the deprivation of a minor's liberty as more harmful for the minor than it would be for an adult.'[6] The report goes on to cite a Supreme Court ruling[7] illustrating how seriously Israel regards the imprisonment of minors:

> The conditions of detention and prison, even without the characteristics of such places, are liable to cause severe emotional shock and trauma. More often than not, a minor is liable to encounter a world of drugs and serious crime. The court must become a 'father to minors', and preserve them – whenever possible – from this experience.[8]

According to this report, in the year 2000 Israeli courts dealt with 4,940 cases involving children,[9] sentencing only 291 (5.9 per cent) to prison and giving to the rest alternative sentences such as fines, supervised probation, or placement in a special residential facility for juveniles.[10]

The military court system does not utilise such forms of alternative sentencing. Only one military order, No. 132 (July 1967), deals with the sentencing of Palestinian children, and it contains two serious flaws that ultimately undermine any potential protections. First, although this order defines terms such as child, adolescent and teenager, it only covers teenagers aged 14–16, omitting those aged 16–17. Later military orders amended the definition of teenager to those aged 14–18, but in practice children 16 and 17 continue to be treated as adults.[11] Second, the apparent distinction between sentencing provisions for children as opposed to adults is overridden by considerations of the nature of the offence. On the one hand, Article 5 of Military Order No.132 states: 'If a court finds a teenager (defined as someone over 14 and under 16) guilty of an offence and sentences them to prison, the prison sentence will not exceed 1 year.' But this distinction is undermined in the same article by the reservation, *'unless the crime for which the teenager is charged carries a maximum sentence of more than 5 years'* [authors' emphasis].

This escape clause has serious implications for sentencing provisions if one considers the 'crimes' that most Palestinian children are accused of committing. For example, Military Order No. 101, 'Order Concerning Prohibition of Incitement and Hostile Propaganda', issued on 27 August 1967, allows for a maximum sentence of ten years for those found guilty of the following acts:

- Conducting a protest march or political meeting with ten people or more without permission from the Israeli military commander;
- Raising a flag or other symbols;
- Distributing or publishing a political article or picture with political connotations;
- Attempting to influence public opinion in a way detrimental to public order/security.

As virtually every arrested Palestinian child is accused of an offence that fits into one of the above categories, carrying maximum sentences greater than five years, the provisions in Military Order No. 132 limiting prison terms for juveniles do not apply. Moreover, these acts constitute basic democratic rights of freedom of expression, participation and organisation. This example demonstrates how military orders offer a semblance of legality to the restrictions and control of the lives of Palestinians under occupation.

As we saw, Israel's 2001 report stated that less than 6 per cent of Israeli children found guilty of an offence had received a prison sentence.[12] In contrast, military courts pass sentences on Palestinian children which are out of all proportion to the charges. This contrasts sharply with international standards that call for the shortest appropriate periods of detention for children. There is no comprehensive database recording the sentences given to Palestinian children by the Israeli military court system. However, according to records kept by DCI/PS since 1992, the military courts sentence the vast majority of convicted Palestinian children over 14 years old to prison – alternative sentences are extremely rare.

The discrimination in sentencing is starkly exposed in a comparison of the sentences typically given to Palestinian children with those given in two notorious Israeli criminal law cases. (See Box 8.1.)

Child-specific procedures

Israel's own civil legislation distinguishes between Israeli children and adults in the judicial system, and contains specific provisions for treating Israeli juvenile offenders.[18] Relevant authorities in contact with Israeli children must follow internal directives setting out child-specific procedures covering the functioning of juvenile courts, arrest and pre-trial proceedings, punishment and modes of treatment.[19] The Israeli government prides itself on employing professionals who have been specifically trained to deal with juvenile

---

Box 8.1   Discrimination in Sentencing

A stone throwing and a killing

On 15 December 2000, the Israeli military arrested 17-year-old Murad Rashad Abu Judeh and charged him with throwing stones at Israeli military jeeps and soldiers. The military court sentenced him to 10 months in Megiddo Military Prison, a one-year suspended sentence if he committed any offence within the next five years and a fine of 3,000 NIS (approximately US$690).[13]

On 30 September 1988, a Jewish Rabbi, Moshe Levinger, opened fire with live ammunition in the centre of Hebron killing one Palestinian and wounding another. On 12 April 1989, an Israeli court indicted him on charges of manslaughter, causing serious bodily injury in aggravated circumstances, and causing malicious damage. On 1 May 1990, following a plea bargain between the Jerusalem District Attorney's Office and Levinger's lawyer, Levinger was convicted of causing death by negligence, wounding in aggravated circumstances, and causing malicious damage. In the end Levinger served only three of a five-month sentence.[14]

A stone throwing and an assassination plot that killed the Israeli Prime Minister

Israeli soldiers arrested 14-year-old Sami Issa Qandeel on 15 November 2000, accused him of throwing stones, and took him to the Givat Ze'ev settlement in handcuffs and blindfolded. There the police interrogated Sami, hit him on the face and said they would not stop beating him until he confessed. After Sami confessed, the Israeli soldiers took him the next day to the Beit El detention centre, held him for three days, then moved him to Etzion detention centre near Bethlehem where he stayed for two weeks. He was then moved to Telmond and placed with Israeli juvenile criminal prisoners, who stole his clothes on the first day. His lawyer's complaint to the administration only resulted in further beatings from the Israeli prisoners. Eventually the military court sentenced Sami to six months in prison and a ten-month suspended sentence. He spent two months in the Israeli criminal prisoners' section where he was afraid to sleep for fear of being attacked.[15]

In 1998, Margalit Har-Shefi was convicted of knowing and failing to report that her former boyfriend, Yigal Amir, was planning to assassinate Israeli Prime Minister Yitzhak Rabin in 1995. Har-Shefi was sentenced to nine months in prison, which she began serving in March 2001. In July 2001 Israeli President Moshe Katsav commuted her sentence to six months,[16] defending his decision by noting that Har-Shefi 'has paid her debt to society, has been punished, and is pained by the horrible assassination and has denounced it'.[17]

---

suspects,[20] and in their 2001 report to the UN Committee on the Rights of the Child noted:

In most cases, minors are handled by people who are specially trained for the task. In all systems, there are rules that aim to provide special protection for minors, including protection of their privacy and prevention of their stigmatisation as criminals. Therapeutic professionals accompany a minor from the initial stages of criminal proceedings; the majority of decisions regarding the fate of the minor are made in consultation with these professionals, and with preference given to treatment and rehabilitation.[21]

This report also noted that every Israeli police station has a special youth unit responsible for contacting child suspects. These units are 'composed of police officers who undergo special training and in-service refresher courses on interrogation of youth, and who receive information on the distinct laws and procedures for handling youth and on community services for minors and youth'.[22]

Under Israeli civil law, Israeli children must be brought before a juvenile court, or a court sitting as a juvenile court, presided over by a juvenile judge.[23] The military courts in the OPT have no such system – Palestinian children appear before the same military courts that try Palestinian adults.[24]

Several military orders address the issue of juveniles; however, most are revisions to two main orders: Order Concerning the Trial of Juvenile Offenders (1967),[25] and Order Concerning the Conduct of Minors (Imposition of Bond) (Temporary Provisions).[26] The former provides theoretical sentencing guidelines for juvenile offenders which do not apply in practice, as discussed above. The latter stipulates the financial penalties imposed on the parents of Palestinian children convicted of violating Israeli military orders.

Authority to arrest children

A police officer may detain Israeli children in only eight specific circumstances, including situations in which minors commit an offence in the presence of a police officer, escape from lawful custody, or refuse to identify themselves or accompany the police officer.[27] In such cases, arrests of minors must take into account the severity of the offence and the degree of certainty that they committed the offence.

In contrast, the powers to arrest Palestinian children are very broad, both in relation to who has authority to arrest and for what offences. Military Order No. 378 allows any Israeli soldier or police officer to detain a Palestinian child merely on the suspicion that the child has violated a military order, regardless of the severity of the offence or the likelihood that the child actually committed it. Military Order No. 898 gives Israeli settlers the right to detain any Palestinian, including children, whom they deem to be 'acting suspiciously'. Military orders are couched so broadly that, in effect, any Israeli soldier, police officer or settler can detain a Palestinian child at any time.

Detention before sentencing

Israeli civil law stipulates that the maximum initial detention period of an Israeli minor is ten days. This period can be extended for a further ten days, but within the 20-day limit the child must be indicted unless the Attorney General requests an extension.[28] Thereafter, the rules for children are the same as for adults. After 75 days, they must be released unless charges have been filed against them.

The military court can imprison a Palestinian child for up to six months without an indictment.[29] The military court can also issue an administrative detention order, detaining Palestinian children up to six months without trial or charge. Administrative Detention Orders can be renewed every six months, and do not require the detainee to ever appear before a court.

Right to see a lawyer

Under Israeli law a detainee has the right to see a lawyer as soon as possible. In very exceptional circumstances (such as threats to state security or human life, or in order to prevent a crime) a police officer may request in writing that this be delayed a few hours for purposes of interrogation. These delays can be extended several times by increasingly senior police officers or Shabak commanders to a maximum period of 15 days. According to the Israeli human rights organisation B'Tselem, this authority is rarely invoked.[30]

In contrast, Military Order No. 1500 automatically denies Palestinian detainees from the OPT the right to see a lawyer for 18 days. A Shabak officer or a military court judge can extend this period to 90 days,[31] justified on the basis of the 'security of the region or for the sake of the interrogation'. The criteria for determining what constitutes such a justification are kept secret.[32] Thus, Palestinian detainees often face the most violent means of interrogation, including torture, during the very period when they are denied the right to see a lawyer.

Appointment of a lawyer

Israeli legislation contains provisions entitling children to legal representation under The Public Defenders' (Entitlement of Additional Minors to Representation) Regulations of 1998.[33] In addition, Section

18(a) of the Youth (Trial, Punishment and Modes of Treatment) Law 1971 mandates juvenile courts 'to appoint counsel for the defence of a minor, if it believes this to be in the best interests of the minor'.[34]

Palestinian children have no such right. If the family of the child cannot afford an attorney, military court proceedings simply proceed without one.

Detention before being brought before a judge

The Youth (Trial, Punishment and Modes of Treatment) Law 1971 and the Criminal Procedure (Enforcement Powers – Arrests) Law 1996 stipulate that Israeli minors aged 14 to 18 must come before a judge within 24 hours of being detained. In exceptional circumstances this can be extended for a further 24 hours. In contrast, Military Order No. 1500 allows Palestinian detainees (including children) to be held for up to 18 days without being brought before a judge.

Detention until termination of legal proceedings

In 1998, 4,131 Israeli minors were arrested. Of those, 216 (5.3 per cent) remained in detention from the moment of arrest until legal proceedings finished.[35] Palestinian children are almost always in detention from the moment of arrest until the end of legal proceedings. In one very rare case, in October 2001 a 14-year-old girl, Sawsan Abu Turki, who suffered from serious psychological problems, was arrested and accused of attempting to stab an Israeli soldier. She was imprisoned for just over four months and then released into the custody of her parents who had to put up a bail sum of 15,000 NIS (US$3,500). The terms of her bail placed Sawsan under house arrest. She had to attend a secure rehabilitation centre and otherwise could only leave home to go to the hospital or court if accompanied by a chaperone aged over 30. After 13 months of house arrest Sawsan was released, but the court imposed a fine of 15,000 NIS which her parents had to pay, and gave her a suspended sentence of seven months should she offend again within five years.

Education while in prison

The right of children to education is confirmed in Article 28 of the UN Convention on the Rights of the Child. This right extends to children deprived of their liberty, a principle made clear by Point 38 of the UN Rules for the Protection of Juveniles Deprived of their Liberty:

Every juvenile of compulsory school age has the right to education suited to his or her needs and abilities and designed to prepare him or her for return to society...Special attention should be given by the administration of the detention facilities to the education of juveniles of foreign origin or with particular cultural or ethnic needs.

These rules also stipulate that detained children 'should have the right to receive vocational training' to help them get work on their release.[36]

Israeli juveniles in prison follow the formal curriculum of the Israeli Prison Service, delivered over three twelve-week trimesters per year.[37] There are four hours of formal study daily, sometimes combined with work, at the prison education centre.[38] At the end of each trimester, the IPS submits prisoners' grades to Israel's Minister of Education and 'certificates issued receive a legal seal of approval from the Ministry of Education and Culture via the Head of IPS Inmate Schooling and Education Division'.[39] Describing these educational and vocational services, the IPS says:

Imprisonment in fact offers an opportunity to acquire important skills. Through the education, care, and employment systems prisoners can complete their formal schooling to various levels, entertain and enrich themselves in a variety of activity groups, learn a trade and regular work habits, and contribute to their family budget.[40]

The IPS describes education in Ramle (Neve Tertze) prison as follows: 'Classes are offered at different levels within the formal educational system, from basic elementary education up to high school level.'[41] It provides a fuller description of educational services provided in Hasharon:

Study classes enable completion of formal education at different levels. A less formal educational system offers a range of courses, workshops and many other activities, along similar lines to a community centre. Overall educational activity aims to enrich the prisoners' knowledge base and encourage the acquisition of tools for increased development and awareness, as a basis for an eventual change in behavioural and thought patterns.[42]

Only one prison provides Palestinian children with any formal education. In November 1997 the Central Court in Tel Aviv ruled that detained Palestinian children have the right to education and that this should be provided according to the Palestinian syllabus. The court ruling admitted: 'There exists discrimination between Palestinian and Israeli children in regards to access to education and cultural matters.'[43] While this ruling appeared to grant Palestinian children the right to education, the court decision also noted that nothing in the ruling should be seen as *detrimental to matters of security*. The effect of this escape clause is to continue to deny Palestinian children the right to education, claiming 'security interests'. The prison system further punishes Palestinian children by forbidding access to books, newspapers, television and telephones. As with Military Order No. 132, a ruling that appears to promote the rights of Palestinian children actually discriminates against them.

Currently, Palestinian children receive *no formal education* whatsoever in Megiddo, Ramle and Ketziot prisons. In Ofek lessons are conducted in Hebrew, which they do not understand. In Hasharon, the prison authorities teach Palestinian children three subjects, Hebrew, Arabic and Mathematics, in violation of the 1997 ruling that prison education should follow the full Palestinian curriculum of eight subjects. When the DCI/PS attorney queried why the remaining subjects such as history, geography and religion were not taught, he was informed that they are viewed as 'detrimental to security'.

Palestinian children receive no vocational training in Megiddo and Ketziot. In Ramle, vocational training exists for Israelis, but there is none for the Palestinian girls. Most of the vocational training for juveniles in Telmond compound is located in Ofek, but Palestinian children rarely get to participate.

The experience of lawyers

Previous chapters have described the obstacles lawyers routinely encounter in trying to defend Palestinian children. Of course, Palestinian lawyers have the greatest difficulties. They routinely encounter institutional discrimination. A structural power imbalance infuses the entire system and treats them as part of the occupied population. Unlike their Israeli colleagues, they must be careful not to antagonise the court and in particular the judges. All have to apply for a special letter confirming they are lawyers, and for special travel permits which since 2000 have been very difficult to obtain. Since they are not allowed to be members of the Israel Bar, they cannot take cases to the Israeli high court, and have to go through Israeli lawyers.

The Israeli lawyers who represent Palestinian detainees are part of the Israeli legal system and know how it works. This is often important – if there are gaps in the military legal regulations, the military legal establishment tends to refer to Israeli civil law for guidance. It is also easier for Israeli lawyers to get hold of the case files and material for their cases. As Israeli human rights attorney Lea Tsemel notes:

> Palestinian lawyers in the West Bank have a much more difficult time. They have no rights and they can't represent Palestinians in Israel. They have the language issue and can't access material easily. They don't know the Israeli legal system so well or the rules of the game. I have all those advantages. In addition I can be very extreme and demanding and not obey all the rules.[44]

A SYSTEM OF STATE-SANCTIONED VIOLENCE

Israel's harsh treatment of Palestinian child prisoners is not a new phenomenon resulting from the escalation of current hostilities, nor is it accidental or arbitrary. The question remains however, what does Israel hope to achieve by subjecting children to such treatment?

During interrogation various branches of the Israeli state try to coerce Palestinian children into quick confessions using physical and psychological methods calculated to disorient and terrify. This is accompanied by direct and repeated accusations that the child is guilty of an offence. The combined abuse frequently results in signed confessions that serve as the basis for their prosecution through the military court system.

The continuation of harsh treatment beyond the period of interrogation suggests another pattern of coercion. The entire edifice of the military order and military court system outlined in Chapter 3 is directed towards maintaining Israeli control of the OPT. Any form of resistance to this military occupation is defined as a threat to the security of the state of Israel. The fact that Palestinians universally reject Israel's occupation makes *any* Palestinian a security threat by definition.

Israel's treatment of Palestinian children is central to a policy of intimidation designed to quash all resistance to Israel's system of control. On the surface, Palestinian children may seem like any other juvenile offenders charged with offences that violate the law. However, these Palestinian children do not fit the textbook definition of adolescents in conflict with the law over offences such as theft, drug abuse or vandalism. Instead, the Israeli state charges them with violating military orders that have been established to maintain an illegal occupation and punishes them for protesting Israel's presence in the OPT. Certainly, the majority of the former prisoners interviewed by DCI/PS in 2003 believed that these harsh policies were aimed at discouraging them from resisting the occupation. This reality is made clear in cases where the military court lists the charge against the child under the umbrella term 'Intifada activities'.

However, imprisonment serves another more explicitly political agenda. It is used to gather information about and control Palestinian political activity. During interrogation, Israeli state agents put pressure on both children and adults to provide information about, and names of, other Palestinians. At times, they also attempt to recruit these children to long-term collaboration with Israeli security services in exchange for lighter sentences or early release.

Israel ultimately regards Palestinian children as members of a population rejecting Israel's control of the OPT. During the mass arbitrary arrests of 2002 and 2003, Israel punished hundreds of children simply for being Palestinian. Israel also targets these children's national and religious identity during detention. Sworn testimonies from children recount being forced to curse Palestinian leaders or God, to stamp on the Qur'an and to destroy pictures of leaders or commemorative posters of Palestinian political activists and civilians killed during the Intifada.

Israel's arrest of Palestinian children also exerts pressure on the population as a whole. When the political situation on the ground deteriorates, Israel increases the rate of arrests. In 1999 Israel started to detain increasing numbers of Palestinian children and sentenced them to longer prison terms.[45] When widespread demonstrations against Israel's occupation broke out in September 2000, Israel initiated wide-scale arrests of Palestinian children. As the uprising continued, arrests increased culminating in the mass arbitrary arrests of thousands of Palestinian males in 2002 and 2003.

Political activity is not a prerequisite for arrest; being Palestinian, particularly a male, is the major risk factor. The likelihood that any Palestinian male can be arrested at any time exerts a psychological toll on the entire population. This stress is compounded by the knowledge that family visits are denied, prisoners' access to legal recourse is restricted, and conditions of detention are abusive. The dramatic rise since 2002 of administrative detention orders, and the spectre of indefinite detention, further exacerbates the stress. Thus the effects of arrests extend far beyond the numbers of those imprisoned. Through these policies Israel sends a strong message to the Palestinian population: resistance to the occupation comes at a heavy price. The violence with which children are treated underlines this message.

In this context Israel's treatment of Palestinian child political prisoners must be viewed as part of a state-sanctioned policy of violence in which torture plays a central role. Torture goes further than violations against individuals; it is used by one group against another as a means of domination and control and as a means of undermining sources of strength and resistance. In discussing torture, the US-based Center for Victims of Torture states: 'The purpose of torture is to control populations by destroying individual leaders and frightening entire communities.'[46] Likewise, in its *Stop Torture* campaign, Amnesty International US used a number of sources to outline the purpose of torture. It coincides closely with Israeli state practices:

> Torture is the systematic destruction of person, family, neighborhood, school, work, formal and informal organisations, and nation, with the purpose of controlling a population the state perceives to be dangerous. ...Torture's purpose is to change the behavior, the thinking patterns, and the personalities of the victims – many do not survive it. By taking advantage of the person's values and fears, torturers cut the sources of personal strength needed to resist and recover.[47]

Many branches of the Israeli state regularly participate in the systematic maltreatment of Palestinian children and the violations of their human rights. Soldiers routinely violently arrest and abuse children while transporting them to detention/interrogation centres, which are always located in alien and hostile environments. In these centres Israeli state employees from different branches of the military and security subject Palestinian children to physical and psychological torture, including beatings, sleep and food deprivation, isolation, and position abuse.

Detention facilities are substandard: filthy, unhygienic and overcrowded, and the prison authorities fail to provide essential supplies. The food is poor and often insufficient and medical care is perfunctory and negligent. Prison authorities for the most part deny these children access to any education or vocational training. Prison guards, and Israeli prisoners with whom some Palestinian children are detained, frequently beat and psychologically abuse them. Particularly since the beginning of the second Intifada, Palestinian children lack the protection of any external monitoring, given restrictions on family and lawyer visits.

Trials, presided over by Israeli military judges, do not guarantee anything approximating a fair and impartial hearing. The system is weighted against the defence, secret evidence is used, and lawyers' access to their child clients is denied or severely limited.

Such mistreatment is neither random nor an occasional departure from established good practice – it applies to all Palestinian prisoners including children. It is a deliberate policy that is supported by the institutional discrimination that underpins the framework of military orders. Many security branches implement these policies including the army, police, border guard, prison staff, and the Shabak, which reports directly to the Israeli Prime Minister. The abuses occur in facilities supervised by the Israeli military and those under the control of the Ministry of Public Security.

Local and international organisations have widely documented this long-standing pattern of abuse, and have repeatedly raised their concerns with the Israeli government. The state of Israel has consistently failed to change its policies and treat Palestinian prisoners humanely. Instead it continues with practices that are tantamount to a thoroughly institutionalised system of state-sanctioned violence.

9
Psychological and Social Impacts of Prison and Torture

Detention had a bad impact on my life, socially and psychologically. I was depressed and lost trust in other people and this affected my relationships with them. I can't work now since I can be arrested at any time. I have had health problems as a result of torture.

> *M.A., now 27 years old, arrested in 1991*
> *at 15, detained for 3 years for stone throwing*

I needed help to get back to school. It was a very difficult experience. For a long time afterwards I was left with feelings of depression and mistrust. I had pains in my head from the beating but eventually this got better after treatment.

> *M.O., now 31 years old, arrested in 1987*
> *at 15, detained for a year for writing slogans*

I became stronger and a more patient person and this helped me deal with my parent's divorce. I still remember the experience all the time. It was positive. It strengthened my personality. But I did have insomnia and a tendency to keep apart from others.

> *M.Z., now 31 years old, arrested in 1988*
> *at 16, detained for 22 months*
> *for throwing stones during a demonstration*

Almost all Palestinian children detained in Israeli prisons and detention centres are subject from the moment of their arrest to extreme forms of harsh treatment, including systematic mental and physical torture. The torture takes place in a broader context of social violence[1] – violence which results in psychological terror over and above any physical injury. This chapter looks at the psychological and social effects of this experience – how Palestinian children respond to, cope with, and survive this severe trauma, and the subsequent impact it has on their lives.

When children are imprisoned and tortured they are at a critical stage in their cognitive and physical development, and especially vulnerable to short- and long-term effects. They may tend to confess sooner than adults because of their vulnerable psychological state during interrogation, and so they may be punished less severely than adult prisoners, but this does not negate the brutality of the treatment these children may have faced. The effects of imprisonment and torture extend well beyond the period behind bars, and can seriously disrupt their education, social relationships and future life chances and choices.

Individual personality plays a significant role in coping and survival strategies, but there are other important factors. To understand Palestinian children's responses to the prison experience and the long-term impact on their lives, we must put it in the context of Palestinian society.

First, Palestinian children have all grown up under an occupation, frequently marked by armed conflict. Most of the casualties are civilian, and the Israeli military has continued to target children for attack.[2] Palestinians have lived with occupation and its consequent chronic stress for several generations now. The cumulative effect of this history fundamentally affects the relationships between Palestinian child prisoners and their families and the wider society.

Second, although Palestinian society is by no means homogeneous, it is characterised by strong family and local loyalties and deeply held ideologies and beliefs.[3] The extended family is a central element in this society and prioritises the collective over the individual. The deep-rooted community spirit and sense of collective responsibility means that the suffering and stress of individual members affects everyone; it is also a primary source of emotional and psychological support. Both religion and nationalism are important sources of patience and stoicism.[4] This cultural context has an important bearing on Palestinian children's responses to the trauma of prison.

Third, the cultural, political and social context of imprisonment can mitigate some of the psychological effects. Social and political events in the wider community outside prison, as well as detainees' own social and political backgrounds, can influence their coping and survival strategies and forms of resistance. For instance, during the first Intifada Israel imprisoned a much larger proportion of the Palestinian population, and strong social networks were established in prison, promoting political education and particular social values.

This affected how prisoners felt and often helped them readapt after release. The first Intifada also changed traditional social conceptions about children, who began to participate in the wider national liberation struggle, having had little previous social or political voice.

TRAUMA AND TORTURE

The experience is out of the imagination. The prison administration wants to break your spirit.

G.A., now 35 years old; imprisoned
five times since 1982, when he was 14

According to the American Psychiatric Association,[5] imprisonment and torture are beyond the range of normal experience and amongst the most frightening and psychologically damaging events that an individual can experience.

As a form of state violence, torture has been used for centuries as a tool of war to systematically inflict mental and physical suffering. Currently it is practiced in more than half the countries in the world to achieve a number of physical, psychological, political and social outcomes, all of which are relevant to Palestinian children. The ostensible purpose is to extract information through confessions, but in the process torture also aims to undermine and crush the victim's personality and identity for political purposes.[6]

Torture can also be viewed as a means 'to achieve social control through coercion and terror'.[7] By targeting specific individuals, particularly children, it also seeks to undermine the community, its solidarity, leadership and future. The suffering and distress of the tortured person is not a personal affair, it also deeply affects their family, neighbours, friends and community. In specifically targeting children for torture and imprisonment, the state also attacks the actual and symbolic future of a community. Former child prisoners repeatedly stressed this point in interviews.[8] They discussed why they thought they had been imprisoned: 'The aim is to depress and torture and abolish the national feeling'; 'The aim of detaining me was to undermine my spiritual feelings and make me lose trust in myself and others'; and 'to terrorise the other children to prevent them from participating in the Intifada and to stop them getting educated'. These children will have interpreted their jailors' intentions in part from the explicit comments and threats of those who arrested and interrogated them.

Research into connections between the trauma of war and torture and subsequent psychological disorders among adult civilians intensified following World War II. By 1980, Post-Traumatic Stress Disorder (PTSD) was classified as a distinct category in psychological and psychiatric diagnosis. It comprises three groups of symptoms:

1. *recurrence/intrusion*, in which the traumatic event is repeatedly experienced, for instance in dreams;
2. *avoidance/numbness*, ignoring stimuli or avoiding people, places or situations associated with the trauma;
3. *increased arousal* such as sleep difficulties or extreme caution.

PTSD is now generally used to identify trauma in combination with other approaches, which take account of its limitations when used alone and its Western cultural bias. The UK Medical Foundation for the Care of Victims of Torture has adopted this more eclectic and multi-disciplinary approach in an attempt to reconstruct the torture survivor's world, drawing on individual and community resources and networks.

Research studies have linked exposure to torture to a range of psychological consequences including PTSD, depression, anxiety, antisocial behaviour and non-specific physical complaints.[9] Some of the most common psychological outcomes are sleep disturbances, nightmares, impaired memory, lack of concentration, guilt, low self-esteem, a change in identity, and sometimes psychosis. Other consequences include fatigue, emotional instability and social withdrawal and a range of psychosomatic complaints such as headaches and stomach pain.

Disturbed patterns of sleep are a very typical reaction. Survivors commonly relive the torture through nightmares, in which survivors try to escape but cannot protect themselves. Certain sensory signs can also trigger memories of the torture.

Unlike neurosis, the anxiety of the victim is associated with conscious memories, tentatively but never really repressed. The anxiety is evoked by sensory, auditory or visual signals or experiences, which symbolise torture and persecution...and they are overwhelmed by panic.[10]

Some research suggests that as many as 90 per cent of torture survivors suffer from chronic psychological symptoms such as emotional instability, depression, passivity and disturbed sleep.[11] Another review indicated that 70 per cent of torture survivors suffered from PTSD.[12] The more extreme the experience, the more severe are the consequences.

Research in the OPT has revealed high PTSD scores. For instance, 50 per cent of males injured during the first Intifada met all the diagnostic criteria for PTSD,[13] and a survey of 550 male former political prisoners from Gaza found that more than three-quarters reported intrusive memories and nearly one half had repeated nightmares.[14] Those who were most severely tortured, by chemical or electrical means, had the highest prevalence of PTSD symptoms, including intrusive thoughts, numbness, withdrawal and hyper-arousal.[15]

While there may be shared symptoms among those who experience similar kinds of trauma, after-effects are not universal and are mediated by a range of factors such as age, gender and the nature and intensity of the event. Coping and survival strategies also derive from the meaning people give to their experience, the internal and external resources upon which they draw to maintain their sanity and integrity as well as context-specific social, political and cultural factors.

In looking at impacts and responses to torture, it is essential to acknowledge that it is not the responses of survivors that are 'pathological' or abnormal, but their oppressive political environment in which stress has become the norm. Therapeutic and other forms of rehabilitation and support need to include environmental resources that can empower individuals and communities.[16]

CHILDREN FACING EXTREME VIOLENCE AND CONFLICT

The psychological effects of extreme violence and conflict on children have received widespread attention in the past 20 years, with the intensification of military conflicts which directly and indirectly involve children in Africa, the Middle East, Southeast Asia, former Yugoslavia and Latin America. Research there shows that children who have been tortured usually have experienced other and repeated forms of brutality, including social and political conflict and poverty. There may also be a lack of parental care, with children taking on adult roles as parents disappear, are killed violently, or simply die. Often the child is not the only person in the family who has been tortured, and may well have witnessed parents or older siblings being humiliated, a common experience of children in the OPT.

Children growing up in violent environments and war zones live in conditions of chronic traumatic stress, in addition to their more acute episodes of trauma. This is an important distinction, as they do not return to a safe environment after experiencing trauma. Such chronic stress can lead to delayed PTSD and long-term mental health impacts, such as emerged for children in Cambodia long after the end of the Pol Pot regime.[17] The physical and emotional drain of living with chronic stress and danger depletes their resources and affects their ability to cope. They have to make developmental adjustments in interpreting and coping with their daily reality. They may experience persisting PTSD symptoms as well as significant changes in behaviour and personality and interpretations of their world.[18]

All this can elicit different adaptations and responses in children. A 1987 [19] study investigating children living in conditions of violent conflict noted the development of an enhanced 'moral sensibility' as an adaptive mechanism. However, other research has highlighted the physical damage, emotional trauma and development impairment that often results and can lead to reactions involving violence, hatred and fear.[20]

Vulnerability of adolescents to torture

Research identifies personality and age as significant factors in children's responses to traumatic or violent experiences, both protecting them and posing risks. While secure relationships are particularly important for younger children, traumatisation in adolescents can reduce their ability to form long-lasting personal relationships and make plans.[21]

Adolescents are especially vulnerable to torture for a number of reasons – their specific stage in development places them at especially high risk. In the extensive experience of the Danish Rehabilitation and Research Centre for Torture Victims:

Because their personality structure is not fully developed, children tortured at the age 12–16 are particularly severely damaged. The combination of their being deprived of a normal development combined with the experience of long periods in refugee camps or in the constant insecurity of civil war makes treatment very complex and time consuming.[22]

Going though normal physical and emotional changes, adolescents can feel insecure and emotionally volatile, as they attempt to distance themselves from their families, developing a separate identity while consolidating social and psychological resources. They are involved in planning for the future, in education, in creating intimate relationships and in developing a world view as their abstract thinking becomes increasingly sophisticated and they engage in more complex analysis. Although expected to function more as adults, they lack emotional maturity, and often have a strong belief in their invulnerability and their ability to change the world.

Experience from other contexts shows that teenagers who have been tortured may feel guilty and depressed, believing that they did not do enough to protect their families or friends.[23] This corresponds with a key objective of torture: to undermine, disempower and attack self-confidence, and can be particularly damaging for adolescents whose self-identity is fragile.[24]

Trauma and Palestinian children

Palestinian children grow up in a context of chronic violence and danger, and it should not be surprising if many display a range of psychological symptoms in direct response. They will have been exposed to repeated, not single, traumatic episodes. On the one hand, daily exposure to traumatic events such as gunfire, that in other contexts would be extreme and 'abnormal', can become 'normalised'. On the other, events which might seem 'normal' in other contexts, such as a knock at the door at night – which could signal the Israeli army entering their house – might be extremely distressing.

Research from the 1980s before the first Intifada, based on reports from Palestinian mothers, indicated that Palestinian children had higher levels of aggression, withdrawal and nervousness symptoms, anxieties, and phobias with increased exposure to trauma.[25] A 1990 study during the first Intifada[26] confirms these findings and highlights children's widespread fear of soldiers (nearly 50 per cent), fear of leaving the house (28 per cent) and increased aggressive behaviour (45 per cent).[27] More recently, a third of male and a half of female children who lost a parent in the 1994 Hebron massacre[28] met PTSD criteria.[29]

On the other hand, interviews with Gazan children aged 9 to 16 during the first Intifada[30] challenged the Western correlation between stress and decline in self-esteem and highlighted the positive challenge of these events. Although they had high scores for depression and anxiety at the height of the Intifada, they did not exhibit the loss of self-esteem or disempowerment normally associated with exposure to stressful events. Compared to their Arab peers they felt in control of their future, possibly because of Palestinian society's support of their active participation in the Intifada. The violent crises were seen as positive challenges as children moved from being passive bystanders to active participants.[31]

Nonetheless, the severity of the trauma is critical. A 1995 study of Palestinian children[32] suggests that those exposed to the most extreme traumatic events, such as torture, had depressed self-esteem scores. The severity of the trauma overcame potential 'mediating' factors such as social and family support for their participation. Similar findings have been reported from other conflict zones such as Angola. [33] More recent data from Palestine confirms the powerful link between exposure to trauma and negative psychological impacts,[34] with exposure to torture rating highest of all.

> The Palestinian experience clearly showed that children and youth who were exposed to extreme forms of traumatic events displayed the highest rates of PTSD and other stress-related symptoms...The Palestinian experience has also shown that torture produced the highest rate of induced PTSD and its related symptomology among Palestinian youth...Furthermore, children and youth who were repeatedly exposed to traumatic events were more likely to develop PTSD symptoms than their peers...These findings are similar to those emanating from other war-torn regions.[35]

DCI/PS staff who have worked with hundreds of young ex-prisoners both individually and in groups are in no doubt that these children suffer a range of psychological symptoms following torture and imprisonment. After-effects include sleep disorders, low self-esteem, social withdrawal, learning disorders and lack of concentration, anxieties and fears, and nervousness. Many develop stomach pains and headaches which, when examined, show no physical basis. In certain instances teenage boys start bed-wetting. Some children are afraid to go to sleep at night because of constant nightmares, and teachers report finding them asleep in the classroom.

Interviews with a group of 18 young men imprisoned as children between the mid-1980s and the mid-1990s and who had all been tortured revealed a range of psychological and physical effects.[36] Many reported some of the more extreme aspects of trauma, such as continually reliving the details of their experience and constant nightmares. More than 20 years later, N.A., imprisoned for 13 days in 1981 when he was 16 says: 'I still dream and have nightmares that they are coming to arrest me. I still remember the first person that interrogated me. I remember all the body details, facial and body movements after 20 years.'

Half of those interviewed said they suffered from depression after leaving prison, and two had nervous breakdowns. One was S.N., arrested for three years in 1991 at the age of 17: 'After my release I had a breakdown and needed psychological treatment and am still suffering from the impacts of that now.' One-third said that they had lost self-confidence and became more withdrawn as well as more generally suspicious or afraid of others. Time and again detainees described similar symptoms and long-term effects. M.H., arrested for 19 months in 1996 at 16, reported, 'I started feeling more afraid and I mistrusted others and became more isolated.' His words were echoed by E.A., arrested for three years in 1991 when he was 16: 'After prison I felt withdrawn and that pushed people away from me. I became more afraid of people and more cautious in dealing with others. I was very alone.'

More than half said they had problems sleeping after being in prison. M.Z., arrested for 22 months in 1988 at age 16 said: 'The detention still affects me and causes problems like insomnia as well as difficulties in making friends.' These quotes are from children who had long sentences, so it is not surprising that their detention should have long-lasting impacts. However, shorter periods in prison can also have long-lasting and devastating impacts, as with M.O., arrested at 15 in 1987 and detained for 48 days: 'It was such a hard experience and so difficult to forget. I spent a long time afterwards being depressed and lost my self-confidence.'

Over half of the interviewees still suffered from long-term physical problems directly resulting from torture or other maltreatment, including leg pains, muscle and joint problems and vision deterioration. O.O., arrested at 17 in 1992 and detained for six months, suffered a heart attack and still has heart problems and pains in his legs from his torture. A.J., arrested at 16 in 1989 for a year and a half, still suffers from headaches resulting from heavy beatings.

COPING STRATEGIES

Coping and survival strategies employed by imprisoned and tortured adults may also be relevant to older children. Political activists who are mentally prepared for arrest, detention and torture and have the support of their communities may cope better with that experience than others.[37] In South Africa, young political activists under the apartheid regime often accepted pain and suffering as part of their political engagement.[38]

A survey of 79 young, male, former political prisoners in the Gaza Strip, jailed before and during the first Intifada, looked at three aspects of their prison experience: the subjective meaning they gave to their imprisonment; their coping strategies; and how their appraisal of the experience and their coping strategies affected their mental well being.[39] The study identified seven types of prison experience, of which only one was entirely negative, stressing disillusion and suffering. The other six were seen as relatively rewarding. They included: a useful and necessary task for their personal development; a normative stage in a Palestinian man's life (risk is part of the struggle for independence); a means of heroic fulfilment (of deeply held beliefs); a period of personal insight and growth; a struggle between weakness and strength; and (the least-cited experience) a crystallisation of religious experience.

The wider social and political context both inside and outside prisons at that time, as well as public support for the Intifada, undoubtedly influenced coping strategies. For many, the experience had some positive aspects, including character building, camaraderie, collective actions to improve prisoner conditions, and informal study organised by adult prisoners or political parties within the prison. Moreover, there was social acceptance that engagement in the struggle for national liberation was an appropriate role for young men – prison as a price for this involvement did not carry a stigma. As Amira Hass, writing about Gaza in the mid-1990s, notes: 'For Palestinians, serving time has played much the same role as the Palmach, the Jewish combat corps of pre-statehood days, did in Israeli society; a gruelling shared rite of passage that forged lifelong bonds among a sizeable number of Palestinians.'[40]

How Palestinian children coped with prison

There is a growing body of research on how children cope with the violence of prison, harsh treatment and torture. An extensive recent review of the psychological effects of political and military trauma on children suggests that three generic factors provide some insight into their capacity to cope: their individual personality and perceptions, their 'indigenous milieu', and the types of political and military tools used to traumatise them.[41] Amnesty International's review of children and torture highlights the role of cultural norms that can shape children's perceptions of what constitutes ill-treatment or torture.[42] Children who have never slept alone at night, therefore, might find this isolation much more difficult to bear than some physical abuse, or girls from a conservative tradition will experience even partial exposure of their bodies as deeply humiliating.

DCI/PS social workers highlight a similar range of factors that helped children survive their time in prison. Children's personalities were key – whether they were happy, outgoing, open-minded, self-confident and independent, and how they related to others was more important than their age. Their family background, strength of local community, wider networks and political convictions were also significant. Some children were more prepared than others for prison, and had encountered more direct confrontations with the Israeli army. Being detained with adult prisoners could provide an enormous support structure and encouragement to study, although it could push a child to behave more like an adult.

The primary factor helping these children survive was their peer group, especially if they were with people they already knew or who came from the same place. Interviewed former detainees noted that: 'being with detainees from my own town was most important'; 'being with my two brothers'. Some specifically mentioned adult detainees who were role models, and a critical source of care and support in a very hostile environment: 'The adult detainees helped me a lot. They developed my character and I benefited from their experience of culture and life. They made me feel comfortable. Without their support I would have been lost in prison'; 'The children lived with adults who took a lot of care of us. Support was strong and detainees discussed their problems. I am still in touch with friends I made in prison even though they are much older than me.'

The love, support, endorsement and encouragement of their families was particularly important for Palestinian children. The rare contact with families was especially valued as families faced so many obstacles in attempting to visit children in prison, or having any communication with them at all. One can only imagine how precious such visits were for these two young people of 17 and 16, each jailed for three years: 'My family was the main support that helped me survive, especially when they visited me and kept encouraging me', and 'My family gave me the most support especially when they were able to visit. They were proud of me and encouraged me to be "steadfast" because it was a source of pride for Palestinians to be detained.'

Political conviction and involvement in political groups and activities inside the prison was the third most-often-mentioned sustaining factor. Political groups in prisons played a number of roles. They provided structure through organised activities such as study circles and meetings, solidarity through collective actions, friendship and support, and above all a confirmation of collective values in harsh circumstances. The following quotes from two prisoners shows the importance of this involvement in confirming their political ideology, which sustained them while under extreme stress: 'The things that helped me through were my sense of national identity, of true belonging, and the loyalty from home', and 'My greatest support came from my political awareness and belief in social justice.'

RETURNING TO SOCIETY

Every arrested child is traumatised because he is a child, is immature and not an adult, even if he has an adult's physique. The community doesn't allow child prisoners to be dealt with as children as they are considered heroes and political prisoners.

DCI/PS social worker

Former child prisoners confront a host of serious social and economic problems in adjusting to life outside prison. They return to a society with virtually no economy or specialised rehabilitation and support services. Returning home, to school or work and to their friends and communities is so difficult precisely because they were children when they were arrested. Their external world will inevitably have changed, just as life did not stand still for their families, friends and communities.

The survey of 550 Palestinian former political prisoners from the Gaza Strip[43] also investigated children's ability to reintegrate into their families and communities. The results highlight some quite dramatic difficulties. For instance, 42 per cent experienced problems in adapting to family life and 45 per cent in socialising, 20 per cent had sexual and marital problems and 77 per cent had economic difficulties.

The main challenges facing children after prison are building a positive connection with their family and friends, returning to school or getting vocational training, and obtaining work. Many have problems establishing relationships and participating in the community. A high proportion drop out of school and cannot find or hold down jobs. This type of experience is common among refugee child survivors of torture or conflict.[44]

Returning to family and community

During any conflict situation, families may undergo dramatic change and face financial pressures because parents are involved in the conflict, imprisoned, even killed. The family has had to continue functioning without the imprisoned child, although the child's absence is always strongly felt. Siblings may have taken on different roles and resent the returnee. The child is a changed person, who will have moved or been pushed into a maturity and independence beyond his or her years. Too often their families and friends cannot comprehend what they have been through or relate to their fears and worries. The longer the child has been away, the more dramatic the change and the more difficult the adjustment; as we saw in earlier chapters, short sentences are increasingly rare.

In a society rooted in traditions of children's respect for and obedience to older generations, issues of discipline and control may surface both at home and at school. Parents often find it difficult to deal with children when they have been in prison where, despite the physical constraints, they have gained a degree of independence. Families often respond by wanting to be overly protective for fear that the child might be rearrested. The child is perceived as difficult to control. After their return, former prisoners are often aggressive towards their siblings, like M.Z., arrested in 1988 at 16 and detained for 22 months: 'It is true that there were positive aspects in that my personality was strengthened and I became more responsible, but there were more negative impacts...I tried to impose prison rules at home and got into many arguments with my brothers.'

For returning child prisoners, re-entering their communities brings a range of other problems. The very political conviction and engagement in political struggle that had sustained many during their time in prison rebounds on their return. Especially during and immediately after the first Intifada, child ex-prisoners were glorified for being part of the collective resistance. Though younger than most prisoners, they had proved themselves by surviving prison, an experience regarded by many in their society as a significant stage in normative development for young Palestinian men. They were regarded as heroes and role models, not as children. It was no longer possible to cry or express emotions. As Amira Hass notes: 'For all the talk about jail, however, most ex-prisoners say little about the legacy of trauma, precisely because the experience is so common and widespread and also because Gazans rarely talk about the emotional aspects of their hardships.'[45]

In a group discussion with three young men imprisoned as children during the 1980s, all agreed that the community did not know how to respond to a child's violent experience of prison. 'Prison is for "men", so a child becomes a man after prison. Even the families failed to treat them as children.' In turn they could not express their real feelings for fear of appearing weak: 'My family, school and friends all reacted as if I was a hero. But this wasn't what I felt. I had to hide my feelings and present myself as being strong', and 'I couldn't express what I really felt in case they thought I was weak. I don't feel that the community at that time encouraged children to talk about their feelings.'

In ways similar to the spirit of activism in South Africa during the apartheid era, this inability to express emotions was reinforced by the collective spirit of resistance to the occupation. People took it for granted that everyone would suffer. One of this group of three young men noted:

The activists in the community promoted a culture that the children who went to jail were freedom fighters; they too were resisting the occupation to get freedom for the people. There was an ethos that people needed to be strong and that everyone needed to face the prospect of being arrested or expelled. Everyone had to bear the burden.

Friendships

Picking up the threads of old friendships and forming new ones after a period away is very hard. For some, the experience of torture and prison left an enduring legacy of depression, anxiety, social withdrawal and loss of self-confidence that stood in the way of forming relationships. The previously cited clinical observation of detained Palestinian children aged 13 to 15 suggests that traumatisation in adolescence is a risk factor in forming intimate, lasting relationships and in planning for the future: both tasks require trust in others and goodwill, which is often shattered in extreme situations like torture.[46]

Being in prison can affect social relationships in two main ways. First, the period away disrupts friendships and networks. This can happen also if children have been in prison for short periods. For instance, O.O., who was detained at 17 for six months, lost his school friends: 'My friendships were very much affected. I had lots of school friends but after I left prison I felt they didn't want to know me.' Also, the psychological and other impacts of detention and torture compound the difficulties in continuing old and establishing new relationships. M.S. was imprisoned for 19 months when he was 16, and his relationships suffered: 'Detention affected my friendships. Many broke up after I was released because I didn't trust others and tended to keep to myself.' M.D., who was detained at 16 for two and a half years, was left with very few friends: 'After I left prison my friendships were limited to a very small group.'

Getting back to education

Chapter 7 described the lack of any structured education using the Palestinian syllabus in Israeli prisons. A hiatus in education is particularly serious for children in their middle to late teens who are preparing for their graduation examinations; this can critically damage their future life chances. Many ex-prisoners finally drop out of school. A number of those interviewed felt that this was one of the purposes of the whole detention process.

Any student who has missed more than 70 days is required by the Palestinian Directorate of Education to repeat the whole school year. Many then opt not to continue in school, as they feel uncomfortable in classes with younger children. This happened to M.K., who was arrested at 16 for two years: 'I missed two years of school and that affected my attitude towards studying as my peers finished two years before me. I also had to work after school and during the holidays to help support the family.' M.K.'s situation also highlights the wider issue of poverty and high rates of unemployment. As the majority of imprisoned children come from poorer families, they need to work to supplement the family income. The experience of R.A., arrested at 17 for 16 months, is typical. 'I was at school, but when I was released I couldn't continue studying because of my family's difficult economic situation.'

It is often difficult for child ex-prisoners to return to their old school. Schools themselves are increasingly stressful and unsafe environments, given the ongoing and escalating violence of the occupation, especially since the second Intifada. For instance, throughout the OPT in the early part of 2002, the Israeli military requisitioned many schools, entering them without warning and closing them down for prolonged periods during 24-hour curfews. Sudden curfews, incursions, sieges and the ongoing restrictions on travel, affected teachers and pupils alike. Schools now report that pupils have become more fearful, find it difficult to concentrate and display feelings of insecurity and violent behaviour.[47] Teachers coping with the disruptive occupation conditions constantly juggle with timetable changes to make up lost time and ensure the syllabus is completed. They have little extra energy or time to respond to students with particular needs, such as child ex-prisoners, and there is a general shortage of school-based counsellors and social workers to respond sensitively or appropriately to such students, many of whom feel more adult, are often difficult to control, or lack self-confidence and are withdrawn.

Former child prisoners returning to school may find it difficult to focus and concentrate or have other physical or psychological difficulties that make study difficult. Again, the impact of imprisonment is not necessarily related to the length of time in prison. This is particularly significant for younger children where the after-effects of even a few weeks or months in prison can be very traumatic. O.M., who was detained at 17 for six months, recalls that 'the detention affected my life in general and my education in particular because I couldn't finish my education after I was released. I felt depressed and lacked self-confidence.' M.O., arrested at 15 for seven weeks, eventually completed his education but with great difficulty. 'I also needed help in returning to school, as I felt so anxious. In the end I managed to finish school and university but I am now unemployed.'

Undoubtedly, some former child prisoners, especially those held with adult prisoners during the first Intifada, regarded prison as a literal 'school' or 'university' of life. But for too many others looking back, the theft of the opportunity to complete their education assumed much greater significance.

Work

Securing work on leaving prison is equally difficult. Unemployment among former prisoners is a major problem, especially in the Palestinian context of economic collapse and widespread unemployment. Former child prisoners face a range of obstacles, including lack of education and skills, fierce competition for jobs, restrictions on movement, and fear of re-arrest. R.R.'s experience after being detained at 17 for three years is a common one: 'I couldn't get a job for four years after I left prison.'

There is a shortage of vocational training places. Particularly since the second Intifada, much more stringent restrictions on movement mean that vocational students studying away from home have to live on campus, resulting in further separation from families and increased financial burdens. Enen if they do manage to get some training, most need some initial capital to start up their own businesses. Again O.O.'s experience is a common one: 'I got a truck driving license, but that support wasn't enough as I needed financial support to start a business.'

On their release from prison, ex-prisoners are issued an identity card that is different from those of other OPT residents. The card's distinctive colour marks them as former prisoners. Even before the current Intifada when Palestinians could get permits to work in Israel, this was always difficult for former prisoners, who routinely encountered problems with the border guards and police. F.K., arrested at 17 for six months, describes his experience: 'I wasn't able to finish my education so I joined a course through the detainees rehabilitation programme and got a bus-driving license. It was better than nothing, but I couldn't go to Israel to work as I was given a green identity card.'

At present, the Israel employment route is closed for most Palestinians, and the stringent restrictions on movement even make it difficult to travel for work between population centres within Palestine.

Others cannot work because of long-term physical health problems resulting from torture or other maltreatment. This is M.H's situation following his arrest at 16 in 1996 and 19 months detention, 'I can't work now and have a lot of health problems from the position torture. I have permanent pain in my back.' The sheer practical difficulties of finding and keeping work are further compounded for those with long-term psychological problems.

The children who are the subject of this book have known nothing but the Israeli occupation, a harsh regime that penetrates the entire social fabric of Palestinian life, and sanctions violence against individuals through physical attacks, imprisonment and torture. Under this regime and in this conflict they have been targeted for attack specifically as children.

The experience of sustained physical and mental torture, which is routine for the majority of Palestinian child prisoners, is beyond the imagination of those unfamiliar with the situation on the ground.

As adolescents, they are particularly vulnerable to brutalising and traumatic experiences. Their ability to cope depends on a complex interplay of personal resources, peer support and social and political factors inside and outside prison. However, even these mitigating factors can be neutralised and fail to 'buffer' the traumatic after-effects of such extreme assaults on their identity.

Most of the children also grew up in the period following the Oslo Accords and the advent of the PA, which was distinguished by widespread disillusionment in the political process and feelings of disempowerment. The current Intifada reflects this change in public mood and experience and, unlike the first, is not characterised by the same mass popular uprisings or extensive social support networks inside prisons. This changing social and political context, and the deterioration in the conditions and experience of imprisonment, has resulted in increasingly negative social and psychological effects.

One outcome of the continuing decline in social and economic conditions is a serious lack of services or resources to support these ex-prisoners when they return home. Families, communities and schools that could provide a source of support and empowerment are exhausted and over-stretched. The serious longer-term effects of imprisonment and torture thus result for many in lifelong psychological, social and economic problems.

10
Myths and Politics – The Foundation of Israel's Impunity

How has Israel been able to conduct its programme of state-sanctioned violence with apparent immunity from internal or external censure and pressure? We will address this fundamental question by looking beyond individual acts of violence and abuse to the wider political context.

The answer lies in part with Israel's ability to manipulate international human rights and humanitarian law and the UN bodies responsible for overseeing compliance. Ever since the Israeli occupation began in 1967, reports to UN bodies and member governments have thoroughly documented Israel's treatment of Palestinian prisoners. In response, Israel consistently claims that various international treaties and human rights instruments are not applicable to the OPT, and simply refuses to cooperate with fact-finding bodies or UN missions attempting to investigate their behaviour.

The answer also involves the powerful 'security' rationale that Israel has elevated into a compelling ideology to sustain the occupation and justify its consequences. Claiming that its policies and practices in the OPT are motivated and justified by security concerns, Israel has largely succeeded in convincing the vast majority of Israeli society and the international community that its actions are legitimate. An indiscriminate rallying call of 'security threat' is applied to all acts of resistance against the occupation, including stone-throwing by children.

Israel uses the security argument as camouflage to obscure its ultimate goal of controlling land, resources and people. The routine detention of Palestinians, including children, plays a key role in crushing resistance and in undermining national identity and any aspirations contrary to Israel's policy objectives for the OPT.

Finally, to understand why international and local human rights institutions have failed to stop these ongoing abuses or to challenge the 'security' discourse effectively, we will look closely at the broader political interests influencing decisions by the international community to take, or decline to take, action.

APPLICABILITY OF INTERNATIONAL LAW IN THE OPT

On 11 May 1949 the United Nations received Israel as a member state. Since then Israel has ratified the main international humanitarian and human rights treaties discussed in Chapter 4, including the Fourth Geneva Convention, the International Covenant on Civil and Political Rights (ICCPR), the Convention Against Torture and Other Cruel, Inhuman or Degrading Treatment or Punishment (CAT), and the Convention on the Rights of the Child (CRC).[1]

Despite its status as a State Party to these treaties, Israel consistently denies their applicability to the OPT. The international community repeatedly insists that they do indeed apply. The Palestinians continue to suffer.

International humanitarian law

Israel accepts the Hague Regulations as binding on its practice in the occupied territories since they form part of customary international law, which 'constitutes part of the municipal law of Israel'.[2] Although Israel is a State Party to the Fourth Geneva Convention, it denies that the Convention applies to the OPT, while claiming to apply the humanitarian and customary provisions of the Convention there. Many reports from human rights organisations and the UN have strongly contested these claims, documenting in detail Israel's systematic violations: blocking access to medical care; attacks on medical personnel, vehicles and institutions; indiscriminate attacks in civilian areas; arbitrary arrests; torture; extra-judicial killings; restricting civilian freedom of movement; etc.[3]

Without going into the details of Israel's detailed arguments regarding applicability,[4] it is enough to say that Israel claims that no sovereign state was replaced in 1967 when it assumed control of the West Bank, East Jerusalem, and Gaza Strip, and therefore these territories are not 'occupied' but 'administered'. In addition, since 1994 Israel has contested the issue of applicability by arguing that the Palestinian Authority has held effective control in the 'Area A' enclaves, despite the fact that these areas constitute only 17 per cent of the OPT.[5]

Human rights treaties

Israel similarly rejects the applicability of various human rights treaties in reporting to the UN Committee Against Torture and to the UN Committee on the Rights of the Child, among others. First,

Israel argues that the Palestinian Authority's control over Area A absolves Israel of responsibility to implement there any human rights treaties to which it is bound. Second, Israel claims: 'Pursuant to Article 29 of the 1969 Vienna Convention on the Law of Treaties, a State's jurisdiction is not binding beyond its national territory unless otherwise determined in the treaty.'[6] Finally, Israel claims that, despite similarities between international humanitarian law and international human rights law, they are in fact two distinct bodies of law and are not designed for concurrent application – during periods of armed conflict, only international humanitarian law applies.[7] Israel has frequently invoked this last argument in relation to the period after September 2000.

Response of the international community

The international community has consistently rejected these arguments, maintaining that Israel occupied the West Bank, East Jerusalem and Gaza Strip in 1967 and that the Fourth Geneva Convention applies to these territories. This position is clearly stated in numerous UN Security Council and General Assembly resolutions, and in statements by the High Contracting Parties, or State Parties, to the Convention.[8]

John Dugard, the UN Special Rapporteur and international legal scholar, was explicitly critical of the State of Israel's two-fold argument seeking to justify the inapplicability of the Fourth Geneva Convention:

Neither of those arguments is tenable in law. The first, premised on a strained interpretation of Article 2 of the Geneva Convention, fails to take account of the fact that the law of occupation is concerned with the interests of the population of an occupied territory rather than those of a displaced sovereign. The second, that Israel is no longer an occupying Power because it lacks effective control over 'A' areas of the Occupied Palestinian Territories, is likewise unacceptable. The test for the application of the legal regime of occupation is not whether the occupying Power fails to exercise effective control over the territory, but whether it has the ability to exercise such power…The Oslo Accords leave Israel with ultimate legal control over all of the Occupied Palestinian Territories and the fact that for political reasons it has generally chosen not to exercise this control over the 'A' zones, when it undoubtedly has the military capacity to do so...cannot relieve Israel of its responsibilities as an occupying Power...The international community therefore rejects the argument that the Fourth Geneva Convention is inapplicable to the Occupied Palestinian Territories.[9]

International legal experts, including those serving on UN committees, have similarly rejected Israel's arguments. Both the UN Committee Against Torture and the UN Committee on the Rights of the Child have affirmed the applicability of their respective treaties to the OPT.[10]

Israel uses inconsistent logic in relation to these treaties. On the one hand, its policies and actions show that it believes all areas of the OPT come under its jurisdiction, and that its military orders apply equally to all areas of the West Bank and Gaza Strip. It regularly arrests Palestinian children even from Area A, prosecuting them through the Israeli military court system, and charging them with offences allegedly committed in areas under the administrative control of the Palestinian Authority. The fact that Area A comes under Israel's ultimate jurisdiction has been particularly evident since 2002 with the Israeli army's wide-scale invasions into these areas, exercising its ability to directly control them, as Special Rapporteur Dugard highlighted above.

On the other hand, Israel clearly considers that human rights treaties are applicable in the OPT, but only to Israeli settlers illegally living there. However, with the exception of settlements in the Jerusalem area, Israel has not annexed the territory on which the settlements are located. In 2001, Israel submitted its 381-page first report to the UN Committee on the Rights of the Child outlining measures it had taken in compliance with the CRC. It justified the total absence of information on Palestinian children in the OPT by arguing that the CRC is not applicable to those areas and it is thus not required to report on them.[11] Following this logic the report should also have excluded settler children living in the OPT. However, the Israeli population statistics included in the report concur exactly with population figures provided by the Israel Central Bureau of Statistics that include the Israeli settler population.[12] While it reports on settlement children living in the OPT despite arguing that the CRC is not applicable to these areas, Israel excludes any information on Palestinian children from the OPT whom it imprisons in facilities inside Israel.

This inconsistent reporting is a clear example of the discrimination and racism inherent in Israel's treatment of Palestinian children. By including only settlement children, Israel recognises the applicability of the CRC to the OPT, but on the basis of nationality, rather than territory as required by the Convention.[13] The report demonstrates publicly that Israel considers that CRC rights apply to Israeli children wherever they might live, but not to Palestinian children, whether they remain in the OPT or are detained in Israel.

So far, we have focused on the theoretical applicability of the international legal framework to the OPT. Whether the provisions of a treaty *have been applied* to that territory is a separate question – states can acknowledge the legal applicability of a treaty while failing to apply its provisions, or deny its applicability yet implement the provisions. Recognising applicability is nevertheless the crucial first step, since if a state denies the legal applicability of a treaty, it can then argue that it is not bound to apply the treaty's provisions or to report on territories to which the treaty is not applicable. Israel's arguments highlight how a state can manipulate the legal discourse of 'applicability' to avoid acknowledging non-compliance with their legal obligations and reporting requirements.

We will now go beyond the theory of applicability to consider what happens when a state does not comply with its treaty obligations. A brief look at the history of Israel's manipulation of the UN system will provide some insight into how the situation in Israel and the OPT has evolved, and reveal some critical weaknesses in the UN's human rights and humanitarian law framework.

Translating theory into practice: manoeuvring through the UN system

Since 1967 Israel's conduct in the OPT has been characterised by institutionalised discrimination and widespread, systematic violations of international humanitarian and human rights law. Grave concerns about these violations led the UN to establish two mechanisms expressly to monitor Israel's conduct in the OPT. In 1968 a UN General Assembly resolution established the first, the *UN Special Committee to Investigate Israeli Practices Affecting the Human Rights of the Population of the Occupied Territories* (Special Committee). Israel has consistently objected to the existence of this Special Committee and has refused to cooperate with it.[14] Consequently, the Special Committee meets each year in surrounding Arab countries to hear from human rights defenders and victims who have travelled from the occupied territories to testify. A report is subsequently submitted to the General Assembly.

In 1993, the UN established the second mechanism, the *Special Rapporteur of the Commission on Human Rights on the Situation of Human Rights in the Palestinian Territories Occupied Since 1967* (Special Rapporteur). The Special Rapporteur is mandated to 'investigate Israel's violation of the principles and bases of international law, international humanitarian law and the [Fourth] Geneva Convention'. Israel also objects to the Special Rapporteur's mandate and refuses to cooperate with it.[15]

Over the years, Israel has also refused cooperation with other UN initiatives. In April 2002, Israel rejected a delegation mandated by the UN Human Rights Commission to gather information about the human rights situation in the wake of Israel's wide-scale March–April 2002 military offensive.[16] At approximately the same time, it refused to cooperate with the fact-finding mission proposed by the UN Secretary-General, and endorsed by the Security Council, to gather information about conditions in Jenin Refugee Camp before and during Israel's military operations there in April 2002.[17] Because of Israel's non-cooperation, the Secretary-General had to disband this fact-finding team. The UN General Assembly then commissioned its own report on Jenin, but Israel failed to provide any relevant information despite a specific request from the Secretary-General. Neither of these delegations set foot in the occupied territories.

Israel displays a similar pattern of non-cooperation in its interaction with various UN committees whose brief is to monitor implementation of major human rights treaties. Article 20 of the Convention Against Torture (CAT) authorises its Committee to launch an inquiry into a State Party's practice, if the State Party has agreed to accept this article, and if the Committee receives 'reliable information which appears to [the Committee] to contain well-founded indications that torture is being systematically practiced in the territory of a State Party'. However, when it ratified the CAT, Israel declined to accept this article, stating: 'Israel hereby declares that it does not recognise the competence of the Committee provided for in article 20.'[18] As a result, the Committee is not empowered to undertake such inquiries vis-à-vis Israel.

Articles 21 and 22 of the CAT also provide a mechanism permitting the Committee to receive complaints about a State Party's failure to comply with its obligations, either from other States Parties or from individuals subject to the jurisdiction of the State Party. The

Committee can then request the State Party in question to address whatever concerns have been submitted in writing. This mechanism can only be invoked if the State Party in question accepts these articles. Israel has chosen not to accept either of the articles, though the Committee has urged it to do so.[19]

Human rights treaties may contain certain requirements that cannot be rejected, such as the obligation to report on measures taken to comply. In the face of such compulsory requirements, Israel's approach has been evasive and delaying. This was illustrated in its interaction with the Committee on the Rights of the Child in 2002. Not only did it take seven years to report, but using circular legal arguments Israel ultimately refused to provide the Committee with any information or comment on its actions in the OPT, even when directly requested to do so.

Although the Committee on the Rights of the Child affirmed the applicability of the Convention to the OPT and expressed a number of 'concerns' about Israel's conduct, the discussion essentially ended there. The reporting requirement included in treaties is not a means of enforcing the treaties' provisions, so the issues are left to discussion with no means of redress. Israel argues it is not responsible and Palestinian children are left unprotected.

Palestinian child prisoners effectively do not exist as far as the various human rights mechanisms and structures are concerned. Israel has excluded them from its report to the CRC, and they have no state to represent or protect them. International legal bodies designed to monitor human rights treaties are stymied by the Israeli government argument that the treaties do not apply. When the international community tries to address gross violations of human rights and humanitarian law, Israel either refuses to cooperate, as in the case of the Special Committee, the Special Rapporteur, and other UN initiatives, or it refuses to provide information or comment on its conduct in the OPT.

THE SECURITY DISCOURSE

In addition to using wide-ranging legal arguments and non-cooperation tactics in evading international law and monitoring mechanisms, Israel harnesses the powerful ideology of the security of the state to justify its practices in the OPT.

Palestinian activists and human rights workers are often asked about the extent of opposition within Israel to the government's policies in the West Bank and Gaza Strip. Such opposition is sadly limited. There are a few highly dedicated Israeli human rights organisations such as B'Tselem and Physicians for Human Rights (Israel) which actively document, report and publish human rights abuses, as well as a number of individuals and organisations who have expressed considerable solidarity during the recent Intifada; but the vast majority of Israeli society supports or silently acquiesces in the policies of their government.

In part this is due to the Israeli public's ignorance about what occurs in the West Bank and Gaza Strip. These areas could be thousands of miles away, rather than a few kilometres. Most Israelis know little about conditions in the OPT in general, and will know almost nothing about the topic of this book. The role of the media in constructing – as opposed to reporting – the news is critical in Israel as elsewhere. In his study of how the media shape public opinion, Daniel Dor demonstrates how newspaper editors in Israel are driven by emotions, beliefs and opinions.[20] Only one Israeli newspaper, *Haaretz*, reports on a daily basis about the situation in the OPT and has a reporter based there. In addition, the Israeli government places heavy restrictions on access by foreign journalists and independent observers to the OPT.

However, there is another rarely acknowledged or understood aspect. Successive Israeli governments have skilfully constructed an ideological discourse within Israeli society to gain support for and justify a wide array of human rights abuses under the broad umbrella of 'security'. The media has willingly colluded in representing all Palestinians, including children, as the enemy, and increasingly as 'terrorists' who pose a security threat to the State of Israel. In such a climate *Yedioth Ahronoth*, the Israeli daily mass circulation newspaper, in January 2003 was able to print the headline: 'Eight-year-old terrorist captured', referring later in the report to this child as 'the youngest Palestinian'.[21] Commenting on this change in mood, Israeli human rights attorney Leah Tsemel notes:

In the last two years things have got much rougher. Palestinian children are seen less as children and more as Arabs and there is more indifference towards them. This is reflected in newspaper reporting. Now an eight-year-old is reported as a 'Palestinian that got shot' and youngsters as 'mechabelim' (Hebrew for terrorists). Now you hardly see any separation on the basis of age. They are as dehumanised as the adults, dehumanised and feared by Israeli society.[22]

Terror and security have become two sides of the same equation, and the definitions of both have become extremely broad:

An attack on a military post is defined as a terror attack and the attackers are deemed terrorists – the exact same term used to describe the suicide bombing in Israel. This is the prevailing Israeli view: Israeli soldiers are always involved in 'combat', even when they bomb a refugee camp and kill children. Palestinians are always terrorists, even when they face a tank, even when their targets are Israeli soldiers in an Israeli army base, even when one of the missions of that base is to make sure that Jews are allowed to settle without obstruction in lands conquered by Israel in 1967.[23]

From the onset of the occupation in 1967 when Israel issued Military Proclamation No. 1, and in the thousands of military orders issued since then, Israel has used the security argument to justify its policies in the OPT. In the name of security successive military orders have confiscated Palestinian land, demolished Palestinian homes, censored the press, closed Palestinian schools, prevented Palestinians from travelling, placed hundreds of thousands of civilians under house arrest and imposed numerous other repressive measures. Despite the well-documented impact of these policies of collective punishment, Israeli society has by and large accepted the security argument.

Zionism, Israel's dominant ideology, is a major factor in Israeli society's ready acceptance of the security argument, since it justifies a variety of discriminatory laws and practices. Israel's 1948 Declaration of Independence explicitly defines Israel as a Jewish state, committed to the 'ingathering of the exiles'. While the Declaration of Independence refers to the democratic rights of all citizens, a number of rights are defined on the basis of being Jewish and do not apply to Israel's non-Jewish citizens, such as the Palestinians who remained after 1948.

In Israel, citizens are classified according to whether they are Jewish, Arab, Christian or Druze, which must be registered on their identity cards. Jewish Israeli citizens have special rights and privileges. For example, over 90 per cent of land in Israel is earmarked for Jewish citizens, who also enjoy preferential access to employment, education, educational loans, home mortgages, etc. As Israeli journalist Gideon Levy points out: 'What sort of a democracy is this, if exactly half the state's residents don't benefit from it? Indeed, can the term democracy be applied to a state in which many of the residents live under a military regime?'[24]

A series of Basic Laws passed by the Israeli parliament (Knesset) underpins the Jewish character of the state. Thus, the Law of Return (1950) grants every Jew, anywhere in the world, the right to settle in Israel and automatically gain citizenship, but excludes Palestinians who were forced to flee their homes in 1948 and 1967. While there are no laws that explicitly discriminate between a Jew and a non-Jew, this practical objective is achieved through legal sleight-of-hand – by stating that certain privileges and rights are granted to those 'to whom the Law of Return applies', discrimination against non-Jews is embedded in the law.

This fundamental Jewish character of the Israeli state leads inexorably to viewing any non-Jew as threatening it. Indeed, in a ruling on the precise meaning of the 'Jewish State', the Israeli Supreme Court explicitly defined this as meaning the maintenance of a Jewish majority.[25] Even many liberal Israelis consider this imperative of a Jewish majority a suitable justification for discriminatory practices against non-Jews. Ruth Gavison, former Chair of the Association of Civil Rights in Israel and a professor of Law at Hebrew University, argued that laws and practices around land-use designed to maintain Jewish control and majority were justifiable because Jews were 'a small minority in a hostile region'.[26]

A very particular ideological environment thus characterises Israel. The state defines itself on the basis of one particular ethno-religious group and seeks to maintain the control and majority of that group through a legislative framework designed to that end. The state perceives anyone from outside that group as a potential threat to its demographic make-up. So Israel is not a state equally for all its citizens – the interests of its Jewish citizens are paramount: 'Democracy exists only for the state's (proven) Jewish residents.'[27] It is a state where democratic values are on the decline, particularly since the current Intifada began.[28] In such an environment, the concept of security does not mean the individual, physical security of the Israeli citizen, but rather the security of Israel as a Jewish state.

It is a very short step from accepting this viewpoint as the paramount organising principle of Israeli society to subordinating universalistic notions of human rights, equality and respect for others to the perceived security needs of the state. Israel's Association for

Civil Rights hosted a Human Rights Day in Jerusalem in 2001; Israeli Attorney Allegro Pachecco describes the discussions:

> The persistent theme heard was that human rights are limited: 'You don't observe human rights to the point where you destroy yourself.' In essence they were saying, 'We must balance human rights with the preservation of Israel as a Jewish state.' The discussion was not about all human beings, universal good and rights, or the protection of human liberty and dignity. Rather, this was ignored to emphasise that these issues are precisely not universal or absolute, but rather are limited to the point of whether 'we the Jews, as victims' are threatened...The emphasis was not on human rights, but rather on how to balance these rights with a Jewish state.[29]

Many Israeli citizens are willing to justify or turn a blind eye to human rights abuses because they were brought up being told that everything is subordinate to the supposed security threat facing Israel. Security is used as a justification for all manner of practices – demolition of houses, confiscation of land, restriction of movement, censorship of the press, and, of course, the treatment of child prisoners.

Israel is certainly not unique in using the security discourse as a justification for human rights abuses or military aggression; one need only look at the actions of the US government since September 11 2001. In Israel, however, this argument has been completely bound up with the self-identity of the state since its establishment in 1948. It is directly related to perceiving any non-Jew as a potential threat – fertile ground for justifying, permitting, and committing abuses.

The security discourse has been highly successful in manufacturing the consent of the Israeli public – and many outside the country – for the continuing occupation and its oppressive practices. More specifically, this discourse has been used in conjunction with denial and cover-up to justify the continuing use of torture against Palestinian prisoners.

Torture and the security discourse[30]

The debate around torture in Israel is at the core of discussion about Palestinian political prisoners, especially children. The international community (UN committees, foreign governments, human rights organisations) and Palestinian prisoners say that Israel practices torture. Israel denies it. The debate has been ongoing for at least 30 years.

Previous chapters have documented Israel's use of torture against detained Palestinian children and its cumulative longer-term impact. Here the concern is with Israel's justifications for using torture, which is an indictable war crime, a crime against humanity, and absolutely prohibited by international human rights law. Israel's concept of the 'ticking bomb' – a person who is about to carry out, or has knowledge of, an imminent attack against Israeli civilians – lies at the heart of this debate.

Israel has used torture against Palestinians in the OPT since the start of the 1967 occupation, and its practice can be divided into three phases: 1967 to 1977, 1977 to 1999, and 1999 to the present. In the first phases, during the 1960s and 1970s, Israel used extreme forms of physical violence. Initially, public awareness within Israel that Israeli state agents utilised torture was limited to a few lone voices in left-wing circles and lawyers working with Palestinian clients. In 1974 Israeli attorney Felicia Langer petitioned the Israeli High Court of Justice against the use of torture by the General Security Service (the Shabak), as did her colleague attorney Leah Tsemel a little later. Such voices were generally dismissed in the mainstream Israeli debate as 'PLO sympathisers', traitors, and enemies of the Jewish people.[31] The absence of public debate within Israeli society was matched by silence from the international public and the mainstream media, despite reports in 1970 from the United Nations and Amnesty International accusing Israeli authorities of practicing torture in the OPT.[32]

This silence was eventually broken on 19 June 1977, when the London *Sunday Times* published a four-page article by two respected journalists following interviews with 44 Palestinians who stated they had been tortured during interrogation to extract confessions.[33] The article noted that torture was so 'systematic that it cannot be dismissed as a handful of "rogue cops" exceeding orders'. All branches of the Israeli state were implicated. Torture was seen to be so widespread as to require a substantial level of bureaucratic organisation and infrastructure (such as the construction of special cells and the apparatus for electric shock torture), pointing to the systematised, planned nature of this practice. This evidence corroborated many of the arguments presented by Israeli lawyers such as Langer and Tsemel.

The Israeli government responded with outright denials of these allegations, branding the evidence 'fantastic horror stories'.[34] When a Swiss human rights organisation drew similar conclusions in a report published soon afterwards,[35] the Israeli government responded in the same fashion, labelling its critics as Palestinian sympathisers. But information about its torture practices was reaching wider audiences. Between 1977 and 1979, the US consulate in East Jerusalem sent more than 40 cables to the State Department in Washington reporting the common use of torture by Israelis to extract confessions and to punish Palestinian prisoners.[36]

Throughout the 1970s and 1980s, and particularly following the 1982 Israeli invasion of Lebanon, Israel's torture practices gained an increasingly high international profile. In 1984 Shabak operatives beat two Palestinians to death following a failed bus hijacking in Gaza. This incident marked a turning point in both local and international recognition of Israeli torture. The Shabak officers initially claimed the two were killed during the storming of the bus, but photographs of one of the men being taken away in handcuffs, which later appeared in the Israeli press, proved that they had been killed during interrogation.[37] The scandal and subsequent Israeli government cover-up of this incident led to the establishment of the Landau Commission in October 1987, just a few months before the start of the first Intifada.

The Landau Commission, headed by Moshe Landau, a former Justice of the Israeli High Court, was set up as an official government inquiry into interrogation methods. Its report (LCR) confirmed that, at least since 1971, Shabak agents had routinely used violent methods in their interrogations of Palestinian detainees. The LCR is remarkable for its attempt to justify these practices on security grounds, stating that the use of coercive tactics is necessary in the fight against 'hostile terrorist activity'.[38] It recommended that ' "moderate physical and psychological pressure" be permitted to extract confessions from political detainees',[39] so that interrogators would not be encouraged to lie in the courts.[40] In effect, the outcome of this Commission was to officially endorse the continuing practice of torture in interrogation and to conceal the specific interrogation techniques that were permitted.

The UN Committee Against Torture rejected the LCR's sanction of 'moderate physical and psychological pressure' and in June 1994 stated that:

165.[41] There is real concern that no legal steps have been taken to implement domestically the Convention against Torture. Thus, the Convention does not form part of the domestic law of Israel and its provisions cannot be invoked in Israeli courts.

166. The Committee regrets the clear failure to implement the definition of torture as contained in article 1 of the Convention.

167. It is a matter of deep concern that Israeli law pertaining to the defenses of 'superior orders' and 'necessity' are in clear breach of that country's obligations under article 2 of the Convention.

168. The Landau Commission Report, permitting as it does 'moderate physical pressure' as a lawful mode of interrogation, is completely unacceptable to this Committee.[42]

In 1997, the UN Committee Against Torture noted that reports from human rights organisations provided evidence that Israel's methods of interrogation 'appear to be applied systematically' and 'constitute torture as defined in article 1 of the Convention'.[43] In January 1999 Amnesty International stated: 'Torture is used systematically against hundreds of Palestinians every year, even in situations where no "ticking bomb" is involved.'[44] Directly addressing the 'ticking bomb' argument, Amnesty International noted: 'The mockery of this argument is shown by the fact that in the majority of cases interrogators take weekends off, using interrogation methods constituting torture only from Sunday to Thursday.'[45]

Finally, on 6 September 1999, years of persistent efforts by human rights organisations and increasing international pressure bore fruit. The Israeli Supreme Court, sitting as the High Court of Justice, issued a ruling that a variety of interrogation methods used by the Shabak were not legal. The ruling stated that the Shabak did not have the authority to utilise specific methods, such as shaking a suspect, forcing him to crouch for long periods of time, tying him to a small chair (*shabeh*), covering his head with a sack, painfully handcuffing him, or intentionally depriving him of sleep.

Though many perceived the ruling as a definitive ban on torture, this was not the case. The court ruling did not proscribe torture as defined in the CAT but only prohibited the Shabak, as one particular security branch, from carrying out specific methods of interrogation. The High Court refused to take responsibility for sanctioning particular methods of interrogation, proposing instead that this should be dealt with through legislation in parliament. Security concerns formed a core part of the reasoning of High Court Justice Barak:

> The question of whether it is appropriate for Israel – in light of its security difficulties – to sanction physical means in interrogations, and the scope of these means – which deviate from the 'ordinary' investigation rules – is an issue that must be decided by the Legislative branch, which represents the People.[46]

Another High Court presiding judge, Justice Y. Kedmi, used the security argument more explicitly as his rationale for advocating a one-year delay in prohibiting the use of torture by the Shabak:

> Deriving from the will to prevent a situation where the 'time bomb will tick' before our eyes and the State's hand will be shortened to help, I suggest that the judgment be suspended from coming into force for a period of one year. During that year, the GSS [Shabak] could employ exceptional methods in those rare cases of 'ticking time bombs', on the condition that explicit authorisation is given by the Attorney General.[47]

In this way, the security argument dominated the debate and offered a ready excuse for Israel's actions. Subsequent efforts to regulate torture employ the term 'explicit authorisation' as if this legitimises its use. Since the 1999 High Court ruling, public officials including former Prime Minister Ehud Barak and current Prime Minister Ariel Sharon have continued to propose and submit legislation allowing the use of torture during Shabak interrogation.[48]

In November 2001, in its Concluding Observations to Israel's Third Periodic Report about measures taken to implement the CAT, the Committee Against Torture welcomed the September 1999 ruling but noted that:

> a) While acknowledging the importance of the September 1999 Supreme Court decision, the Committee regrets certain consequences of it:
>
> i) The ruling does not contain a definite prohibition of torture
> ...
> iii) The [Israeli] Court indicated that GSS [Shabak] interrogators who use physical pressure in extreme circumstances (ticking

bomb cases) might not be criminally liable as they may be able
to rely on the 'defence of necessity'.
b) Despite the Israeli argument that all acts of torture, as defined
in Article 1 of the Convention, are criminal offences under Israeli
law, the Committee remains unconvinced and reiterates its
concern that torture, as defined by the Convention, has not yet
been incorporated into domestic legislation.[49]

Since the 1999 ruling, lawyers and human rights activists have
witnessed a decline in the use of some torture methods but also report
the frequent use of new methods including psychological techniques
such as isolation, and attempts to recruit collaborators. Child
detainees have been no exception to this trend. These developments,
however, continue to be masked by the priority accorded to Israel's
'unique security situation'.

In each of the three phases in the evolution of its use of torture
against Palestinian prisoners, Israel has shifted its position from one
of initial outright denial to the legalised codification of redefined
forms of torture, and has altered its practices and arguments in
response to international and local public pressure. At every stage,
however, Israel has evaded taking the necessary legislative and
executive decisions to halt the practice of torture and has couched
its justifications in the language of security.

In answering the question of whether most cases of Shabak torture
prior to the 1999 ruling involved cases of 'ticking bombs', the Israeli
human rights organisation Public Committee Against Torture in Israel
addressed the danger of the 'ticking bomb' terminology. They note:

The use of this term is dangerous because it acts emotionally on
all Israelis, who see themselves as potential victims of a terrorist
act…As a result of this the Israeli public agrees to the employment
of torture and disregard [sic] the inhuman, immoral and illegal
aspects of these actions.[50]

One of the most disturbing aspects of the public debate about
Israel's practice of torture is the minimal attention paid to the
widespread and systematic use of torture against Palestinian child
detainees. The debate about torture in Israel highlights two critical
points. First, the routine torture of Palestinian children by Israeli
soldiers or police has been sidelined in the debate and in court rulings,
which focus almost exclusively on the issue of interrogation methods

practiced by the Shabak. Second, by framing the debate in terms of 'ticking bomb' scenarios, the issue of torture in Israel is repeatedly placed within the context of Israel's security needs, while minimising or ignoring the widespread use of torture against the vast majority of prisoners, including children, who are not 'ticking bombs'.

PROBLEMS IN THE HUMAN RIGHTS FRAMEWORK

The political reality of Israel's incarceration polices is obscured if one only measures these practices against the supposedly neutral yardstick of human rights. The human rights framework locates the issue of prisoners within a body of law addressing the rights of persons deprived of their liberty. The emphasis is thus on the extent to which their rights *as prisoners* are upheld and whether or not their treatment is in accordance with international standards. In the Israeli case, what is often missing, is a discussion of why children are detained in the first place and what Israel hopes to achieve by detaining them. While the superficial 'excesses' of Israel's practices are criticised, the underlying premise is not challenged. Without this understanding of 'why', the door is opened to the security argument. Instead of questioning the very premise of the security discourse, the debate is restricted to balancing children's rights against Israel's 'legitimate security concerns'.

Each year, a number of organisations submit reports to UN bodies and other agencies documenting systematic violations of international human rights and humanitarian law by Israel. Human rights organisations repeatedly issue press releases calling for action by the international community, and undertake advocacy and lobbying to bring about concrete, positive change in the situation. The attempts of Palestinian organisations to address rights violations within the internationally accepted framework of the UN is but one example of the many Palestinian initiatives to resist the occupation through non-violent means which adhere to international law. However, these efforts have not succeeded in providing protection to Palestinian civilians.

The failure of international human rights law to impact on Israel's continuing human rights violations in part is explained by Israel's use of complex obfuscating arguments to explain why most human rights protections do not apply to the OPT. However, it has only been able to do this because of an inherent weakness in the application of this international framework. Standards might be 'objective' but the test lies in their application, which requires a conscious political will.

In addressing general issues concerning the applicability of the Fourth Geneva Convention, the International Committee of the Red Cross (ICRC) notes that 'when confronted with situations in which the Convention should be applied, the States party to it almost invariably cite some grounds or other on which, in their view, it is not applicable'.[51] This practice is not limited to the field of international humanitarian law, as illustrated by Israel's arguments about the applicability of various human rights treaties. Nor is Israel alone in using such arguments.

The ICRC also criticises certain States for using complex legal arguments as a form of political exercise to justify their unwillingness to apply international law in situations to which they are a party.[52] In its commentary, the ICRC goes on to state: 'What counts is actual protection for the victims of armed conflict...Political considerations should under no circumstances be allowed to weaken the protection to be enjoyed by civilians under hard law.'[53] But that is precisely what happens in the OPT.

States have a number of means at their disposal which could be used to put pressure on Israel to fulfil its obligations under international human rights and humanitarian law. In failing to take action, and in some cases in facilitating Israel's violations, governments around the world have violated both their obligations under international law, and at times their own domestic legislation.

Article 1, common to all four Geneva Conventions, requires High Contracting Parties (HCPs) to respect and ensure respect for the Conventions in all circumstances. While Article 1 does not define the means or methods by which HCPs not party to the conflict should act in order to fulfil this duty, there are steps State Parties can take to fulfil their Article-1 duty, namely by maintaining a 'Clean Hands' policy.[54] This requires HCPs to refrain from participating in violations of the Convention and to ensure that their policies vis-à-vis the Occupying Power do not help it to commit violations of the Convention.

While the European Union has theoretically made respect for human rights and humanitarian law a cornerstone of its policy-making, it has 'dirty hands' in its dealings with Israel. Article 2 of the European Community's bilateral trade treaty with Israel – the Association Agreement – requires both the EC and Israel to respect human rights in the conduct of their policy.[55] Both parties chose to condition the trading privileges of the agreement upon compliance with human rights and Israel freely chose to accept those conditions when it signed the agreement. Both parties placed such importance on respect for human rights that Article 2 is an 'essential element' of the agreement. As such, a breach of that article constitutes a material breach, giving either party the right to suspend the agreement unilaterally.

The EU has failed to act despite repeated Israeli violations of Palestinian human rights. By continuing to offer Israel trading privileges while it commits gross violations of human rights and humanitarian law the EC not only violates provisions of its own treaty, it also provides Israel with political legitimacy and the economic means to continue its occupation. Consequently, it has crossed the line and implicated itself in weakening the Convention by failing to uphold its Article 1 duty.

As an HCP to the Geneva Conventions, the US also has 'dirty hands'. In its repeated attacks on the Palestinian civilian population, the Israeli military has used US-supplied weapons and ammunition, including F-16 fighter jets and Apache and Cobra attack helicopters. The US Arms Export Control Act governs the export of military weaponry to other countries, and requires that military hardware provided be used only for defensive purposes or to maintain internal security.[56] In using this weaponry to attack a civilian population, Israel has violated conditions of the Arms Export Control Act.[57] By continuing to provide weaponry, the US not only violates its own legislation but also fails to meet its obligation to ensure respect for the Convention. Aside from the arms issue, maintaining a Clean Hands policy would require the US government to ensure that it is not contributing to violations of the Convention. By providing Israel with the largest US annual foreign-aid package, the US government is assisting the state of Israel to maintain both its economic viability and its occupation.[58]

In summary, for human rights and humanitarian law to be enforced, government decision-makers need to display the political will to take concrete action ensuring that international standards are upheld. However, major political and economic considerations govern these decisions, usually at the expense of human rights. Until now, the Palestinians have not had powerful sponsors, nor has the systematic violation of their rights posed a threat to international equilibrium, or to political and economic interests, sufficiently compelling for States to actively intervene.

The passive acceptance of Israel's violations of international law – revealed in the lack of political will to enforce it – is coupled with active military and financial support to the Israeli state that enable its actions in the OPT. It is indeed ironic that the vast amounts of military grants and hardware supplied to Israel by the US are used to destroy Palestinian infrastructure, most of which has been funded by foreign donors, who will also support the rebuilding. Israel's continuing occupation would quite simply not be possible without this political, economic and military support. Both the US and the European Union are in a prime position to exert sufficient pressure to compel Israel to stop violating international human rights and humanitarian law, but to date neither has done so.

While governments have participated on the political level in efforts ostensibly designed to bring about an end to hostilities, they have not engaged in such a way as to ensure implementation of human rights standards. These political interventions ignore dynamics of power, and place occupier and occupied on the same level. In fact, many provisions of these agreements have actually been counter-productive to upholding human rights and humanitarian standards. For example, Israeli settlements in the OPT, constructed in violation of the Fourth Geneva Convention, were subject to negotiation through the Oslo process and its later incarnation, the 'Road Map'.

The lack of political will to enforce the provisions of international humanitarian and human rights law has left Palestinians as a stateless people living under occupation, with absolutely no means of protection. Moreover, it sends a very strong message to Palestinian civilians: international law does not apply to you; it does not protect you. International law has little resonance for Palestinian civilians, who know they are theoretically protected by it, but day after day fail to see those protections implemented. Instead they witness the failure of the international community to rise to its obligation to enforce these protections. Israel's success in absolving itself of any responsibility for its conduct in the OPT since 1967 and the lack of any concrete international measures of enforcement thus have much wider implications. The international community's inaction in the face of Israel's activities in the OPT highlights one of the failures of international law and weakens efforts to promote societies based on respect for human rights and the rule of law.

11
Conclusion

Israel's occupation is about control: control of land, control of resources, and control of lives. The issue of prisoners in general, and child prisoners in particular, is thus one pillar of a system of oppression systematically applied by successive Israeli governments to serve the political strategy of occupation. This inherently racist strategy aims to undermine the social and political ties binding Palestinian society together.

This is why the authors of this book consciously chose to locate the issue of child political prisoners within the political context of occupation. Without this approach it is impossible to understand the reasons behind Israel's incarceration policies. This book has aimed to answer questions such as: why does Israel arrest Palestinian children? Why are child detainees subject to systematic patterns of abuse and discrimination? Why do military courts function in the way they do? Answers to these questions cannot be found in a purely human rights framework. An understanding needs to go beyond a descriptive approach of individual *experiences* to an interpretative analysis of the strategy behind these policies. If the policies are to be halted they must be tackled within this political framework, not solely through appeals to a supposedly neutral body of international law.

ISRAEL'S HUMAN RIGHTS RECORD

Israel is an image-conscious country, and highly sophisticated in its understanding and use of public relations techniques. While it patently and grossly violates international humanitarian and human rights law in its treatment of Palestinian prisoners, it certainly recognises the importance of these standards, and indeed generally acts to uphold them in dealing with its own citizens. Rather than denounce or reject particular treaties or principles, Israel simply denies these standards apply in the OPT, or tries to veil its behaviour in secrecy. For the media, the government arranges carefully crafted sound bites that present Israeli violations in the OPT as necessary for 'security' in the fight against 'terror'. These approaches have been sufficiently successful to allow Israel to continue its gross transgressions of human rights, while manufacturing the consent of the Israeli public and the world and presenting itself as a country founded on democratic principles and respect for the rule of law.

This can be seen most clearly in Israel's arguments related to its use of torture. Israel initially denied allegations of torture in the 1970s. When the facts became undeniable, Israel attempted to define its practices as something other than torture, insisting torture had been abolished, despite the overwhelming evidence to the contrary.

Israel argues that its brutal practices, repressive policies and discriminatory legal system are essential given the special threat of 'terrorism', that is, 'for security reasons'. While the word 'terrorist' has been popular in Israeli discourse for years, it resonates very conveniently since 11 September 2001, drawing dangerously misguided parallels between the situation in Israel and that of other countries around the world.

The Israeli concept of extensive 'security' threats is ideologically loaded. For years, Israel has routinely applied the 'terrorist' label to any Palestinian who carries out an attack against Israelis, making no distinction between Palestinian attacks on Israeli civilians and those against armed Israeli soldiers implementing Israel's illegal occupation of the OPT. Israel applies the word to any Palestinian perceived as threatening its system of control.

Clearly, if one extends the definition of a 'security' threat to any act or individual that threatens the life and limb of Israeli soldiers and civilians, then some Palestinian children may conceivably pose a security threat. Nevertheless, whatever the act allegedly committed by a child, he/she has rights to minimum standards of protection under international law. These laws are not relative or negotiable. They are universal, with a legitimacy rooted in their widespread endorsement by the international community.

The vast majority of detained Palestinian children pose no threat to soldiers or civilians. They are civilians rounded up en masse simply because they are Palestinian males, or arrested because they have engaged in an act of protest against an illegal occupation, continued with impunity for decades. Palestinian teenagers armed with stones pose no significant threat to well-armed Israeli soldiers backed by tanks, armoured personnel carriers, helicopter gunships, F16s, and a wide array of highly advanced military hardware.

All Palestinian child prisoners are subject to the system of institutionalised discrimination that lies at the heart of Israel's occupation.

Israel employs two vastly different bodies of law, one for Palestinian residents of the OPT and one for Israeli citizens. Palestinian children who are arrested are denied all the basic rights mandated for juvenile offenders under Israel's domestic legal code. While the Israeli system of military orders and courts provides a public face of legitimate legal proceedings, in reality it is nothing but a complex bureaucracy specifically designed to enforce the occupation.

The human rights attorneys struggling to represent detained Palestinian children are essentially powerless within this system. In principle, they should have an important role in their clients' court defence. In practice, with little room to manoeuvre, they are effectively reduced to damage control involving some mitigation and plea bargaining: most children have already confessed, the cases against them are based heavily on third-party testimony, 'secret' evidence is often introduced, and judges tend to accept the prosecution's arguments. Court statistics show how rare it is for convicted children to get a penalty other than prison, such as a suspended sentence, release or a fine.

While Israel's actual practices grossly violate international standards, in its public statements it presents the image of a state which firmly supports the rights embodied in international human rights and humanitarian law. However, although Israel acknowledges that the Hague Regulations of 1907 apply to its rule over the occupied territories, it denies to Palestinians the relevance of other treaties containing new provisions of international humanitarian and human rights law that have evolved since the Hague Regulations were framed nearly one hundred years ago. The international community accepts these additional provisions, and Israel accepts them for its own citizens by ratifying major human rights treaties, but it denies that these rights apply to the 3 million Palestinians living under its military occupation. What emerges is a discriminatory legal system that provides preferential treatment to one group of human beings, while systematically abusing the human rights of another.

MOVING PAST RHETORIC TOWARDS ENFORCEMENT

Local and international mechanisms that should ensure compliance with international law and respect for the rule of law and human rights have largely failed to offer any significant protection to the Palestinian civilian population. Since the 1970s, human rights attorneys and organisations have tried to use the military court system,

Israel's domestic legal system, and UN mechanisms to bring Israel into compliance with international standards. Some of these efforts have resulted in specific, temporary changes in practices and procedures. They have totally failed to bring about any major policy changes.

Israel's manipulation of the UN human rights system is a major factor, bolstered by the acquiescence of Israeli society. Despite the close proximity of the OPT to their homes and communities, Israelis remain largely ignorant or apathetic about these gross violations of Palestinian human rights. However, responsibility also lies with governments around the world. They have repeatedly failed to muster the necessary political will, in the face of Israel's intransigence, to pressure Israel to abide by its obligations under international human rights and humanitarian law.

Israel's public relations efforts account in part for this lack of political will to enforce human rights obligations. To the extent that people around the world – particularly in the US, Israel's staunchest supporter – believe Israel to be a law-abiding country, they will not apply sufficient pressure on their governments to ensure that Israel actually does comply. Common (mis)understandings of the conflict as one of Muslim vs. Jew, and disproportionate media coverage emphasising Israeli civilian casualties while minimising or ignoring Israeli violence against Palestinian civilians contribute to the lack of pressure on governments.

Although the world's citizens may be largely ignorant of the facts, their governments' failure to act is not due to ignorance at the official level. The human rights situation in the OPT has been clearly and thoroughly documented for decades in government and UN reports, and by local and international human rights and humanitarian organisations. It has been the subject of much international debate, particularly in the United Nations. Governments' failure to act stems not from ignorance but from a conscious political decision not to act, reflecting undeniable double standards in the international legal system.

This book has argued that there is a fundamental problem in an international legal framework which in principle sets objective standards but enforces these standards selectively. In such an environment, the human rights discourse can actually become self-defeating. We are continually told that we live in a world that respects human rights, democracy and freedom. As the Palestinian population has long understood, these terms are often used as a smokescreen for injustice, violence and occupation. Such hypocrisy undermines the very ideals which motivated the development of international humanitarian and human rights law.

This is starkly illustrated in the case of children's rights. Despite overwhelming international support for the Convention on the Rights of the Child, 14 years after its creation there has been little improvement globally in the conditions of children's lives. Such improvements are unlikely to occur as long as enforcement requires political will, and that will is absent. Concrete steps are needed to create this political will.

Individual governments around the world have typically offered lip-service in support of international humanitarian and human rights law, but have failed to act in support of that body of law. Indeed, Israeli practices in the OPT are enabled by the active support of other governments. For this reason, the task of generating political will depends on the international public. Governments regularly provide both covert and overt support to unjust regimes, even where their nature is well documented. One strong example is British and US support for the apartheid South Africa government, including active opposition to economic and political boycotts of that oppressive regime. Successive Australian governments provided military, political and economic support to the Indonesian dictatorship over several decades, including the period following its bloody invasion of East Timor in 1975 that resulted in the deaths of one-third of East Timor's population. In both these situations, sustained movements by the public eventually proved effective in ending their government's support of unjust regimes.

Like these other struggles the Palestinian struggle is one of liberation. Support by other governments for the Israeli regime allows the human rights abuses described in this book to continue. Tragically, this support continues despite documented proof that Israel is among the most serious violators of international law in the world.

Change must be sought on the streets and not simply in the parliaments and halls of government. Activists must move beyond information dissemination confined largely to like-minded groups and build strategic alliances that will create an environment where governmental support for criminal regimes becomes impossible to sustain. An important part of this process is grassroots dissemination of information challenging the official 'story' as promoted by mainstream media and governments. Forms may vary from country to country through awareness raising, demonstrations, boycott campaigns, networking, coalition building and lobbying among other tactics. Key however, is an emphasis on the dynamics of power that enable and sustain human rights abuses. Related to this is an understanding of the common links between the Palestinian struggle and other struggles against oppression around the globe.

A major problem with the human rights framework to date is its appeal to neutrality, while disavowing any notion of the political. This leads to the practice of cataloguing or documenting human rights abuses and measuring them against an international standard. However, violations of human rights do not occur in a vacuum; they are almost uniformly the result of power politics. While the process of documentation is undoubtedly important as part of building an argument against injustice, it does little to reveal the underlying causes of that injustice. Without this understanding, it is difficult to tackle the problem at its root.

There is a definite and unfortunate trend within international human rights forums to reduce struggles for equality to a checklist of 'violations' in which the record of the oppressed is compared with that of the oppressor. This is clearly demonstrated in the Palestinian case, where the just cause of national liberation has been elided into the nebulous and apparently neutral term 'the Israeli–Palestinian conflict'. In other words, a struggle against oppression has been reduced to a dispute where both sides are equally at fault, and some kind of power equality is assumed. This claim of objectivity serves to obscure the dynamics of power, turns the oppressor into a 'party to the conflict', and often leaves readers with a confused understanding of the issue.

For human rights work to be an effective framework for the twenty-first century, it must move out of the confines of legal discourse and directly acknowledge and address the power imbalances and strategic interests that enable human rights abuses. The authors of this book have tried to expose the political reasons underlying Israel's detention policies. The book has made it very clear that Israel's practices *do* violate international law and internationally accepted standards of detention – but this understanding does not go far enough. Rather, these policies are deliberate and state-backed, designed to achieve the political aim of maintaining occupation. We have presented concrete evidence of the ways detention policies are directed towards this goal.

The authors hope this book will serve as a useful guide to the ways in which the human rights discourse can be successfully woven into a larger discussion of the political motivations behind rights abuses.

Most importantly, it is hoped that the book will be a powerful tool in mobilising the public will that is necessary to generate concentrated pressure on governments to bring their policies into accord with international human rights and humanitarian law.

RESISTING OCCUPATION

While the situation on the ground in the OPT is often portrayed simply as a 'conflict', the reality is a military occupation where an internationally recognised state power exerts total control over every aspect of the lives of over 3 million civilians. The abuse detained Palestinian children experience as a result of this system of control is not haphazard or a product of their captors' lack of training or ignorance of human rights standards. It is an integral part of a system designed with specific purposes in mind. Ultimately, each phase forms part of a coercive process designed to extract quick confessions, recruit collaborators, demonstrate the overwhelming reach of state power and force Palestinians into submitting to Israeli control of their land, their resources, and their lives. It constitutes a policy of state torture, complemented by a wide range of other measures of collective punishment employed in the OPT.

Whether controlling the movement of persons and goods, confiscating land, demolishing homes, or assassinating activists, Israel seeks to achieve its underlying goals of punishment, intimidation, and coercion. By targeting the most vulnerable sector of society, children, in its campaigns of arrest, Israel sends a message that no one is beyond its reach.

Throughout this book we have stressed that Palestinian children are not merely victims of Israel's incarceration policies, but are actors in their own right. They are part of a national movement against occupation which tries to organise and find ways to resist these policies. Inside prison, Palestinians attempt to organise by launching hunger strikes and resisting attacks by prison guards and soldiers. Outside the prison, ex-detainees and the Palestinian people as a whole offer considerable solidarity to those behind bars. The prison experience, seen as part of the national struggle, is an integral part of the self-image of the Palestinian movement. Indeed, one of the key factors that mitigate the negative psycho-social effects of imprisonment and torture in the Palestinian context is this feeling of peer support, of belonging to a broader struggle.

During the current Intifada, the occupation has escalated into an overt war by Israel against a civilian population in order to achieve and maintain total power and control over all aspects of civilian life, undermine economic, political and institutional development, and to suppress resistance.

As long as the system of occupation, as described throughout this book, remains, Israel can reinstate the same policies at will, at any time. The case of prisoners during the second Intifada has clearly illustrated this; thousands of Palestinians have been arrested, old military orders and torture methods reinvigorated and old detention facilities reopened. The treatment of Palestinian child prisoners in 2003 largely mirrors that of children detained prior to the second Intifada.

Israel's policies of arrest and imprisonment also serve a wider political function. By using mass arrests and administrative detention of increasing numbers of Palestinians who are not charged with any specific offence, Israel is able to artificially inflate the prison population. Thus, when Israeli and Palestinian negotiations take place, Israel is able to use the large prison population as a powerful bargaining chip.

This motive behind Israel's arrest policies was clearly demonstrated following the resumption of political negotiations around the Road Map in May 2003, when the issue of prisoners was a major priority of the Palestinian population. Israel consistently presented the release of prisoners as a 'concession', although the vast majority of those initially released were just about to complete their sentences or were being held under administrative detention orders without charge. Indeed, in early July *Haaretz* reported: 'Security sources said that the number and rate of prisoners released would be relative to the Palestinian's progress in battling and preventing terror.'[1] Even while these releases were occurring, new arrests were taking place including the arbitrary round-up of 180 Palestinian males from the Hebron region in June 2003 alone. Many of those were subsequently released, which Israel presented as a concession and a demonstration of its good faith.

This same pattern of 'prisoners as bargaining chips' was witnessed many times during the years of the Oslo Accords.[2] Indeed, Israel's staged releases of prisoners who had only a few days left in their sentences or had been arrested for criminal and not political offences constituted a major source of Palestinian discontent prior to the September 2000 Intifada.

In the future, Israel may well choose to release large numbers of prisoners and halt the arrest campaign against children and others. However, past experience has demonstrated that such easing of incarceration practices is too often temporary and linked to applying political pressure on the Palestinian population; prisoners become a 'bargaining chip' in a familiar carrot-and-stick routine. The policies of incarceration exist to stifle resistance against occupation and will be brought to bear when needed. As long as the system, which motivates and facilitates the arrest of Palestinians, particularly children, remains in place, Israel is more than able to re-arrest large numbers of Palestinians when it serves their political interests. This conclusion points to an undeniable fact – Israel's policies of detention will be halted only when the occupation which they are designed to support is also ended.

Notes

1 INTRODUCTION

1. B'Tselem, *Torture of Palestinian Minors in the Gush Etzion Police Station* (Jerusalem 2001) p. 16.
2. Excerpt from DCI/FS case study, 16-year-old Rami Zaoul. Arrested in 2000.
3. Although there are a small number of Palestinian children arrested for non-political reasons, their experience differs vastly from children arrested for political reasons.
4. James A. Graff, *Palestinian Children and Israeli State Violence* (Toronto: Near East Cultural and Educational Foundation of Canada, 1991), p. 110.
5. The age range of those detained varied between areas but consistently included children 15 years and over.
6. B'Tselem, *Death in Custody, The Killing of Murad 'Awaisa, 17, in Ramallah, 31 March 2002, Case Study no.14* (Jerusalem 2002).
7. Amos Harel, 'Disorder in the Court', *Haaretz* (18 December 2001).
8. Israeli detention facilities distinguish between 'criminal' and 'security' prisoners in their classification of detainees. The use of the word 'criminal' in reference to juveniles is problematic and has come under criticism within the international child rights movement for its stigmatisation of children. Throughout this book, unless otherwise specified, references to Israeli prisoners are to those who have come into conflict with the law because of civil offences, including children.
9. DCI/PS, *Needs Assessment of Child Ex-Prisoners from the Hebron and Bethlehem Areas* (Ramallah 2002), (unpublished).
10. According to Human Rights Watch, the incarceration rate in the West Bank and Gaza Strip during the first Intifada was 'by far the highest known anywhere in the world: close to 1,000 prisoners per 100,000 population, or one prisoner for every 100 persons'. Middle East Watch, *Prison Conditions in Israel and the Occupied Territories* (New York: Human Rights Watch, 1991), p. 16.
11. *Facts About Torture*, www.irct.org.

2 THE POLITICAL CONTEXT

1. Yezid Sayigh, *Armed Struggle and the Search for State, The Palestinian National Movement 1949–1993* (Oxford: Oxford University Press, 1997), p. 539.
2. Israel expanded the borders of municipal Jerusalem in 1967 to include East Jerusalem which it placed under Israeli civil law. In 1980 it formalised this incorporation by annexing East Jerusalem to Israel. Despite this annexation, Palestinians living in East Jerusalem are not Israeli citizens but carry 'permanent' residency cards which can be revoked.

3. Raja Shehadeh, *Occupier's Law: Israel and the West Bank* (2nd edn, Washington DC: Institute for Palestine Studies, 1988), pp. viii, 114–15.
4. Ibrahim Matar, 'Israeli Settlement and Palestinian Rights', in Naseer Aruri (ed.) *Occupation: Israel Over Palestine* (Belmont, MA: AAUG Press, 1983), p. 131.
5. Military Order No. 92, 15 August 1967, Military Order No. 158, 11 November 1967, and Military Order No. 291, 19 December 1968.
6. Military Order No. 947, 8 November 1981.
7. Raja Shehadeh, *Occupier's Law*, pp. ix–x, 91–5.
8. This section is largely drawn with the publishers' permission from Adam Hanieh and Catherine Cook, 'A Road Map to the Oslo Cul-de-Sac', *Middle East Report Online*, 15 May 2003. Available online at www.merip.org.
9. Hisham Shirabi, *Clashes in the West Bank and Gaza Strip: The Underlying Causes* (Washington, DC: Centre for Policy Analysis On Palestine, May 2000); B'Tselem, *Oslo Before and After* (Jerusalem, May 1999).
10. See Interim Agreement, Annex I, Article XII (Security Arrangements Concerning Planning, Building, and Zoning), Paragraph 2a: 'Buildings or installations shall not be constructed or erected and natural and artificial culture shall not be altered, on either side of the roads delineated in blue on map No. 7 up to a distance of 50 meters from the centre of these roads.'
11. Shirabi, *Clashes in the West Bank and Gaza Strip*.
12. According to the Oslo agreements, Area A referred to areas under the civil and internal security control of the Palestinian Authority, Area B to areas in which the PA held civil responsibility but Israel maintained security control, and Area C where Israel held sole responsibility for security and public order and some control of civil issues was transferred to the PA. Area C constituted the majority of the West Bank (59 per cent) while the majority of the Palestinian population lived in Area A.
13. Import and export figures are percentages of total value in US$ in the year 2000. Figures from Palestinian Central Bureau of Statistics.
14. For more background on the deliberate de-development of the OPT see Sara Roy, *The Gaza Strip: The Political Economy of De-development* (Washington, DC: Institute for Palestine Studies, 1995).
15. While a Palestinian communications company, Paltel, provides the direct phone service to Palestinians in the West Bank and Gaza Strip, phone lines ultimately pass through Israel.
16. B'Tselem, *Oslo Before and After*.
17. World Bank, *Poverty in the West Bank and Gaza Strip* (January 2001), p.14. Available online at http://lnweb18.worldbank.org/mna/mena.nsf/Attachments/Poverty+Report+WBG/$File/poverty+report.pdf.
18. Ellis Shuman, 'Israel's "Ongoing Military Pressure" on Palestinians to continue', *IsraelInsider* 5 March 2002, www.israelinsider.com.
19. Detailed breakdowns of civilian deaths and injuries are available from the Palestinian Red Crescent Society, www.palestinercs.org.
20. *Answers to Frequently Asked Questions: Palestinian Violence and Terrorism, The International War against Terrorism* (Updated – August 2002). Israel Ministry of Foreign Affairs, www.mfa.gov.il.

21. DCI/PS Documentation Unit, *Breakdown of Child Deaths in 2002*, www.dci-pal.org.
22. See DCI/PS *A Generation Denied*, 2001, for a detailed discussion of these deaths and the various reports of the demonstrations in which they occurred, www.dci-pal.org.
23. Adam Hanieh, 'Israel's Clampdown Masks System of Control', *Middle East Report Online*, 14 February 2003. Available online at www.merip.org.
24. Gideon Levy 'A Checkpoint Turns on its Creators', *Haaretz*, 24 February 2002.
25. Hanieh, 'Israel's Clampdown'.
26. *Palestinian Census 1997*, Palestinian Central Bureau of Statistics, 1997.
27. Hanieh, 'Israel's Clampdown'.

3   ISRAEL'S SYSTEM OF CONTROL

1. The content of military orders for the West Bank and Gaza Strip is generally the same although the numbering differs.
2. Until 1980 military orders were not generally available to the public or to lawyers trying to operate within the system. Following 1980, collections of orders were issued retroactively in both Hebrew and Arabic in official gazettes.
3. Military Order No. 854, 6 July 1980.
4. Raja Shehadeh, 'The Changing Juridical Status of Palestinian Areas Under Occupation: Land Holdings and Settlements', in Naseer Aruri (ed.), *Occupation: Israel Over Palestine* (Belmont, MA: AAUG Press, 1983), p. 108.
5. Military Order No. 1342, 7 July 1991.
6. Military Order Nos 33 and 49.
7. Military Order No. 818, 22 January 1980. While this example may seem trivial, it serves to illustrate how these orders have concerned themselves with the intricate details of control. The intention of this order was to prevent Palestinian farmers competing with the Israeli market for flowers. Following the Oslo Accords, Israeli producers began to subcontract Palestinian farmers in the Gaza Strip to produce decorative flowers such as sunflowers for export and for the Israeli market.
8. For further information and analysis of the military court system, see Lisa Hajjar, *Courting Conflict: The Israeli Military Court System in the West Bank and Gaza* (Berkeley, CA: University of California Press, forthcoming).
9. Authors' interview with Attorney Khaled Quzmar, December 2002.
10. Chapters 5 and 6 detail the regulations and obstacles facing lawyers visiting detention centres and prisons.
11. Birgitta Elfstrom, *Palestinian Children in Israeli Detention Centres and Prisons: Report on Trials in the Israeli Military Court Beit El Settlement Ramallah 7–12 July 2001*, International Commission of Jurists, Swedish Section, available at www.dci-pal.org.
12. Authors' interview with Attorney Khaled Quzmar, in Ramallah, March 2003.
13. Amnesty International, *Broken Lives – a Year of Intifada* (AI Index: MDE 15/083/2001), p. 64.

14. Authors' telephone interview with Attorney Tamar Pelleg, 16 March 2003.
15. Authors' interview with Attorney Khaled Quzmar in Ramallah, 12 December, 2002.
16. Authors' interview with Attorney Sahar Francis in Ramallah, 18 March 2003.
17. Authors' telephone interview with Attorney Andre Rosenthal, 16 March 2003.
18. Authors' telephone interview with Attorney Leah Tsemel, 14 March 2003.
19. DCI/PS case file No. 1999/119C.
20. Authors' interview with Attorney Khaled Quzmar in Ramallah, May 2003.
21. See www.child-soldiers.org.
22. B'Tselem, *Collaborators in the Occupied Territories: Human Right Abuses and Violations* (Jerusalem, 1995), p. 5.
23. Ibid., p. 26.
24. Ibid., p. 26.
25. Ibid., p. 27. The B'Tselem report contains further case studies of Palestinians (including children) recruited as collaborators during their interrogation.
26. Palestinian business people often find it easier to obtain permits because of their role as intermediaries between the Israeli and Palestinian economies – a relationship also characterised by dependency as outlined in the previous chapter.
27. DCI/PS case study, A.A., 17 years old, Old City, Hebron. Arrested 9 January 1998 near Ibrahimi Mosque.
28. Quoted in B'Tselem, *Collaborators in the Occupied Territories*, p. 39.

4   INTERNATIONAL LAW AND CHILD DETENTION

1. For a principle to be considered part of CIL it must be a general practice that States feel they are obliged to follow.
2. There are 165 State Parties to the Geneva Conventions of 1949. The widespread endorsement of the Conventions is one factor supporting the view that the Conventions, in whole or substantially, constitute part of customary international law. See Adam Roberts, 'Prolonged Military Occupation: The Israeli-Occupied Territories, 1967–1988', in Emma Playfair (ed.), *International Law and the Administration of Occupied Territories* (Oxford: Clarendon Press, 1992), p. 35.
3. Article 4, Fourth Geneva Convention.
4. The overwhelming majority of Palestinian children arrested for 'security' offences by the Israeli military do not fit the description of a combatant as outlined in international humanitarian law, nor are they detained as prisoners of war.
5. Such declarations include UN 'rules' and 'guidelines'. Some of the provisions outlined in these instruments are also incorporated into binding treaties.
6. The Optional Protocol on the Involvement of Children in Armed Conflicts entered into force on 12 February 2002. The Optional Protocol

on the Sale of Children, Child Prostitution and Child Pornography entered into force on 18 January 2002.

7. The latter principle is also found in the UN Rules for the Protection of Juveniles Deprived of their Liberty and The Beijing Rules. The Beijing Rules further outline in 18.1 that: 'A large variety of disposition measures shall be made available to the competent authority, allowing for flexibility so as to avoid institutionalisation to the greatest extent possible.'

8. CAT; ICCPR, Article 7; UDHR, Article 5; CRC, Article 37a; UN Declaration on the Protection of All Persons from Being Subjected to Torture and Other Cruel, Inhuman or Degrading Treatment or Punishment; European Convention on Human Rights, Article 3; the American Convention on Human Rights, Article 5.2; the African Charter of Human and Peoples' Rights, Article 5.

9. The Rome Statute stipulates in Article 7 that torture is a crime against humanity 'when committed as part of a widespread or systematic attack directed against any civilian population, with knowledge of the attack'. Article 8 includes torture in its definition of war crimes. The Rome Statute entered into force on 1 July 2002.

10. See UN Human Rights Committee, *General Comment 20* (1992), regarding Article 7 of the ICCPR.

11. See *Outcome Document of the International Conference on Children, Torture, and Other Forms of Violence: Facing the Facts, Forging the Future*. Conference of the World Organisation Against Torture, in partnership with the Mannerheim League of Child Welfare (27 November–2 December 2001) p. 37.

5   ARREST AND TRANSFER

1. DCI/PS case file 43B/2001.

2. Prior to the current Intifada, and for the period immediately following, around 95 per cent of arrested children were charged with throwing stones. Beginning in 2001, and increasing in 2002, greater numbers of children were arrested on more serious charges such as making and/or throwing Molotov cocktails, weapons possession, and planning or carrying out attacks on Israeli civilians. In April 2003, DCI/PS attorney Khaled Quzmar estimated that more than 15 per cent of cases represented by the organisation were arrested on such charges.

3. B'Tselem, *Torture of Palestinian Minors in the Gush Etzion Police Station*, p. 12.

4. DCI/PS case file 17A/2001.

5. B'Tselem, *Torture of Palestinian Minors*, pp. 18–19.

6. Ibid., pp. 21–2.

7. Name of child has been changed and abbreviated by authors. DCI/PS case file 1999/111c.

8. Su'ad was wearing a head scarf worn by many Muslim women for religious reasons. Removal of the scarf in public is a culturally and

religiously significant insult and viewed as a measure of extreme disrespect.

9. DCI/PS case file 2001/046.
10. Affidavit of Riham As'ad Muhammad al-Shaikh Musa provided to DCI/PS attorney.
11. Quoted in Haim Shadmi, 'Wounded Palestinian Teen Shackled to her Israeli Hospital Bed', *Haaretz English Online Edition* (26 February 2003).
12. DCI/PS Child Prisoner Briefing, No. 13 (12 March 2003).
13. Amnesty International, *Mass Detention in Cruel, Inhuman and Degrading Conditions*, CAI Index: MDE 15/074/2002, p. 1.
14. Authors' interview with Attorney Sahar Francis in Ramallah, 13 March 2003.
15. Amnesty International, *Mass Detention*, pp. 5–6.
16. For more information on conditions of detention during the 2002 mass arrests, see: DCI/PS and Addameer Prisoners Support and Human Rights Association, *Palestinian Prisoners' Day: Thousands of Palestinians Blindfolded, Handcuffed and Tortured* (17 April 2002); B'Tselem, *Daily Updates* (12, 13, and 15 April 2002), and *Operation Defensive Shield, Soldiers Testimonies, Palestinian Testimonies* (September 2002).
17. Amnesty International, *Mass Detention*, p. 8.
18. Ibid., p. 12.
19. Statement of Samih Sameeh Atta Judeh provided to DCI/PS.
20. Amnesty International, *Israel/Occupied Territories: Amnesty International Calls for a Commission of Inquiry into Mass Arbitrary Detention of Palestinians*, AI Index: MDE 15/089/2002.
21. See Arnon Regular, Yossi Verter, *et al.*, 'IDF Ends Tul Karm Operation After Key Arrests', *Haaretz English Online Edition* (4 April 2003), and UNRWA Press Release, *Israeli Military Forcefully Occupies UNRWA School*, No. HQ/G/04/2003 (3 April 2003). Available online at www.un.org/unrwa.
22. UNRWA, *Selected Refugee Statistics, Total Registered Camp Population as of 31 March 2003*. Available online at www.un.org/unrwa/publications/pdf/population.pdf.
23. A number of media reports gave 14 to 40 as the age range of those ordered to report.
24. Camp residents placed the figure at close to 2,000, while the Israeli military asserted that only 1,000 were detained. Figures reported in the media varied between these two.
25. For additional information, see Nathan Guttman, *Haaretz* Correspondent, Haaretz Service and Agencies, 'IDF Launches Counter-terror Raid in Tul Karm Refugee Camp,' *Haaretz English Online Edition* (3 April 2003); Arnon Regular, *et al.*, 'IDF Ends Tul Karm Operation'; BBC News Online, *Six Killed in Israeli Raids* (3 April 2003); Sharmila Devi, 'Israel Quizzes up to 2,000 Palestinians in West Bank', *Financial Times* (3 April 2003); Chris McGreal, 'Six Killed in Israeli Raids on West Bank: 1,000 Boys and Men Detained in Seized UN School', *Guardian* (4 April 2003).
26. IDF Spokesperson's Announcements, *IDF Ends Operations in Tulkarem* (4 April 2003). Available online at www.idf.il.
27. Amnesty International, *Mass Detention*, p. 1.

28. Such fears are not unfounded. The concept of 'transfer', which is a euphemism for ethnic cleansing, is a topic of regular discussion within Israeli political circles. Several prominent Israeli politicians support it, including those serving in Ariel Sharon's administration. For discussions of this discourse, and of Palestinian reactions, see Amira Hass, 'Horror Scenarios Coming True', *Haaretz English Online Edition* (27 March 2003); 'As War Approaches Palestinian Fears Rise', *Haaretz English Online Edition* (20 March 2003); 'Threats of Forced Mass Expulsion', *Le Monde Diplomatique* (19 February 2003); and Norman Finkelstein, *Image and Reality of the Israeli–Palestinian Conflict*, 2nd edn (Verso, 2003), pp. xi–xxvi.

29. Though detainees were allowed to return to their homes, the temporary expulsion of Palestinian civilians engendered concerns that the Tulkarem incident was a test. See Palestine Monitor Update, *The Threat of 'Transfer' Becomes Temporary Reality for Thousands from Tulkaram Refugee Camp* (5 April 2003).

30. Ibid.

31. For more information see: DCI/PS press release *Israel's Campaign of Arrests Against Palestinian Children*, ref: 00200 (15 January 2000), *Israel's 'Gift' to Palestinian Children: 16 Children Arrested on the Eve of Eid al-Fitr*, ref: 00100 (6 January 2000), and *Annual Report 1999*.

32. B'Tselem, *Torture of Palestinian Minors*, pp. 14–15.

33. DCI/PS case file 225/2002.

34. Name has been charged and abbreviated. DCI/PS case file1999/119C.

35. Authors' interview with Attorney Yossi Wolfson, Hamoked in Jerusalem, 22 February 2003.

36. Ibid.

37. Authors' interview with Attorney Khaled Quzmar, in Ramallah 12 December 2002.

38. See Chapter 1.

39. Arnon Regular, 'Jeep Ride to the End of the Road', *Haaretz English Online Edition* (18 April 2003).

40. Arnon Regular and Roni Singer, 'Four Border Police Suspected of Killing Hebron youth', *Haaretz English Online Edition* (19 April 2003).

41. Baruch Kra, '8 Border Police Officers Suspected of Killing Palestinian', *Haaretz English Online Edition* (21 April 2003).

42. Regular, 'Jeep Ride'.

43. Kra, '8 Border Police'.

44. For more information, see B'Tselem press release, *B'Tselem Welcomes Arrest of Border Policemen Suspected of Killing 'Imran Abu Hamdia* (Jerusalem, 18 April 2003).

6   INTERROGATION AND DETENTION

1. Testimony of Mufid Hussein Muhammad Hamamreh, 15 years old, B'Tselem. *Torture of Palestinian Minors*, pp. 14–15.

2. Association for Civil Rights in Israel, *'Security Concerns do not Justify Sub-Standard Conditions of Detention'* (Jerusalem, 18 December 2002).

3. HCJ 3239/02 *Iyyad Ishaq Mahmud Mar'ab et al.* v. *Commander of IDF Forces in the Judea and Samaria Area et al.*, 5 February 2003.
4. LAW, The Palestinian Society for the Protection of Human Rights and the Environment, press release, *New Year's Strike: Palestinian Prisoners Refuse to Attend Court* (Jerusalem, 2 January 2003).
5. Palestinian Prisoner Society, *Palestinian Prisoners During the Al Aqsa Intifada* (Bethlehem, January 2002), www.ppsmo.org.
6. Amnesty International, *Medical Concern/Detention Without Charge*, AI Index: MDE 15/030/2003.
7. DCI/PS Child Prisoner Briefing, No. 14, 20 May 2003.
8. Ibid.
9. DCI/PS Child Prisoners Briefing No. 6, February 2002.
10. DCI/PS Child Prisoners Briefing No. 16, 8 July 2003.
11. DCI/PS case file 2001/63C.
12. DCI/PS case file 1998/027.
13. DCI/PS case study of 17-year-old S.M. from Ramallah, arrested on 30 March 2002 and detained for 10 days.
14. DCI/PS Child Prisoner Briefing No.13, 8 April 2003.
15. B'Tselem, *Torture of Palestinian Minors* (Jerusalem, July 2001), p.4.
16. Based on DCI/PS Press Release, 16 May 2002, *DCI/PS Lawyer Visits Child Detainees in Ofer Detention Centre: Conditions Sub-Human and Barbaric.*
17. Based on DCI/PS Press Release, 16 May 2002. Edited for language with DCI/PS's permission.
18. Human Rights Watch/Middle East, *Torture and Ill-Treatment: Israel's Interrogation of Palestinians from the Occupied Territories* (New York, 1994), p. 161.
19. See 'The Prison Factory: An Interview with Adv. Allegra Pachecco', *Between the Lines* (Jerusalem, July 2001).
20. See Human Rights Watch *World Report, 1993, Israeli-Occupied West Bank and Gaza Strip* (New York, 1993) for details on this case.
21. See Rami Zaoul case study, Chapter 1. Rami eventually lost consciousness and was transferred to hospital as a result of his torture. He had been accused of throwing stones.
22. See Ismail Sa'batin case study, Chapter 1 and A.A. case study Chapter 3 for examples of *shabeh* used against children.
23. US State Department 2000, 2001, and 2002 annual 'Country Reports on Human Rights Practices' contains allegations by Israeli human rights organisations that shaking continues to be used against detainees.
24. Unpublished DCI/PS survey, 2001.
25. B'Tselem, *Routine Torture: Interrogation Methods of the General Security Service* (Jerusalem: B'Tselem, 1998), p. 8.
26. George Abu Zulof, BA Seminar Thesis, Bethlehem University, 'Psychosocial Impact of Detention on Palestinian Prisoners in Israeli Jails', 1994.

7   IMPRISONMENT

1. For example, in June 2003, the Israeli press noted the instrumental role of Palestinian political prisoner Marwan Barghouti in launching cease-

fire talks between the Palestinian Authority and Palestinian armed factions. He was involved both in mobilising support among the prison population for a cease-fire, and in lobbying through intermediaries with representatives of armed groups, locally and regionally. See Arnon Regular, Baruch Kra *et al.*, 'Palestinians: Israel to Swap Barghouti for Azzam Azzam', *Haaretz English Online Edition* (18 June 2003).

2. DCI/PS case file 0217/2002.
3. DCI/PS case file 020/2002.
4. DCI/PS case file 053/2002.
5. DCI/PS case file 021/2002.
6. DCI/PS case file 031/2002.
7. Amnesty International, *Mass Detention in Cruel, Inhuman and Degrading Conditions*, p. 1.
8. Israel's prisons and detention centres are sometimes known in the OPT by a different label from their official Hebrew name. For example, Palestinians use 'Telmond' to refer to Hasharon, Ofek and Hadorim prisons. Also, some variances occur due to linguistic or translation differences. This book uses the names as they are known in the OPT. Megiddo and Ketziot correspond with the official names of the prisons. In this chapter, Ramle consistently refers to Neve Tertze. In referring to Telmond, we have distinguished between the two different facilities that detain Palestinian children, using their official names in Hebrew, under the umbrella of 'Telmond Compound'.
9. Article 76 of the Fourth Geneva Convention requires that protected persons be detained inside the occupied territory and, if convicted, serve their sentences therein.
10. See Jonathon Cook, 'A Shameful Legacy Returns', *Al-Ahram Weekly Online* (18–24 April 2002); Associated Press, 'Israeli Detention Camp Open', *MiamiHerald.com* (17 April 2002); Palestinian Centre for Human Rights press release, *Israel Reopens Notorious Desert Prison Camp* (14 April 2002); *BBC News*, 'Israel in Prisoner Transfer Row' (21 April 2002).
11. Palestinian minors with Israeli citizenship and those from East Jerusalem who have come into conflict with the law for criminal offences are detained in Ofek.
12. Palestinian child political prisoners given administrative detention are also detained in Ofer.
13. DCI/PS Child Prisoners Briefing, No. 11 (9 February 2003).
14. Decision of the Tel Aviv Central Court, *Mohammed Mahmoud Farheeyat et al. v. Prison Services Authority* (17 November 1997).
15. Verbal report of DCI/PS attorney recorded by the authors in DCI/PS Child Prisoner Briefing, No. 9 (21 May 2002).
16. See Mary E. Howell 'Ansar III: Camp of the Slow Death, An Eyewitness Account', in Jay Murphy (ed.), *For Palestine* (New York: Writers & Readers Publishing, Inc., 1993), pp. 121–4.
17. DCI/PS Child Prisoner Briefing, No. 12 (12 March 2003), and No. 13 (8 April 2003).
18. Addameer Prisoners Support and Human Rights Association press release, *General Information on Conditions of Detention* (23 October 2002).
19. Ibid.

20. Addameer press release, *Ketziot Military Prison Authorities Endanger the Lives of Palestinian Detainees: Detainees Protest Attack and Continuing Human Rights Violations* (4 November 2002).
21. Addameer, *General Information.*
22. See DCI/PS Child Prisoner Briefings No. 11 and No. 13.
23. Gideon Alon, 'Meretz MK: Hasharon Detention Centre Violates Human Rights', *Haaretz*, English print edition (20 September 2001).
24. See DCI/PS Child Prisoner Briefing, No. 6 (18 February 2002).
25. DCI/PS Child Prisoner Briefing, No. 13.
26. DCI/PS case file 2000/18A. This incident occurred during Islam's holy month of Ramadan when Muslims fast from sunrise to sunset.
27. Affidavits taken by DCI/PS attorney. For additional information, see DCI/PS report, *Summary of Attacks on Palestinian Child Political Prisoners by Israeli Prison Guards, Army and Riot Police in 2001* (September 2001).
28. LAW, The Palestinian Society for the Protection of Human Rights and the Environment press release, *Palestinian Children in Israeli Jails Face Hardship and Racism* (30 January 2003).
29. Ibid.
30. George Abu Zulof, 'Psychosocial Impact of Detention on Palestinian Prisoners in Israeli Jails'.
31. Authors' interview with former child prisoner N. J. in Ramallah (July 2003).
32. Quoted in Gideon Alon, 'Meretz MK'.
33. See DCI/PS Child Prisoner Briefings, No. 3 (22 September 2001) and No. 13.
34. See memo of Allegra Pachecco, attorney for the Palestinian Prisoners' Society, regarding visit to Ramle (Neve Tertze) Prison (12 May 2002) and DCI/PS Child Prisoner Briefing, No. 13.
35. See DCI/PS Child Prisoner Briefing, No. 11.
36. Adalah [Legal Centre for Arab Minority Rights in Israel], News Update, *Adalah to Prisons Authority: Cancel Decision to Stop Providing Political Prisoners with Personal Hygiene Supplies* (23 April 2003).
37. Pachecco memo.
38. Verbal report of DCI/PS attorney recorded by authors in DCI/PS press release, *14-year-old Sanaa' Amer Receives Excessive Sentence Following Beating and Maltreatment in Ramle Prison*, ref: 0017/01 (16 July 2001).
39. Ibid.
40. Pachecco memo.
41. See DCI/PS Child Prisoner Briefing, No. 4 (10 October 2001).
42. Ibid.
43. DCI/PS case file 2000/18A.
44. Verbal report of DCI/PS attorney (July 2001), recorded by the authors.
45. The case was brought by DCI/PS, Association for Civil Rights in Israel (ACRI), Public Committee Against Torture in Israel (PCATI) and Hamoked.
46. Name has been changed by authors. DCI/PS questionnaire completed by A.J.
47. Name has been changed by authors. DCI/PS questionnaire completed by A.A.

48. Name has been changed by authors. DCI/PS case file 1997/051.
49. Name has been changed by authors. DCI/PS case file 1997/13.
50. During the first Intifada, Palestinian residents of WB did not need permits to enter Israel – the requirement was imposed in 1993. During the first three months of the second Intifada the primary obstacle faced by DCI/PS's Palestinian attorney in visiting detained children was the Israeli authorities' refusal to issue him the necessary permit to enter Israel. Checkpoints within the West Bank have also made it virtually impossible to visit children held in detention centres in the OPT.
51. Associated Press, 'Prisons Chief: Palestinian Prisoners Suffer Harsh Regime,' *Haaretz English Online Edition* (25 June 2003).

8   STATE VIOLENCE AND DISCRIMINATION

1. See B'Tselem, *Torture of Palestinian Minors in the Gush Etzion Police Station* (Jerusalem, July 2001); *Comments on the Third Periodic Report of the State of Israel Concerning the Implementation of the UN Convention Against Torture and Other Cruel, Inhuman or Degrading Treatment or Punishment, and its Annex The Treatment of Detained Palestinian Children by the Israeli Authorities*, prepared by LAW – The Palestinian Society for the Protection of Human Rights and the Environment, PCATI – Public Committee Against Torture in Israel, and OMCT – World Organisation Against Torture (October 2001); Amnesty International, *Mass Detention in Cruel, Inhuman and Degrading Conditions*, AI-index: MDE 15/074/2002. See also relevant releases of LAW, PCATI, Physicians for Human Rights, Addameer Prisoners Support and Human Rights Association, Al-Haq, World Organisation Against Torture, and Human Rights Watch.
2. ICCPR, Art. 10.3; CRC, Art 37c and CRC, Art. 40.3.
3. The commentary to the UN Standard Minimum Rules for the Administration of Juvenile Justice is included within the text of the document itself, following each point.
4. Emergency Regulations (Offences in the Occupied Territories – Jurisdiction and Legal Assistance), 5727–1967.
5. Quoted in UN Committee on the Rights of the Child, *Consideration of Reports Submitted by States Parties Under Article 44 of the Convention, Periodic Reports of States Parties due in 1993, Israel* (20 February 2001), CRC/C/8/Add.44, p. 63.
6. Ibid., p. 337.
7. Miscellaneous Criminal Applications 1363/93 *Y.Z. (Minor)* v. *State of Israel*, P.D. 47(2) 71.
8. From Miscellaneous Criminal Applications 1363/93 *Y.Z. (Minor)* v. *State of Israel*, P.D. 47(2)71, quoted in UN Committee on the Rights of the Child, *Israel* (20 February 2001), p. 337.
9. The wording of the report does not make it absolutely clear for which year statistics are quoted, but this does not compromise the overall patterns of arrest and sentencing cited.
10. UN Committee on the Rights of the Child, *Israel* (20 February 2001), p. 335.

11. Military Order No. 132, 'Order Concerning the Trial of Juvenile Offenders', issued for the West Bank on 24 September 1967 defines a teenager as over 14 and under 16; this was amended by Military Order No. 235 (March 1968) to someone over 14 and under 17. In 1969, Military Order No. 311 changed the definition again to someone over 14 and under 18.

12. UN Committee on the Rights of the Child, *Israel* (20 February 2001), p. 335.

13. DCI/PS case file: 2001/017.

14. B'Tselem, *Law Enforcement on Israeli Civilians in the Occupied Territories* (Jerusalem, 1994).

15. DCI/PS Case File: 2001/015.

16. 'Violent Settlers and Extremists Treated Lightly by Israeli Justice', *Agence France Presse* (20 July 2001).

17. 'Rabin Murder Plot Woman Pardoned', *BBC News* (18 July 2001).

18. Penal Law 1977, the Youth (Trial, Punishment and Modes of Treatment) Law 1971 and regulations enacted thereunder; and the Probation Ordinance [New Version] 1969 and regulations enacted thereunder.

19. UN Committee on the Rights of the Child, *Israel* (20 February 2001), p. 318.

20. The Israeli report to the CRC lists the following agencies that are mandated by law to deal specifically with juvenile suspects: 'the Police Force; the Youth Probation Service (a State social welfare service acting under the auspices of the Ministry of Labor and Social Affairs); the Public Defender's Office; the courts; the Youth Protection Authority (also under the auspices of the Ministry of Labor and Social Affairs, and responsible for juvenile residences); and, in a few cases, the Prison Authority', p. 319.

21. UN Committee on the Rights of the Child, *Israel* (20 February 2001), p. 319.

22. Ibid., p. 321.

23. Section 3, Youth (Trial, Punishment and Modes of Treatment) Law, 1971.

24. The specifics of the military court system are detailed in Military Order No. 378, and have been reviewed in Chapter 3.

25. In the West Bank, Military Order No. 132. Revised by Order No. 235 of March 1968, No. 311 of 1969, No. 371 of 1970, No. 417 of 1971, No. 587 of 1975, No. 639 of 1976, No. 863 of 1980, No. 961 of 1982, No. 1083 of 1983, No. 1172 of 1986, No. 1290 of 1989. In Gaza, Military Order No. 424 of 1972.

26. In the West Bank, Military Order No. 1235 enacted 29 April 1988. Revised by: Military Orders No. 1256 of 27 October 1988; No. 1275 of 28 April 1989; No. 1289 of 29 October 1989; No. 1318 of 18 October 1990; No. 1336 of 28 April 1991. In the Gaza Strip, Military Order No. 951, 1 May 1988. Revised by: Military Orders No. 972 of 30 October 1988; No. 992 of 1 May 1989; and No. 1013 of 30 October 1989.

27. Sec. 3 of the Criminal Procedure (Detention and Search) Ordinance [New Version], 1969.

28. Sec. 10(4) of the Youth (Prosecution, Punishment, and Procedures) Law, 1971.

29. Amendment 68 to the Security Provisions Order, Order No. 1378 of Oct. 20, 1992 in the West Bank, and Amendment 70 to the Security Provisions Order, Order No. 1081 of Oct. 11, 1992, in Gaza.
30. B'Tselem, *Law Enforcement on Israeli Civilians*.
31. Ibid.
32. Allegra Pachecco, Esq., *Proving Torture: No Longer Necessary in Israel*, Public Committee Against Torture in Israel (4 March 1999). Available online at http://internationalstudies.uchicago.edu/torture/abstracts/allegra-pacheo.html.
33. UN Committee on the Rights of the Child, *Israel* (20 February 2001), p. 325.
34. Ibid., p. 325.
35. Ibid., p. 341.
36. UN Rules for the Protection of Juveniles Deprived of their Liberty, point 42.
37. Israel Prison Service Schooling and Education Division, *Schooling and Education Programs for Prisoners*, p. 3. Documents available online at www.ips.gov.il.
38. UN Committee on the Rights of the Child, *Israel* (20 February 2001), p. 345.
39. Israel Prison Service Schooling and Education Division, p. 4.
40. *A Glimpse Behind the Walls*, brochure of the Israel Prison Service. Available online at www.ips.gov.il.
41. Israel Prison Service website, *Prisons* section, subsection on Neve Tertze.
42. Ibid., subsection on Hasharon.
43. Decision of the Tel Aviv Central Court, *Mohammed Mahmoud Farheeyat et al.* v. *Prison Services Authority*, 17 November 1997.
44. Authors' telephone interview with Attorney Leah Tsemel (14 March 2003).
45. In 1998, DCI/PS handled 89 cases. In 1999, it handled 202.
46. www.cvt.org/main.php/InsideCVT/WhatisTorture.
47. See Amnesty International USA's *Stop Torture* campaign website for the sources of this definition, www.amnestyusa.org/stoptorture/abouttorture.html.

9   PSYCHOLOGICAL AND SOCIAL IMPACTS OF PRISON AND TORTURE

1. N. Man, *Children, Torture and Power: The Torture of Children by States and Armed Opposition Groups* (London: Save the Children, 2000), p. 34.
2. Between 1990 and 1999 Israeli soldiers, settlers or undercover units killed 289 Palestinian children, which represents more than 20 per cent of total deaths during this period. Between 1997 and 1999 child deaths accounted for more than 50 per cent of all deaths. Between 29 September 2000 and 30 June 2003, 463 of 2407 Palestinians killed were children. See *Alternative Report to the State of Israel's First Periodic Report to the Committee on the Rights of the Child*, submitted by Defence for Children International/Palestine Section and endorsed by The Palestinian Child

Rights Coalition, March 2002, pp. 5–6, and Palestinian Red Crescent Society, www. palestinercs.org.

3. R. Khalidi, *Palestinian Identity: The Construction of Modern National Consciousness* (New York: Columbia University Press, 1997).

4. For instance Islam, the dominant religion, teaches the individual to be patient and accept the will of God who ordains events; whereas within Palestinian nationalism, 'sumud' or steadfastness – peaceful resistance to the Israeli occupation that evolved during the 1970s is highly valued.

5. American Psychological Association (1994). Quick Reference to diagnostic criteria from DSM-IV (Washington, DC: Author).

6. P. Vesti, F. Somnier, M. Kastrup, *Psychotherapy with Torture Survivors: A Report of Practice from the Rehabilitation and Research Centre for Torture Victims* (RCT) (Copenhagen: IRCT, 1992).

7. This useful distinction is made by Helen Bamber, founder of the UK Medical Foundation for the Care of Victims of Torture. H. Bamber, 'The Medical Foundation and its Commitment to Human Rights and Rehabilitation', in Neve Gordon and Ruchama Marton (eds), *Torture: Human Rights, Medical Ethics and the Case of Israel* (London: Zed Books, 1995), p. 120.

8. See Chapter 7 for discussion of the unpublished interviews with former child prisoners detained between the mid-1980s and mid-1990s.

9. For a useful review of the literature see S. Quota and E. El-Sarraj, 'Prison Experiences and Coping Styles Among Palestinian Men, Peace and Conflict', *Journal of Peace Psychology*, 3(1), 1997, 19–36.

10. Vesti, Somnier, Kastrup, *Psychotherapy with Torture Survivors*, p. 28.

11. J.C. Reid and T. Strong, 'Torture and Trauma', *The Health Care Needs of Refugee Victims in New South Wales* (Sydney: Cumberland College of Health Sciences, 1987).

12. B. S. Brigham 'Clinical Interventions with Refugee Survivors of Torture: Some Considerations', Seminar Paper, Capella University, 1998.

13. V. Khamis 'Post Traumatic Stress Disorder among the Injured of the Intifada', *Journal of Traumatic Stress*, 6.555–9 (1993).

14. E. El-Sarraj, R.L. Punamaki, S. Salmi. and D. Summerfield, 'Experience of Torture and Ill-treatment and Post Traumatic Stress Disorder Symptoms among Palestinian Political Prisoners', *Journal of Traumatic Stress*, 9, 1996.

15. The Gaza Community Mental Health Project was established during the first Intifada. Its research department focuses on 'pressing psychosocial issues' that affect Palestinian society, in particular the psychological effects of violence and trauma, the effects of torture and home demolitions and the prevalence of mental disorders in the Gaza Strip.

16. More recently a similar criticism has been levied at global post-conflict reconstruction programmes using Western-based psychosocial interventions. Some maintain that this pathologises entire non-Western populations and marginalises the role of social action and empowerment in promoting recovery and mental health. See D. Summerfield, 1999, 'A critique of seven assumptions behind psychological trauma programs in war-affected areas', *Social Science and Medicine*, 48, 1999, and V. Pupavac 'Post Conflict Reconstruction: Political, Social and Economic. Pathologizing Populations and Colonizing Minds: International

Psychosocia. Programmes in Kosovo', 51st Political Studies Association Conference, Manchester, 2001.

17. Quoted in J. Garbarino, 'What Children Can Tell Us About Living in Danger', *American Psychologist*, 46 (4), April 1991, pp. 376–83.
18. Garbarino, 'What Children Can Tell Us'.
19. R. Coles, *The Political Life of Children* (Boston: Houghton Mifflin, 1987).
20. Quoted in Garbarino, 'What Children Can Tell Us'.
21. R.L. Punamaki, 'The Uninvited Guest of War Enters Childhood: Developmental and Personality Aspects of War and Military Violence', *Traumatology*, 8, 3 (September 2002).
22. Vesti, Somnier, Kastrup, *Psychotherapy with Torture Survivors*, p. 31.
23. M. Macksoud, 'Helping Children Cope with the Stress of War' (New York: Unicef, 1993).
24. A point stressed by Amnesty International in their report, *Hidden Scandal, Secret Shame: Torture and Ill-treatment of Children*, AI Index: ACT 40/38/00.
25. R.L. Punamaki, 'Psychological Stress Responses of Palestinian Mothers and their Children in Conditions of Military Occupation and Political Violence', *The Quarterly Newsletter of the Laboratory of Comparative Human Cognition*, 9. (2), (1987), 76–84.
26. A.M. Baker, 'The Psychological Impact of the Intifada on Palestinian Children in the Occupied West Bank and Gaza; An Exploratory Study', *American Journal of Orthopsychiatry*, 60 (1990), 496–504.
27. Research undertaken in the mid-90s by Qouta, Punamaki and El Sarraj suggests that most of these symptoms may have abated following the Oslo agreement.
28. On 25 February 1994 Israeli settler and reserve soldier Baruch Goldstein randomly fired on Muslim worshippers kneeling in prayer at the Ibrahimi Mosque in Hebron during the Muslim holy month of Ramadan. During the attack 29 Palestinians were killed and dozens wounded. In the six days of protest that followed, Israeli soldiers killed a further 21 Palestinians. Hebron's Palestinian residents were placed under 24-hour curfew for over a month after the settler's attack.
29. A. Baker and N. Shalhoub-Kevorkian, 'Effects of Political and Military Traumas on Children: The Palestinian Case', *Clinical Psychology Review*, 19, 8 (1999).
30. A.M. Baker, 'Gender, Urban-Rural-Camp and Regional Differences among Self-esteem Scores of Palestinian Children', *The Journal of Psychology*, 126 (1992).
31. R.L. Punamaki and R. Suleiman, 'Predictors and Effectiveness of Coping with Political Violence Among Palestinian Children', *British Journal of Social Psychology*, 29 (1990), 67–77.
32. S. Qouta, R.L. Punamaki and E. El Sarraj, 'Impact of Peace Treaty on Psychological Well-being: A Follow-up Study on Palestinian Children', *Child Abuse and Neglect*, 19 (1995).
33. T.M. McIntyre and M.Ventura, 'Children of War: A Study of PTSD in Angolan Adolescents', a paper presented to the 103rd Annual Meeting of the American Psychological Association in New York (August 1995), quoted in Baker, 'Effects of Political and Military Traumas'.

34. Baker and Shalhoub-Kevorkian, 1995; Khamis, 1993; Sarraj *et al.*, 1996, quoted in A. Baker, 1999.
35. A. Baker, 'Effects of Political and Military Traumas', p. 943.
36. Unpublished survey DCI/PS January 2003.
37. M. Basoglu, S. Mineka, M. Paker, T. Aker, M. Livanou and S. Goek, 'Psychological Preparedness for Trauma as a Protective Factor in Survivors of Torture', *Psychological Medicine*, 27 (1997), 1421–33.
38. Man, *Children, Torture and Power*.
39. S. Qouta, E. El Sarraj and R.L. Punamaki, 'Prison Experience and Coping Styles Among Palestinian Men', *Peace and Conflict, Journal of Peace Psychology*, 3(1) (1997), 19–36.
40. A. Hass, *Drinking the Sea at Gaza: Days and Nights in a Land under Siege* (New York: Henry Holt, 1996), p. 210.
41. Baker, 'Effects of Political and Military Traumas', p. 943.
42. AI Index:ACT 40/38/00.
43. El-Sarraj *et al.*, 'Experiences of Torture and Ill-treatment'.
44. L.A. McLoskey and K. Southwick, 'Psychosocial Problems in Refugee Children Exposed to War', *Pediatrics*, (1996), 97, 3.
45. Hass, *Drinking the Sea at Gaza*, p. 211.
46. Punamaki, 'The Uninvited Guest of War Enters Childhood'.
47. R. Giacaman, A. Abdullah, R.A. Safieh and L. Shamieh, 'Schooling at Gunpoint: Palestinian Children's Learning Environment in War-like Conditions', The Ramallah/al-Brieh/Beitunia Urban Center, December 2002.

10   MYTHS AND POLITICS –
THE FOUNDATION OF ISRAEL'S IMPUNITY

1. Fourth Geneva Convention ratified on 7 June 1951. Israel ratified ICCPR, CAT, and CRC on 3 October 1991.
2. Opinion of the Israeli High Court, quoted in Raja Shehadeh, *Occupier's Law: Israel and the West Bank*, 2nd edn (Washington DC: Institute for Palestine Studies, 1988), p. xiii. Also see Military Advocate General's Unit, Israel Ministry of Defense, *Israel, the 'Intifada', and the Rule of Law* (Tel Aviv: Israel Ministry of Defence Publications, 1993) p. 22.
3. See Amnesty International, *Broken Lives – a year of Intifada* (2001) and *Annual Reports*; US Department of State, *Annual Human Rights Report*; Human Rights Watch, In *a Dark Hour: The Use of Civilians during IDF Arrest Operations* (New York, April 2002), *Israel's Closure of the West Bank and Gaza Strip* (July 1996), *Torture and Ill-treatment of Palestinians from the Occupied Territories* (June 1994), and *World Reports* (annual publication).
4. For detailed discussions see Emma Playfair (ed.), *International Law and the Administration of Occupied Territories* (Oxford: Clarendon Press, 1992); Raja Shehadeh, *Occupier's Law, Israel and the West Bank*; Meir Shamgar, 'The Observance of International Law in the Administered Territories', *Israel Yearbook on Human Rights*, 1 (Published under the auspices of the Faculty of Law, Tel Aviv University by Kluwer Academic Publishers, Dordrecht, Netherlands, 1971); Yehuda Blum, 'The Missing Reversioner:

Reflections on the Status of Judea and Samaria', *Israel Law Review*, 3 (1968).

5. John Dugard, *Report of the Special Rapporteur of the Commission on Human Rights on the Situation of Human Rights in the Palestinian Territories Occupied by Israel since 1967*, A/56/440 (4 October 2001) point 5. Submitted to the Fifty-sixth session of the UN General Assembly.

6. Alan Baker and Ady Schonmann, 'Presenting Israel's Case Before International Human Rights Bodies', originally published in *Justice – The International Association of Jewish Lawyers and Jurists*, Vol. 19 (Winter 1998). Re-published on the Israel Ministry of Foreign Affairs website, www.mfa.gov.il, p. 4. A similar argument was made in the State of Israel's response to the list of issues presented by the Committee on the Rights of the Child in 2002. State of Israel, *Implementation of the Convention on the Rights of the Child in Israel, Response of the State of Israel to the Document Titled 'List of Issues to be Taken Up in Connection with the Consideration of the Initial Report of Israel' (CRC/C/8/Add.44)*, (August 2002), p. 19. See also David Kretzmer, *The Occupation of Justice: The Supreme Court of Israel and the Occupied Territories* (New York: State University New York Press, 2002).

7. State of Israel, *Implementation of the Convention on the Rights of the Child*, pp. 20–2.

8. *Declaration of the Conference of High Contracting Parties to the Fourth Geneva Convention*, Geneva, 5 December 2001, point 3. Also see UNSC Resolutions S/RES/237 (14 June 1967), S/RES/446 (22 March 1979), S/RES/465 (1 March 1980), S/RES/641 (30 August 1989), S/RES/904 (18 March 1994); and UNGA Resolutions A/RES/51/223 (13 March 1997), A/RES/45/83 (13 December 1990).

9. Dugard, *Report of the Special Rapporteur*, A/56/440, point 7.

10. See Concluding *Observations and Recommendations of the Committee against Torture: Israel. 23/11/2001*, CAT/C?XXVII/, point 2, and Concluding *Observations of the Committee on the Rights of the Child: Israel. 09/10/2002*, CRC/C/15/Add.195.

11. See State of Israel, *Implementation of the Convention of the Rights of the Child*, p. 22. For complete explanation, see pp. 17–22.

12. Ibid., p. 26. And *Statistical Abstract of Israel 2002*, Section 2, Population, Introduction, p. 1. Available online at www.cbs.gov.il.

13. Article 2.1 of the CRC states: 'States Parties shall respect and ensure the rights set forth in the present Convention to each child within their jurisdiction without discrimination of any kind.'

14. See *Report of the Special Committee to Investigate Israeli Practices Affecting the Human Rights of the Palestinian People and Other Arabs of the Occupied Territories*, A/54/325 (8 September 1999) point 28. Submitted to the Fifty-fourth session of the UN General Assembly.

15. See Dugard, *Report of the Special Rapporteur* A/56/440, point 1.

16. See United Nations press release, *Visiting Mission to the Occupied Palestinian Territories Will Not Take Place* (19 April 2002).

17. See *Report of the Secretary-General Prepared Pursuant to General Assembly Resolution ES-10/10*, A/ES-10/186 (30 July 2002) and Cabinet *Statement on UN Fact-Finding Team, Communicated by the Cabinet Secretariat* (30 April

2002). Available online at the Israel Ministry of Foreign Affairs website, www.mfa.gov.il.

18. Israel's Reservations and Declarations to the CAT.

19. Conclusions and Recommendations of the Committee against Torture: Israel. CAT/C? XXVII/Concl.5.

20. Daniel Dor, *Intifada Hits the Headlines* (Indiana: Indiana University Press, 2003).

21. Roger Alpher, 'Plugged In', *Haaretz Magazine* (17 January 2003).

22. Authors' telephone interview with Attorney Leah Tsemel (14 March 2003).

23. Amira Hass, 'Who in Israel Knows or Cares?' *Haaretz English Edition* (18 June 2003).

24. Gideon Levy, 'Half a Democracy', *Haaretz English Edition* (26 January 2003).

25. E.A. (Election Appeal) 2/88 Ben Shalom v. Chairman of Central Elections Committee *Piskei Din*, 43(2) (1988) 221.

26. Ruth Gavison, quoted in Tikva Horning-Parnass, 'Freezing the Druckman Law Israel's Actual Apartheid Land Policy Will Continue', *Between the Lines* (August 2002).

27. Levy 'Half a Democracy'.

28. Joint press release of Palestinian Centre for Policy and Survey Research Ramallah and Harry S. Truman Research Institute for the Advance of Peace, Hebrew University, Jerusalem (November 2002).

29. Quoted in 'The Prison Factory: An Interview with Adv. Allegra Pachecco', *Between the Lines* (July 2001).

30. Portions of the discussion on torture here and in Chapter 6 are adapted with the author's permission from a University of Chicago MA Thesis, 'Discipline, Punish and Position Abuse: The Torture of Palestinians in the West Bank and Gaza Strip' by Lori A. Allen, Dept. of Anthropology (December 1998).

31. Gideon Levy, 'What We Owe the Radical Left', *Haaretz* (13 September 1999).

32. See United Nations Economic and Social Council, Commission on Human Rights, *Report of the Special Working Group of Experts Established Under Resolution 6 (XXV) of the Commission on Human Rights*, E/CN.4/1016/Add.2 (11 February 1970); Amnesty International, Report on treatment of certain prisoners under interrogation in Israel (1970).

33. The two journalists were Paul Eddy and Peter Gilman. For more information, see Noam Chomsky, *The Fateful Triangle: The United States, Israel & the Palestinians* (Boston, MA: South End Press; London: Pluto Press, 1999), pp. 126–7.

34. Ibid., p. 127.

35. Ibid.

36. Stephen Sosebee, 'Speaking About the Unspeakable: Officially Sanctioned Torture', *The Washington Report On Middle East Affairs* (Washington DC, October 1991), p. 41.

37. Ibid.

38. Lisa Hajjar, 'Sovereign Bodies, Sovereign States: Torture and the Nation'. Paper presented at the conference, *Investigating and Combating Torture:*

Explorations of a New Human Rights Paradigm, University of Chicago Human Rights Program (4–7 March 1999).

39. Symposium on the Report of the Commission of Inquiry Into the Methods of Investigation of the General Security Service Regarding Hostile Terrorist Activity, *Israel Law Review*, 23(2–3), 1969, 2.

40. Ibid., p. 171.

41. These numbers refer to numbered points within the UN CAT document.

42. Concluding observations of the Committee against Torture: Israel, A/49/44, paras 159–71 (12 June 1994).

43. Concluding observations of the Committee against Torture: Israel, A/52/44, paras 253–60 (9 May 1997).

44. Amnesty International, *Israel: High Court Should End the Shame of Torture*, AI Index: MDE 15/005/1999.

45. Ibid.

46. 6 September 1999 ruling of the High Court of Justice in cases H.C. 5100/94, H.C. 4054/95, H.C. 6536/95, H.C. 51888/96, H.C. 7563/97, H.C. 7628/97, and H.C. 1043/99 on the legality of General Security Service's (GSS) use of 'physical means' during interrogation.

47. Ibid.

48. Amnesty International, *Fear of the Legalization of Torture*, Urgent Action AI Index: MDE 15/79/99; Nina Gilbert, 'Barak Favors GSS "Pressure Tactics"', *The Jerusalem Post Internet Edition* (15 March 2000).

49. Conclusions and Recommendations of the Committee against Torture: Israel. 23/11/2001 /Concl.5.

50. Public Committee Against Torture in Israel, *Questions and Answers*, www.stoptorture.org.il.

51. International Committee of the Red Cross, *General Problems in Implementing the Fourth Geneva Convention*, Report for Meeting of Experts (Geneva: 27–29 October 1998), p. 4.

52. Ibid., pp. 4–5.

53. Ibid.

54. Portions of the discussion on 'clean hands' and the EC–Israel Association Agreement are adapted, with permission of the author, Stephanie Koury, from the draft statement of the Palestine Delegation to the 27th International Conference of the Red Cross and Red Crescent, addressing agenda item 1, The Protection of Victims of Armed Conflict through Respect of International Humanitarian Law, 31 October–6 November 1999.

55. The EU–Israel Association Agreement was signed on 20 November 1995. After ratification by the 15 Member States' parliaments, the European Parliament and the Israeli Knesset, it entered into force on 1 June 2000.

56. See Amnesty International USA, Israel and Occupied Territories, *Amnesty International Calls for Suspension of US Weapons Transfers to Israel – Supply of Weapons for Suicide Bombings & Attacks on Settlers Must be Halted* (9 April 2002). Available online at www.amnestyusa.org.

57. Ibid.

58. For information on US aid to Israel, see Clyde Mark, *Israel: U.S. Foreign Assistance, Congressional Research Service Issue Brief for (U.S.) Congress* (6

June 2002); and Stephen Zunes, 'The Strategic Functions of U.S. Aid to Israel', *Middle East Policy*, 4, 4 (October 1996).

11   CONCLUSION

1. Amos Harel, 'Arafat Calls Israeli Pullback in Gaza, Bethlehem "Cosmetic"', *Haaretz English Online Edition* (5 July 2003).
2. For a summary of the use of prisoners within the Oslo negotiations see www.nad-plo.org.interim/prisoners.html and www.nad-plo.org/interim/prischro.html.

Index

Compiled by Sue Carlton